The
Complete Book
Of
National Dishes

Over 200 Delicious Recipes
and their Origins from
around the World
(With full Color photo for each recipe)

Henderson Daniel *with* Kristy Khemraj

For general information on our other products and services or to obtain technical support, please contact our Customer Care Department within the United States at email hdtenmediagroup@gmail.com.

Photography: Adobe Stock Photos; Africa Studio, ALF photo, anphotos99, Anuska Sampedro, arska n, asife, barkstudio, Bastiaanimage Stock, Bernd Jürgens, Brent Hofacker, Bruno ismael alves, carles, CCat82, chandlervid85, chokniti, corners74, czamfir, Daniel, Daniel Vincek, Dar1930, David Pimborough, davideb89, derejeb, dinanana, Dmitry Ersler, Elzbieta Sekowska, eqroy, Eun, exclusive-design, fahrwasser, Family Business, Fanfo, far700, fascinadora, FomaA, Fudio, Greg, Grigory Bruev, grimms123, Grinchh, Hansgeel, Herby (Herbert) Me, HLPhoto, irina, Jacek Chabraszewski, Jestin, Joe Gough, Kheng Guan Toh, lcrribeiro33@gmail, leisuretime70, lilechka75, Liv Friis-larsen, lmarc, Lucy Brown, Luis, luisapuccini, LuXpics, M.studio, magicbones, malajscy, manyakotic, Marcos, Maridav, Maxim Khytra, Milton Oswald, montegroov, nadisja, naito8, Nelea Reazanteva, Nik, nito, Olga Iljinich, onajourney, oxilixo, paul_brighton, paulovilela, petiast, PhotoKD, Rafael Ben-Ari, ricka_kinamoto, robert lerich, Ryzhkov, Screaghin, seagull_l, Sergio Martínez, sevaljevic, shooting88, siete_vidas1spaxiax, StockphotoVideo, superfood, svariophoto, Szakaly, travelphotos, tycoon101, uckyo, Unclesam, vasanty, Viktor, Visionsi, vkuslandia, Vladimir Kazimirov, volgariver, vvoe, white78, 성수 한

Library of Congress Control Number: 2019907773

Also Available in the following formats

Hard Cover Color **ISBN:** 978-1733191418
Spiral Full Color **ISBN:** 978-1733191425

Author: Kristy Khemraj/Henderson Daniel
Editor: Kristy Khemraj / Melissa Claxton
Cover Design: Henderson Daniel
Book Layout and Design: Henderson Daniel

DEDICATION
Henderson

To my family without whose sympathy and encouragement, this book would have still been on the hard drive of my computer.

In Loving Memory of My mother Elsa E Blaize for allowing me to spend time with her in the kitchen, and Anthony Bourdain for bringing us his hour-long popular weekend TV series 'Parts Unknown.'

GRATITUDE
Henderson

I wish to thank the following: Great Britain and France for sharing their cuisine during the colonization of my Homeland. P Guiste for the great job she did with The National School Feeding Program (feeding kids in need). G Birmingham for nourishing me with her delicious cooking for many years. (CACFP) The Child and Adult Care Food Program for providing nutritious meals and snacks to children and adults at participating child care centers. To the World Food Programme (WFP) for assisting 91.4 million people in around 83 countries each year... There are many more people I could thank, but humility forces me to stop here.

DEDICATION
Kristy

To my sister, whose passion for cooking inspires me every day.

ABOUT THIS BOOK
The Inside Story

It all began in May 2017. While searching for a cookbook with all the national dishes, their origins, and food culture, I realized there were none to be found. I contacted Kristy, and the rest was history.

The Division

The recipes are divided into seven regions of the world: Asia, Middle East North Africa, and Greater Arabia, Europe, North and South America, Central America and the Caribbean, Sub Saharan Africa, and Australia and Oceania. These seven regions provide a clear division of the world's countries.

The colored edges allow you to locate the different regions of the world quickly, and at the end of each recipe is a section for note taking!

The Color Story
Eating a Rainbow

Fruits and vegetables fall into different color categories; purple, orange, red, green, white, brown, and blue. Each color carries unique disease-fighting substances called phytochemicals. Phytochemicals give fruits and vegetables, their colors, and their healthy properties.

That color?

RED

Lycopene is the natural plant pigment in Red fruits and vegetables. Lycopene is a powerful antioxidant which helps reduce the risk of cancer and keeps our brains, hearts, eyes, and bones healthy.

ORANGE

Carotenoids: Beta-carotene is a well-known carotenoid, and is in pumpkins, carrots, and sweet potatoes. Carotenoids help in decreasing the risk of disease, particularly certain cancers. Lutein is Another carotenoid which helps maintain healthy mucous membranes in the eyes and has been found to prevent cataracts, which can lead to blindness.

YELLOW

Vitamin C: Yellow fruits such as oranges, cantaloupes, pumpkins, grapefruits, Mangos, papayas, and pineapples, are all excellent sources of vitamin C. It is a powerful Antioxidant which may reduce the risk of chronic diseases; such as high blood pressure, and heart disease. It also boosts the immune system, fights the common cold, and reduces inflammation.

GREEN VEGETABLES

Folate: Leafy greens vegetables such as spinach and broccoli are also excellent sources of folate and calcium. Folate helps build healthy cells and boosts heart health

BLUE

Anthocyanins: Is found naturally in several foods such as blackberries, blueberries, cherries, cranberries, eggplant, grape, etc. Anthocyanins boost brain health, destroy free radicals, and have anti-inflammatory, anti-viral, and anti-cancer benefits.

PURPLE

Resveratrol: This is part of a group of compounds called polyphenols. They act as antioxidants, decreasing estrogen production, protecting the body against damage that can put you at higher risk for things like cancer, brain, stroke, and heart disease.

BROWN

Fiber: Some of the benefits of a high fiber diet include, normalizing bowel movement, lowering cholesterol level, helping to control blood sugar, boosting digestion, and promoting weight loss.

Table of contents

Asia

Middle East, North Africa & Greater Arabia

Country	Dish	Page
Afghanistan	Quaboli Palaw	37
Algeria	Saffron & Raisin Couscous	38
Azerbaijan	Yapaq Dolmasi	39
Bahrain	Machboos	40
Egypt	Falafel	41
Iran	Chelo Kebab	42
Iraq	Samak Masgouf	43
Israel	Falafel	44
Jordan	Mansaf	45
Kuwait	Machboos	46
Lebanon	Kibbeh	47
Libya	Usban	48
Morocco	Tagine	49
Oman	Shuwa	50
Pakistan	Biryani	51
Qatar	Machboos	52
Saudi Arabia	Saleeg	53
Somalia	Lahoh	54
Syria	Kibbeh	55
The United Arab Emirates	Biryani	56
Tunisia	Tunisian Couscous	57
Turkey	Doner Kebab	58
Yemen	Saltah	59

Europe

Country	Dish	Page
Albania	Qofte Ferguara	60
Andalusia	Gazpacho	61
Andorra	Escudella De Pages	62
Armenia	Khash or Pacha	63
Asturias	Fabada Asturiana	64
Austria	Weiner Schnitzel Mit Beilagen	65
Balearic Islands	Coca de Trempó	66
Basque Country and Navarre	Marmitako	67
Belarus	Draniki	68
Belgium	Carbonnades Flamandes	69
Bosnia and Herzegovina	Cevapi	70
Bulgaria	Banitsa	71
Canary Islands	Papas Arrugadas	72
Castile and León	Castilian Garlic Soup	73
Catalonia	Crema Catalana	74
Cornwall	Cornish Pasty	75
Croatia	Istrian Yota	76

Cyprus	Fasolada	77
Czech Republic	Vepro Knedlo Zelo	78
Denmark	Frikadeller	79
Estonia	Verivorst with Mulgikapsad	80
Finland	Karelian Pasties	81
France	Pot Au Feu	82
Galicia	Pulpo Gallego	83
Georgia	Khachapuri	84
Germany	Sauerbraten	85
Gibraltar	Profiteroles	86
Greece	Moussaka	87
Hungary	Goulash	88
Iceland	Mjolkursodinn	89
Ireland	Colcannon	90
Isle of Man	Bonnag	91
Italy	Pizza	92
Latvia	Janu Siers	93
Liechtenstein	Kasknopfle	94
Lithuania	Cepelinai	95
Luxembourg	Judd mat Gaardebounen	96
Macedonia	Tavce Gravce	97
Madrid	Cocido Madrileno	98
Malta	Stuffat al Fenek	99
Moldova	Sarmale	100
Monaco	Barbagiuan	101
Montenegro	Kacamak	102
Netherlands	Stamppot	103
Northern Ireland	Ulster Fry	104
Norway	Farikal	105
Poland	Bigos	106
Portugal	Bacalhau	107
Republic of Tatarstan	Echpochmak	108
Romania	Mici	109
Russia	Shchi	110
Serbia	Cevapcici	111
Slovakia	Bryndzové Halušky	112
Slovenia	Belokranjska Povitica	113
Spain	Paella	114
Sweden	Ostkaka	115
Switzerland	Fondue	116
Ukraine	Borscht	117
United Kingdom /Britain & Northern Ireland	Fish & Chips	118
Wales	Cawl	119

North and South America

Country	Dish	Page
Argentina	Carbonada Criolla Stew	120
Bolivia	Picante de Pollo	121
Brazil	Feijoada	122
Canada	Poutine	123
Chile	Pastel de Choclo	124
Colombia	Ajiaco	125
Ecuador	Ceviche	126
Greenland	Suaasat	127
Guyana	Pepperpot	128
Honduras	Plato Tipico	129
Mexico	Chiles en Nogada	130
Paraguay	Sopa Paraguaya	131
Peru	Ceviche	132
Puerto Rico	Mofongo	133
Suriname	Pom	134
United States of America	Apple Pie	135-36
United States Virgin Islands	Fish and Fungi	136
Uruguay	Chivito	137
Venezuela	Pabellón Criollo	138

Central America and the Caribbean

Country	Dish	Page
Antigua and Barbuda	Fungee	139
Aruba	Keshi Yena (Stuffed Cheese)	140
Barbados	Flying Fish and Cou Cou	141
Belize	Boil Up	142
Bermuda	Fish Chowder	143
Costa Rica	Gallo Pinto	144
Cuba	Arroz con Pollo	145
Dominica	Mountain Chicken	146
Dominican Republic	Chicharrones de Pollo	147
El Salvador	Pupusa	148
Guatemala	Fiambre	149
Grenada	Oil Down	150
Haiti	Diri Ak Djon Djon	151
Honduras	Plato Tipico	152
Jamaica	Ackee and Saltfish	153
Nicaragua	Gallo Pinto	154
Panama	Sancocho de Gallina	155
Saint Kitts and Nevis	Saltfish, Spicy Plantains, Breadfruit & Coconut Dumplings	155-156
Saint Lucia	Green Fig and Saltfish	157
Saint Vincent & the Grenadines	Roasted Breadfruit and Fried Jackfish	158
The Bahamas	Crack Conch with Peas & Rice	159
Trinidad and Tobago	Callaloo	160

Sub-Saharan Africa

Country	Dish	Page
Angola	Moamba de Galinha	161
Benin	Kuli Kuli	162
Botswana	Seswaa	163
Burkina Faso	Riz Gras	164
Burundi	Elephant Soup	165
Cameroon	Ndolé	166
Cape Verde	Cachupa	167
Chad	La Bouillie	168
Comoros	Langouste a la Vanille	169
Djibouti	Skoudehkaris	170
Equatorial Guinea	Succotash	171
Eritrea	Zigini with Injera	172
Ethiopia	Fit Fit	173
Gabon	Gabon	174
Ghana	Jollof Rice	175
Guinea	Poulet Yassa	176
Guinea-Bissau	Jollof Rice	177
Ivory Coast	Kedjenou	178
Kenya	Sukuma Wiki	179
Liberia	Dumboy	180
Madagascar	Romazava	181
Malawi	Nsima	182
Mali	Tiguadege Na	183
Mauritius	Octopus Curry	184
Mozambique	Frango a Portuguesa	185
Namibia	Sweet Millet Porridge	186
Niger	Djerma Stew	187
Nigeria	Egusi Soup	188
Republic of the Congo	Poulet a la Moambe	189
Sao Tome and Principe	São Tomé and Principé	190
Senegal	Thieboudienne	191
Seychelles	Ladob	192
Sierra Leone	Cassava Leaf Stew	193
South Africa	Doro Wat	194
Sudan	Ful Medames	195
Swaziland	Karoo Roast Ostrich Steak	196
Tanzania	Ugali na Maharage ya Nazi	197
The Gambia	Benachin	198
Togo	Yeyebessissi	199
Uganda	Matoke	200
Zambia	Nshima	201
Zimbabwe	Sadza	201
The Central African Republic	CassavaSticks / Bâton de Manioc	202

Australia and Oceania

Calorie & Nutritional Comparison

BANGLADESH – CHICKEN KORMA

This dish dates back to the Mughal Empire of South Asia. It is the national dish of Bangladesh and therefore utilizes a unique blend of Ingredients from that part of the world including spices, nuts, and exotic peppers.

SERVES 6

INGREDIENTS

whole chicken (skinned and cut into pieces)	1
plain yogurt (whisked)	1 cup
ginger (grated)	1 tbsp.
garlic (minced)	1 tsp.
liquid ghee	3 tbsps.
olive oil	4 tbsps.
cardamom pods	8
sticks of cinnamon	2
large onions (thinly sliced)	2
salt	2 tsps.
bay leaf	1
lemon juice	1 tbsp.
whole Thai bird chili peppers	4
golden raisins	2 tbsps.
sugar	1 tbsp.
ground almonds	2 tbsps.
slivered almonds	3 tbsps.

DIRECTIONS

1. Trim and wash the chicken pieces thoroughly.

2. Create a marinade for the chicken by combining the yogurt, garlic, and ginger.

3. Marinate the chicken for approximately an hour.

4. Heat the olive oil and ghee in a pan, then sauté the onions until brown.

5. Add the cardamom, cinnamon and the bay leaf. Stir frequently until the spices begin to release their fragrances.

6. Add the marinated chicken and sprinkle in the salt.

7. Increase the temperature to medium-high. Stir and allow the natural juices from the chicken to form a gravy. Monitor and let it cook for ten minutes.

8. Add two tablespoons of hot water to the pan and stir. Slowly add more water until the chicken is partially submerged. Bring to a boil. Reduce the heat, cover the pan and allow it to simmer but remember to stir occasionally.

9. After about thirty minutes, the oil should separate from the gravy. When this happens, add the raisins. Pour in the lemon juice, sprinkle in the sugar and add the ground almonds and whole chili peppers.

10. Stir and cook for five more minutes on medium-low heat.

11. Garnish with slivered almonds and raisins.

12. Serve with biryani or steamed jasmine rice.

NOTES

_____
_____
_____
_____
_____
_____
_____

BHUTAN – EMA DATSHI

Ema Datshi is an extremely spicy cheese and chili dish. The name 'Ema Datshi' is Bhutanese and translates to chili and cheese. This fiery dish is eaten daily in Bhutan usually with red rice. Traditionally, moldy cow or yak cheese was used when making Ema Datshi but feta cheese, blue cheese or Italian gorgon-zola can also be appropriate substitutes. To reduce the spiciness of this dish, the seeds from the chili peppers can be removed. Both fresh and dried chili peppers can be used in Ema Datshi. This signature dish is recognized as the national dish of Bhutan.

SERVES 5–6

INGREDIENTS

Danish Feta Cheese / Italian Gorgonzola / Blue Cheese (crumbled)	8 oz.
slices orange cheddar cheese	4
chili peppers (sliced in halves)	8 oz.
onion (chopped lengthwise)	1
cloves garlic (crushed)	5
leaves cilantro (finely chopped)	3
vegetable oil	2 tsps.
Roma tomatoes (diced)	2
steamed red or white rice	4 cups
water	12 oz.

DIRECTIONS

1. Heat a saucepan and add the vegetable oil. Add the chopped onions and halved chili peppers. Pour in 12 ounces of water. Bring to a boil on medium-high heat. After ten minutes, add the diced tomatoes and crushed garlic cloves. Allow this to simmer for approximately two minutes.

2. Crumble the Danish Feta Cheese/Italian Gorgonzola or Clue cheese. Add the crumbled cheese to the saucepan. Dice the orange cheddar and add this to the stew. The orange cheddar will give the Ema Datshi a beautiful, vibrant color. Stir well and after about three minutes, add the finely chopped cilantro and turn off the heat. Cover the saucepan and let it sit for a few minutes.

3. Serve the Ema Datshi with steamed red or white rice. Red rice is more traditional.

NOTES

BRUNEI –Ambuyat

Ambuyat is a type of starch derived from the trunk of a sago palm and cooked as a delicacy in the country of Brunei. It is consumed with a two–pronged bamboo utensil known as 'chandas'. Ambuyat is eaten with a variety of side dishes such as grilled prawns, fish, beef and an assortment of tropical sauces and vegetables. As the sago starch may be difficult to find outside of Brunei, it can be substituted with potato starch or tapioca starch.

SERVES 2

INGREDIENTS

sago starch / tapioca starch / potato starch	500gs.
water	600 ml
Thai chili pepper	1
shrimp paste	1 tsp.
dried shrimp	1 tbsp.
durian (tempoyak)	2 tbsp.
Salt	

DIRECTIONS

1. Combine the sago, potato or tapioca starch with some cold water and set aside in a bowl for a few minutes. Heat the water in a kettle and then pour boiling water slowly into the container with the starch. Once the starch appears sticky, use a wooden spoon to start whisking it together. When it is ready, the Ambuyat will become firm and starchy.

2. Prepare a shrimp flavored tempoyak durian sauce to serve with the Ambuyat. Use a mortar and pestle to mince the dried shrimp with the Thai chili pepper. Traditionally, a stone bowl called a 'Lasung' is used. Add the shrimp paste to the minced shrimp and pepper mixture. Sprinkle in a bit of salt to taste. Transfer this to a separate serving bowl. Slowly stir in a little hot water to the shrimp and durian mixture.

3. Serve the Ambuyat while hot with the shrimp sauce for dipping. Cooked vegetables, whole grilled shrimp, fried fish fillets, fried belutak (mixed beef) and sweet and sour sauces can also be served with the Ambuyat.

NOTES

_____
_____
_____
_____
_____
_____
_____
_____
_____
_____
_____
_____
_____
_____
_____
_____
_____
_____
_____
_____
_____
_____
_____

CAMBODIA – AMOK

Amok is a popular Cambodian fish dish that is fragrant and flavored with the exotic flavors of lemongrass and lime. This is a slightly sweet curry with the consistency of custard. As it is the national dish of Cambodia, Amok can be found on almost every restaurant menu in the country. Amok is traditionally served in a dish lined with banana leaves and eaten with white rice.

SERVES 2–3

INGREDIENTS

fillets white fish (halibut, cod or mahi-mahi are good choices)	2
can coconut milk	1
stalks lemongrass (finely chopped)	4
Kaffir lime leaves or 1 tsp. Lime juice mixed with ½ tsp. lime zest	2
coconut oil	2 tsps.
basil, mint and coriander leaves (chopped and mixed)	3 tbsps.
cloves garlic (finely diced)	2
fish sauce	½ tbsp.
palm sugar	¼ tsp.
fresh saffron (grated) / ½ tsp. dried saffron	1 tsp.
Galangal or ¾ tsp. fresh ginger (thinly sliced)	½ tsp.
Salt	
Black pepper	
Chili pepper flakes	

DIRECTIONS

1. Cut the fish fillets into cubes. Sprinkle black pepper and salt on the fish, mix well and refrigerate until required.

2. Pour the oil into a medium-sized saucepan. Turn on the heat and sauté the lemongrass, kaffir lime leaves, saffron, garlic, galangal (or ginger) and chili pepper flakes. Stir regularly and allow the flavors of these spices to marry. After about a minute, pour in the can of coconut milk. If using the kaffir leaf substitute of lime zest and lime juice, add this now. Add the fish sauce, palm sugar and bring to a boil and let simmer for ten minutes.

3. Remove the fish cubes from the refrigerator and add the cold fish cubes to the simmering liquid. Cover the saucepan and let the fish cook for four minutes or until tender. Turn off the heat.

4. Ladle the finished Amok into a bowl lined with pieces of green banana leaves. Garnish with finely chopped herbs and a spoonful of coconut cream. Serve with white rice.

NOTES

_____

_____

_____

_____

_____

_____

_____

_____

_____

_____

_____

_____

_____

_____

_____

_____

_____

_____

_____

_____

CHINA – PEKING DUCK

Considered one of China's national dishes, Peking Duck is a whole roast duck seasoned with Chinese spices. There are a few methods to prepare this dish including roasting the duck over an open flame and pumping air between the skin and meat. Traditionally, it is skillfully carved into slices each having a bit of crispy skin attached to the meat. Peking duck is eaten with soft Chinese pancakes. The origins of this succulent duck dish can be traced back to the Yuan Dynasty when Mongol emperors ruled China and domesticated ducks were abundant.

SERVES??

INGREDIENTS

whole plump duck (weighing approximately 1.2 kg)	1
pitted plums	11
granulated sugar	5 tbsps.
minced ginger	1 ½ tbsps.
soy sauce	2 tbsps.
chili powder	½ tsp.
cucumber	½
orange zest	1 tbsp.
bunch spring onions	1
packs pre-made Chinese pancakes	2
Salt	
Chinese five–spice powder	

DIRECTIONS

1. The duck should be plucked, gutted, and washed before preparing it for a meal.

2. Start preparing the Peking Duck by generously rubbing the duck inside and out with salt. Sprinkle a bit of Chinese five–spice seasoning over the skin. Rub the duck with some minced ginger and put any extra ginger inside the Duck.

3. Get a large roasting pan and arrange the duck on it, breast side up.

4. Preheat the oven to 325° F°, then place the pan into the oven. Bake the duck for two hours (2:00), monitoring occasionally and removing any excess fat that accumulates in the pan. For extra crispiness, turn up the oven to 400 F° and bake for a few minutes more.

Make a plum sauce to go with the Peking Duck.

5. Combine the pitted plums, sugar, two pinches of Chinese five-spice powder, soy sauce, chili powder, and a little water and bring to a boil in a saucepan.

6. Let it simmer until the plums soften and turn into pulp, removed the skins from the sauce.

7. Stir in a tbsp of orange zest. Turn off the heat and set aside.

8. Carve the duck into thin slices.

9. Slice the bunch of spring onions and the cucumber.

10. Steam the pre-made Chinese pancakes or microwaved them.

11. Spread a dollop of plum sauce onto a cooked pancake, add cucumber and spring onions, and then place a few slices of duck on top.

12. Serve and enjoy

NOTES

_____
_____
_____
_____
_____
_____
_____

HONG KONG – Sweet and Sour Pork

The cuisine of Hong Kong is greatly influenced by Cantonese cooking. One such Cantonese dish that has become increasingly popular in Hong Kong is Sweet and Sour Pork which can also be found in many Chinese and Hong Kong restaurants across the globe. Spare ribs or pork loins are used in the Hong Kong version of this dish and the traditional scarlet sauce is made with vinegar, preserved plums and hawthorn candy.

SERVES 3–4

INGREDIENTS

For the Sauce

sugar	1 tbsp.
cornstarch	¾ tsp.
plum sauce	2 tbsp.
soy sauce	1 tbsp.
rice wine or dry sherry	2 tsp.
salt	1/8 tsp.
unseasoned rice vinegar	2 tsp.
water	¼ cup

For the Pork

boneless pork shoulder/loin (cut into small cubes)	8 oz.
rice wine or dry sherry	2 tsp.
oyster sauce	½ tsp.
plus 1 tsp. tapioca starch / cornstarch	1/3 cup
soy sauce	½ tsp.
beaten egg	2 tbsp.
small onion (sliced)	¼
fresh or frozen pineapple cubes	3–4 oz.
minced ginger	1 tsp.
bell pepper cubes	3 oz.
small ripe tomato (peeled and cut into wedges)	1
green onion (sliced thinly)	1
Canola oil for frying	

DIRECTIONS

1. Combine all of the sauce Ingredients in a bowl, stir well and set aside.
2. Marinate the pork cubes in a mixture of rice wine, cornstarch, oyster sauce and soy sauce in a covered bowl for thirty (0:30) minutes.
3. Add the beaten egg to the marinated pork.
4. Coat the pork pieces in cornstarch and let sit for four (0:04) minutes.
5. Fill a wok with ¾ inch canola oil and heat thoroughly.
6. Work in batches to fry the pork cubes for about three (0:03) minutes until pale golden.
7. Remove from the oil and set the pork on paper towels to absorb excess oil.
8. Increase the heat and add all of the pork cubes back into the wok.
9. Refry until brown and very crisp, then set on paper towels to absorb excess oil.
10. Heat two teaspoons of oil in a clean wok and sauté the onions and pineapple cubes.
11. Allow the pineapple cubes to develop brown streak marks, then add the minced ginger and bell peppers.
12. Stir constantly for one (0:01) minute until the peppers are crispy.
13. Add the tomato wedges and pour in the sauce mixture.
14. Cook for forty-five (0:045) seconds until the sauce begins to bubble and thicken.
15. Stir in the fried pork in the sauce.
16. Transfer the Sweet and Sour Pork to a serving dish and garnish with green onions.
17. Serve hot with steamed rice.

INDIA – TANDOORI CHICKEN

Tandoori Chicken is considered to be one of India's national dishes. Traditionally, the chicken is cook in a tandoor clay oven.

SERVES 4

INGREDIENTS

pieces chicken (6 drumsticks and 6 thighs)	12
smoked paprika	1 tsp.
plain yogurt	1 cup
lemon juice	1 tbsp.
allspice	1 tsp.
coarse black pepper	1 tsp.
ground cinnamon	1 tsp.
Ground cumin	2 tsps.
minced ginger	1 tsp.
ground cayenne pepper	1 tsp.
Salt	2 tsps.
minced garlic	1 tbsp.
Thai chili paste	1 tbsp.
slices raw onions (separated into rings)	3
lemon (sliced)	½

DIRECTIONS

1. Put the yogurt and lemon juice in a bowl.

2. Add the spices, garlic and the chili paste to the lemon and yogurt, then whisk until smooth and thick.

3. Place the drumsticks and thighs in separate resealable plastic bags.

4. Pour half of the marinade in each bag of chicken and seal shut.

5. Massage the bags of chicken in the marinade until coated.

6. Let out any air from the bags and refrigerate for twenty-four (24:00) hours, turning the bags occasionally during this time.

7. Place aluminum foil inside a large roasting pan and lay a rack over it to allow air to circulate.

8. Preheat the oven to 425 degrees F°.

9. Remove the marinated chicken from the bags and place the pieces onto the rack.

10. Place the pan in the preheated oven and bake for thirty (0:30) minutes, then turn the pieces over and cook for fifteen (0:15) minutes until the meat charred a little.

11. Turn off the heat and let the chicken rest in the hot oven for twenty (0:20) minutes.

12. Remove the pan and put the chicken onto a serving platter.

13. Garnish with onion and lemon slices before serving.

NOTES

_____
_____
_____
_____
_____
_____
_____
_____
_____
_____
_____
_____
_____
_____
_____
_____
_____

INDONESIA – GADO GADO

Gado Gado is a well–known dish in Indonesia. It is a one dish meal, similar to a salad. It is prepared with fresh seasonal vegetables, eggs, tofu and Ingredients native to Indonesia. It is usually paired with a special peanut sauce. Gado Gado means "mix" or "medley" in Indonesian.

SERVES 4–6

INGREDIENTS

Yukon Gold potatoes (peeled and sliced 1/3 inch thick)	1 lb.
medium carrots (sliced ¼ inch thick)	2
hardboiled eggs (peeled and halved)	3
mung bean sprouts	2 cups
Chinese spinach (leaves cut into 2-inch pieces)	5 oz.
firm tofu (cubed)	7 oz.
green beans (cut into 2-inch pieces)	4 oz.
green cabbage (cored and sliced into 1 ½ inch chunks)	¼
cucumber (sliced ¼ inch thick)	1
Indonesian shrimp crackers (fried)	15
Indonesian shrimp paste	1 ½ tsp.
unsweetened coconut milk	¾ cup
roasted, unsalted peanuts	1 ½ cup
rice vinegar	1 tbsp.
dark brown sugar	¼ cup
cloves garlic (peeled)	2
chili pepper (chopped)	1
water	½ cup
Kosher salt	
Peanut oil	

DIRECTIONS

1. Toast the peanuts in a nonstick skillet for about nine (0:09) minutes, then cool.

2. Place the peanuts in a food processor and pulse until fine.

3. Place the shrimp paste in a flat foil packet and toast in a hot skillet for four (0:04) minutes, then cool.

4. Add the shrimp paste to the food processor.

5. Add the brown sugar, chili peppers, and garlic cloves to the food processor and puree.

6. Transfer the puree to a hot skillet and stir in the coconut milk.

7. Cook the sauce for about six (0:06) minutes, frequently stirring until the mixture starts to separate.

8. Add the rice vinegar, water, and salt.

9. Simmer for three (0:03) minutes until sauce thickens, then turn off the heat and set the sauce aside.

10. Deep fry the potatoes in peanut oil until golden brown, then drain and set aside.

11. Fry the tofu cubes until puffed and brown, then set aside.

12. In a pot with salt and water boil and cook the spinach, beans, mung bean sprouts, carrots, and cabbage until tender, in batches.

13. After cooking the vegetables, transfer them to a dish of ice water, then drain, dry with paper towels and set onto the serving platter.

14. Arrange the potatoes, cucumber, and tofu cubes onto the platter.

15. Add the eggs and shrimp crackers.

16. Toss with the peanut sauce and serve.

JAPAN – RAMEN

Ramen is a type of Japanese soup, made with wheat noodles which have been prepared in a savory broth and topped with local vegetables, meat, and eggs. It is considered to be one of Japan's iconic dishes, although it is said to be of Chinese origins. It is a versatile dish and varies in the type of meat and vegetables used, as well as the toppings. Ramen is served by itself, without side dishes or condiments.

SERVES 2

INGREDIENTS

chicken breasts (boneless with skin on)	2
unsalted butter	1 tbsp.
packets of dried ramen noodles	2 (3 oz.)
scallions (finely sliced)	½ cup
large soft–boiled eggs	2
fresh shitake mushroom slices	½ cup
Sesame oil	2 tsps.
Minced ginger	2 tsps.
chicken stock	4 cups
Mirin	2 tbsps.
Minced garlic	3 tsps.
Soy sauce	3 tbsps.
Sea salt	1–2 tsps.
Black pepper	

DIRECTIONS

1. Preheat the oven to 375 degrees F°.
2. Season the chicken breasts with adequate salt and pepper.
3. Melt the butter in a skillet and fry the chicken breasts, skin side down first, for about seven (0:07) minutes or until the chicken skin lifts from the pan.
4. Flip the chicken and let it cook for about five (0:05) minutes on the other side.
5. Remove the skillet from the stove and place it into the hot oven.
6. Let the chicken roast for about twenty (0:20) minutes till it is cooked through, then set aside.
7. Begin making the ramen broth by first sautéing the ginger and garlic in hot sesame oil.
8. Add the soy sauce and mirin and cook for one (0:01) minute.
9. Pour in the chicken stock, cover and bring to a boil.
10. Remove the lid and let the broth simmer for five (0:05) minutes before adding the mushrooms.
11. Season the broth with sea salt and let it simmer.
12. In a separate saucepan, boil the ramen noodles for about three (0:03) minutes until tender.
13. Divide the cooked ramen noodles into four bowls.
14. Pour in the hot broth over the noodles.
15. Slice the roasted chicken and place into each bowl.
16. Slice the eggs into halves and add to the bowls.
17. Top with sliced scallions.
18. Serve hot.

NOTES

_____
_____
_____
_____
_____
_____
_____
_____
_____

KAZAKHSTAN – BESHBARMAK

Beshbarmak is boiled meat with noodles. Traditionally, horse or sheep meat were used. The dish was first prepared by Kazakh nomads. The name of the dish translates to 'five fingers' which refers to the fact that no cutlery is used to partake in Beshbarmak and the meal is therefore eaten with the hand.

SERVES 4

INGREDIENTS

lamb/beef (with bones)	2 ½ lbs.
large onion (peeled and cut into rings)	1
bay leaf	1
eggs (whisked)	2
600g plain flour (sifted)	4 cups
water	¾ – 1 cup
salt	½ tbsp.
Ground pepper	
Finely sliced chives (garnish)	

DIRECTIONS

1. Place the meat in a deep pot with water and half of the onion rings.
2. Bring to a boil, continuously removing the scum from the surface.
3. Reduce the heat, cover the pot, and allow it to simmer for two hours and thirty minutes (2:30) or until the meat is soft and falls off the bone.
4. Prepare the noodles by combining the whisked eggs with the flour in a large bowl.
5. Add the salt and gradually pour in the water to form a dough.
6. Knead the dough well, then roll into a ball and cover with plastic wrap.
7. Allow the dough to sit for about twenty-five (0:25) minutes.
8. Divide the dough into several small balls.
9. Roll each ball into a thin layer, then trim into 10x10 cm noodle squares.
10. Set them aside separate from each other to avoid sticking.
11. Five minutes (0:05) before the meat cook, add the remaining onion rings together with salt and pepper.
12. Use a slotted spoon to remove the meat, bones, and onions.
13. Separate the soft meat, chop into bite-sized pieces, and discard the bones.
14. Bring the stock to a boil and let it boil for about seven (0:07) minutes, then add the noodles and allow it to cook for about eight (0:08) minutes.
15. Arrange the noodles around the serving platter.
16. Lay the meat in the center of the platter.
17. Pour a little of the broth/stock over the meat.
18. Garnish with finely sliced chives and serve.

NOTES

_____
_____
_____
_____
_____
_____
_____
_____
_____
_____
_____
_____
_____
_____
_____

KYRGYZSTAN – LAGHMAN

Laghman is a noodle and broth dish that is very popular in Kyrgyzstan. The noodles are usually handmade and the broth consists of meat and vegetables.

SERVES 8

INGREDIENTS

For the noodles

flour	3 ½ cups
water	9 cups
eggs	2
oil	2 tbsp.
salt	2 tbsp.

For the Broth

beef chuck (julienned)	½ lb.
oil	½ tbsp.
medium onion (diced)	1
green bell pepper (cut into 1 inch thick strips)	1
medium carrot (thinly julienned)	1
small potatoes (peeled and cubed)	3
cloves garlic (chopped)	3
medium tomato (thinly sliced)	1
tomato paste	1 tsp.
black pepper	½ tsp.
ground cumin	1 tsp.
glasses water	8
salt	2 tsp.

DIRECTIONS

For the noodles

1. Warm one cup of water.
2. In a large bowl, combine the flour, warm water, eggs, and salt.
3. Knead for twenty (0:20) minutes into a springy ball of dough.
4. Let the dough rest in a covered container for twenty (0:20) minutes.
5. Divide the dough into halves.
6. Roll out each piece of dough with a rolling pin into a flat circle.
7. Roll the dough into a tube by rolling it over the rolling pin.
8. Slide the rolling pin out of the tube and slice the tube horizontally into half-inch cuts.
9. Loosen the strips into long noodles.
10. Pour the rest of the water in a large saucepan, add a little salt and let simmer.
11. Boil the noodles for three (0:03) minutes, then drain and rinse in cold water.
12. Add the oil to the noodles and mix well to prevent the noodles from sticking to each other.
13. Place the noodles into serving bowls.

For the Broth

1. Preheat a big wok on high heat, then add the oil.
2. Stir–fry the beef in the oil until brown.
3. Add the onions to the wok.
4. Add the black pepper, salt, and cumin, then stir together evenly.
5. Add the tomato paste and slices, along with half of the chopped garlic.
6. Cook until the tomatoes are tender.
7. Add the remaining vegetables and stir–fry for about four (0:04) minutes, stirring continuously.
8. Add the water and reduce the heat.
9. Allow the broth to simmer for twenty (0:20) minutes, then add the remaining garlic.
10. Let the soup simmer for an additional twenty (0:20) minutes, then turn off the heat.
11. Pour some of the broth, meat, and vegetables over the cooked noodles, then serve.

LAOS – TUM MAK HOONG

The national dish of Laos is a spicy papaya salad called Tum Mak Hoong. It is also popular throughout South Eastern Asia. Other terms for this dish are Som Tam and Bok L'Hong. Made from unripe papaya that has been shredded and mixed with savory spices. It is said that this dish encompasses all the five tastes of Laos' local cuisine; tart lime, hot chili, pungent fish sauce, saltiness, and sweetness. "Tum" means to smash or mix in Laos and traditionally, a mortar and pestle are used to combine the Ingredients for this salad. Served the Tum Mak Hoong with sticky rice and grilled chicken.

SERVES 4

INGREDIENTS

cups raw, shredded/grated green papaya	2
hot chili peppers (halved)	3
shrimp paste	1 tsp.
crab paste	¼ tsp.
clove garlic	1
shredded carrots	½ cup
brown sugar	1 tbsp.
snake beans (cut into strips)	1 cup
savory fish sauce	1 tbsp.
cherry tomatoes (sliced in halves)	½ cup
sour lime (sliced in thin circles)	1
pinch salt	1

DIRECTIONS

1. Fill a big mortar with the chili peppers, crab paste, brown sugar, shrimp paste, and salt.

2. Use a pestle to grind these Ingredients and mix all the flavors.

3. Add the chopped snake beans, shredded carrots and the grated green papaya to the mortar.

4. Add the fish sauce, lime slices and the single clove of garlic.

5. Gently grind the Ingredients with the pestle until the papaya absorbs the flavors and begins to darken in color.

6. Mix in the sliced cherry tomatoes.

7. Taste the salad and sprinkle in more salt if necessary.

8. Serve Tum Mak Hoong with a portion of sticky rice and hot grilled chicken or pork crackle.

NOTES

_____
_____
_____
_____
_____
_____
_____
_____
_____
_____
_____
_____
_____
_____
_____
_____
_____
_____
_____
_____
_____
_____

MACAU – MINCHI

The Macanese national dish Minchi is thought to have been named after the English word 'minced.' It consists of a flavorful mix of minced meat and potatoes. Traditionally, the meat was minced by using hand cleavers. The origins of this iconic dish is uncertain but is credited to both the Anglophone community in Hong Kong and Goa, a former Portuguese colony.

SERVES 4

INGREDIENTS

minced meat (beef and pork mix)	500g
medium potatoes (peeled and diced into ½ inch cubes)	2
onion (finely chopped)	1
bay leaves	2
cloves garlic (smashed)	3
Worcestershire sauce	1 tsp.
light soy sauce	3 tbsp.
pinch sugar	1
eggs	4
Salt	
Pepper	
Oil	

DIRECTIONS

1. Heat the oil in a cast-iron skillet and fry the potato cubes until golden brown.

2. Lay the potato cubes on paper towels after frying to absorb excess oil, then set aside.

3. Clean the skillet and heat some oil for sautéing.

4. Add the onion and bay leaves to the skillet.

5. Sauté together until the onions become golden and tender.

6. Transfer the cooked onion and bay leaves to a clean bowl and set aside.

7. Add a teaspoon of oil to the skillet, then fry the garlic to extract the flavor into the oil.

8. Discard the garlic when it becomes brown and add the minced meat to the skillet.

9. Add a pinch of salt to the meat and use a spoon or spatula to break up the larger clumps.

10. Cook for four (0:04) minutes, then add the sautéed onions and bay leaves.

11. Season with pepper and additional salt if required, then cook for two (0:02) minutes, stirring occasionally.

12. Combine the sugar, Worcestershire sauce, and soy sauce in a small bowl, then pour this onto the meat.

13. Stir well for about five (0:05) minutes until the meat is cooked and starts becoming dry.

14. Add the fried potatoes and toss with the minced meat.

15. Turn off the heat and dish out the Minchi in four servings.

16. Fry the eggs one at a time, ensuring the white set, but the yolk remains runny (sunny side up).

17. Top each serving of Minchi with a fried egg.

18. Serve hot.

NOTES

_____
_____
_____
_____
_____
_____

19

MALAYSIA – NASI LEMAK

Nasi Lemak is Malaysia's national dish. The name of the dish translates to "creamy rice." It is a fragrant, coconut infused rice dish and is traditionally served with sambal (a spicy paste), fried anchovies, cucumber slices and hard boiled eggs. This popular dish is sold throughout Malaysia, at markets, food courts and roadside stalls. Customarily, Nasi Lemak is packaged in a banana leaf.

SERVES 3–4

INGREDIENTS

jasmine rice	3 cups
pandan leaves (fresh or frozen)	10
stalks lemongrass (white part only, sliced)	1–2
red shallot (peeled and halved)	1
pieces (5mm) slices of ginger	2
salt	1 ½ tsp.
sugar	2 tsp.
coconut cream	¾ cup
ikan bilis (dried anchovies)	¾ cup
vegetable oil	2 cups
cucumber (halved lengthways and sliced into 5 mm pieces)	1
salted beer nuts	¾ cup
hardboiled eggs (sliced)	4
Banana leaves	

DIRECTIONS

1. Rinse the rice and let soak overnight in a bowl of water, then drain and set aside.

2. Line a bamboo steamer or steam pot with the pandan leaves.

3. Add the lemongrass, shallot, and ginger to the steamer and position the vessel comfortably over a wok or pot.

4. In a separate bowl, mix the rice with salt, sugar and the coconut cream.

5. Pour the rice mixture into the steamer, cover and cook for about twenty-five (0:25) minutes or until the rice is soft, then set aside.

6. Fry the ikan bilis in vegetable oil over medium-high heat until crispy and golden, then set them aside on paper towels.

7. Line the serving plates with banana leaves and baste them with a little vegetable oil for a traditional Malaysian touch.

8. Divide the rice equally and place onto each serving plate.

9. Serve the rice with ikan bilis, slices of cucumber, nuts, and slices of hardboiled egg.

NOTES

_____
_____
_____
_____
_____
_____
_____
_____
_____
_____
_____
_____
_____
_____
_____
_____
_____
_____
_____

MALDIVES – GARUDIYA

One of the most basic and traditional dishes in Maldivian cuisine is Garudiya; a type of clear fish broth. Garudiya is usually made with fresh tuna fish which is commonly caught in the Maldivian waters. This dish is prepared and eaten on a daily basis and as such, it is considered to be the national dish of the Maldives. It is often served with rice or roshi (Maldivian chapatti). Garudiya broth is sometimes used to make a popular condiment called Rihaakuru.

SERVES 6–8

INGREDIENTS

tuna fillets (cut into 2-inch slices)	500 g
dried cherry peppers	4
curry leaves (de-stemmed)	2–3
small onion (thinly sliced)	1
water	1 ½ L
Lime (Juiced)	1
Salt to taste	

DIRECTIONS

1. Fill a pot with the water and turn on the heat.

2. Place the pieces of raw tuna into the pot of water together with the cherry peppers, slices of onion and salt.

3. Add the curry leaves to the pot, and bring to a boil and skim off any scum that rises to the surface of the water.

4. Cook the Garudiya for about twenty (0:20) minutes until the tuna is tender, and turn the heat off and stir in the lime juice.

5. Serve the Garudiya hot, with rice or Maldivian flatbread (Roshi), additional chili peppers and lime slices.

NOTES

_____
_____
_____
_____
_____
_____
_____
_____
_____
_____
_____
_____
_____
_____
_____
_____
_____
_____
_____
_____
_____
_____
_____
_____
_____
_____
_____
_____
_____

MONGOLIA – BUUZ

Buuz are small, steamed dumplings which are filled with minced meat. In Mongolia, these dumplings are eaten year round but are especially prepared and eaten for the Tsagaan Sar or Mongolian Lunar New Year.

YIELDS 15

INGREDIENTS

whole wheat flour	2 ½ cups
lukewarm water	1 ¼ cup
salt	2 tsp.
minced beef/mutton	½ lb.
head of cabbage (finely chopped)	¼
medium sized carrot (finely grated)	1
medium sized onion (finely chopped)	½
cloves garlic (minced)	2
ground black pepper	1 tsp.
caraway seeds	1 tsp.
coriander seeds	1 tsp.

DIRECTIONS

1. Combine the flour, one teaspoon of salt and one cup of water in a large bowl.

2. Knead into a ball of dough.

3. Chill the ball of dough in the refrigerator in a covered container for one (1:00) hour.

4. While the dough is chilling, begin preparing the filling by first combining the meat, onion, garlic, carrot, and cabbage in a bowl.

5. Mix the meat, vegetables, black pepper, and salt.

6. Use a spice grinder to grind the caraway and coriander seeds, then add the powder to the meat and vegetables.

7. Combine the meat filling thoroughly, either using the fingers or a spoon, then set aside.

8. Set the chilled ball of dough onto a lightly floured board

9. Roll out into a long rope, and use a sharp knife to cut the dough into one-inch pieces.

10. Use a rolling pin to flatten each piece into a circle.

11. Place one tablespoon of meat filling in the center of each.

12. Fold each dumpling by pinching two parts of the dough and bringing it to the middle, then bringing the remaining two parts to the center so that the dough covers the filling leaving a small hole in the center.

13. Steam the Buuz in a steamer or stockpot for about fifteen (0:15) minutes until cooked.

14. Serve warm.

NOTES

_____
_____
_____
_____
_____
_____
_____
_____
_____
_____
_____
_____
_____
_____
_____
_____
_____

BURMA – MOHINGA

Mohinga is a flavorful Burmese fish and noodle soup which contains fresh native vegetables such as banana stems and blossoms. In Burma, it is eaten for breakfast. The specific type of river catfish used to make mohinga is native to Burma but any other type of whitefish can be used.

SERVES 4

INGREDIENTS

firm white fish (haddock, catfish or sea bass)	7 oz.
dried thin rice noodles /vermicelli	1 lb.
rice (toasted and finely ground)	2 oz.
fish stock	3 cups
flour	2g
stalks lemongrass (thinly sliced)	2
banana stem / blossom (thinly sliced)	2 oz.
red chili peppers (diced)	2
shrimp paste	2 tbsps.
turmeric	1 tsp.
onion (finely diced)	1
ginger (minced)	1 tsp.
canola oil	1 tbsp.
Lime wedges, coriander leaves, fried onions, sliced boiled eggs to serve	

DIRECTIONS

1. Heat the canola oil in a large saucepan, add the diced onions, minced ginger, turmeric, shrimp paste, chopped chili peppers, banana stem or blossoms, and the lemongrass.

2. Sauté these seasonings in the canola oil until the onion is tender.

3. Pour in the fish stock, gram flour and the toasted ground rice. Whisk to remove any lumps.

4. Reduce the heat and allow the soup to simmer for about fifteen minutes or until the soup thickens.

5. Add the rice noodles to the soup and let it continue simmering.

6. When the noodles are tender, cut the fish into bite-sized pieces and add them to the soup.

7. Stir with a wooden spoon to allow the fish to incorporate in the soup. After five minutes, the fish should be cooked.

8. Turn off the heat.

9. Prepare garnishes to serve with the hot mohinga; slice boiled eggs and ripe limes, chop fresh coriander leaves and fry onion slices. Ladle the mohinga in soup bowls and arrange the garnishes on top.

NOTES

_____
_____
_____
_____
_____
_____
_____
_____
_____
_____
_____
_____
_____
_____
_____
_____
_____
_____

NEPAL – DAL BHAT

Dal Bhat is the national dish of Nepal. It is a vegetarian lentil curry which is eaten with boiled or steamed rice. In Nepal, Dal Bhat is eaten once every day. Silverware is not used; the dish is eaten with the hands instead.

SERVES 4

INGREDIENTS

lentils	1 cup
saffron powder	½ tsp.
Ghee/oil	2 tbsp.
onion (peeled and diced)	1
cloves garlic (minced)	2
(2 inches) piece of ginger (grated)	1
coriander seeds (crushed)	1 tsp.
red chili powder	½ tsp.
water	3 cups
salt	1 tsp.
chopped cilantro leaves / sliced green onion	2 tbsp.
cooked white rice (for serving)	2 cups

DIRECTIONS

1. Rinse the dried lentils, then transfer to a bowl and pour in enough water to cover the lentils.
2. Soak the lentils overnight, then drain and set aside until ready to cook.
3. Heat the ghee or oil in a large skillet.
4. Add the diced onions to the skillet and sauté in the oil until translucent and tender.
5. Reduce the heat and add the red chili powder together with the garlic, ginger, crushed coriander seeds and saffron powder.
6. Cook for three (0:03) minutes, stirring the onion and spices frequently.
7. Add the lentils to the skillet and stir well.
8. Pour in the three cups of water, increase the heat, and bring to a boil.
9. Add the salt.
10. Reduce the heat and simmer for about fifteen (0:15) minutes or until the lentils are tender.
11. Sprinkle in the chopped cilantro leaves or sliced green onion and turn off the heat.
12. Separate the cooked white rice into four equal portions and place on serving plates.
13. Use a large spoon to put the Dal Bhat onto the plates of rice.
14. Serve with fruit chutney.

NOTES

_____
_____
_____
_____
_____
_____
_____
_____
_____
_____
_____
_____
_____
_____
_____
_____
_____
_____
_____

NORTH KOREA – KIMCHI

Kimchi is fermented Napa cabbage and horse radishes. It is considered to be a staple in North Korean cuisine. The cabbage is seasoned with spices and salted seafood, then stored in a jar. It is eaten as a side dish.

YIELDS 1 (2 quarts) jar

INGREDIENTS

Napa cabbage	1 (2 lb.)
kosher salt	½ cup
cold water	12 cups
daikon radish (peeled and cut into 2-inch matchsticks)	8 oz.
medium scallions (cut into 1-inch pieces)	4
fish sauce	¼ cup
Korean red pepper powder / kochukaru	1/3 cup
minced ginger	¼ cup
granulated sugar	1 ½ tbsp.
minced Korean salted shrimp / saeujeot	2 tsp.
cloves garlic (minced)	6–8

DIRECTIONS

1. Slice the cabbage in half, lengthwise, then cut crosswise into two-inch pieces.

2. Discard the root end.

3. Put the cabbage pieces into a bowl and add the salt.

4. Toss the cabbage and salt together.

5. Add about twelve cups of cold water so that the cabbage is submerged.

6. Cover the bowl and let the cabbage sit at room temperature for at least twelve (12:00) hours.

7. Drain the water from the cabbage and rinse.

8. Delicately squeeze the excess water from the leaves and place into a separate container, then set aside.

9. In another bowl, combine the daikon radishes, Korean red pepper, scallions, ginger, garlic, sugar, fish sauce, and salted shrimp.

10. Place the cabbage into the bowl and toss together so that it mixes with the radishes and covered with the spices and seafood flavorings.

11. Pack the mixture into a clean canning jar.

12. Seal the jar with a tight lid and let it sit in a cool, dark place for twenty-four (24:00) hours.

13. Open the jar to release any gas, then seal it again and place in the refrigerator for at least forty eight (48:00) hours before serving.

14. Serve kimchi with white rice or porridge.

NOTES

_____
_____
_____
_____
_____
_____
_____
_____
_____
_____
_____
_____
_____
_____
_____

25

PALESTINE – MUJADARA

Mujadara is a vegetarian rice and lentil pilaf. Bulgur is sometimes used instead of rice. It is a popular Palestinian dish and sometimes referred to as a poor man's dish because of its basic Ingredients that can be found in most households. Mujadara means 'pockmarked' in Arabic as the lentils among the rice grains or bulgur resemble pockmarks.

SERVES 6–8

INGREDIENTS

medium grained rice	3 cups
brown lentils	1 ½ cups
ground cumin	1 tbsp.
extra virgin olive oil	1/3 cup
ghee / clarified butter	1 tbsp.
sumac spice	1 tsp.
red onions (peeled and thinly sliced)	4–5
water for boiling	3 cups
Flour	
Salt	
Additional hot water	

DIRECTIONS

1. Soak the rice in water for twenty (0:20) minutes, then drain and set aside.

2. Fill a pot with three cups of water and bring to a boil.

3. Add the lentils and cumin.

4. Boil until the lentils are tender and cooked through.

5. Add the rice, stir together and season with adequate salt.

6. Pour in enough hot water to cover the rice.

7. Bring to a boil, then reduce the heat and allow to simmer.

8. When the water has evaporated, and the rice becomes tender, turn off the heat.

9. Set the rice and lentil pilaf aside.

10. Pour the olive oil into a shallow skillet or frying pan and heat.

11. Dust the onion slices in flour, then fry them in the hot olive oil until they are brown and crispy.

12. Pour the excess hot oil together with the ghee over the rice and lentil pilaf.

13. Mix the fats well with the rice and lentils.

14. Top the pilaf with the crispy fried onions and sprinkle the sumac spice over it

15. Serve the Mujadara with plain yogurt.

NOTES

_____
_____
_____
_____
_____
_____
_____
_____
_____
_____
_____
_____
_____
_____
_____
_____
_____
_____
_____

PHILIPPINES – ADOBO

Adobo is the most popular stew in the Philippines. It is prepared by marinating and cooking meat in vinegar, garlic and soy sauce. The method of cooking adobo in vinegar is indigenous to this country and it may have originated as a means of food preservation. Adobo is traditionally cooked in small clay pots and served with steamed rice.

SERVES 8

INGREDIENTS

chicken thighs (bone in, skin on)	8
soy sauce	¼ cup
large cloves garlic (chopped)	10
Filipino palm vinegar / white vinegar	1 ¼ cup
canned whole tomatoes (with the juices)	1 cup
bay leaves (broken)	2
freshly ground black pepper	1 tbsp.
medium onions (peeled and thinly sliced)	2
scallions (thinly sliced)	2
Extra virgin olive oil	

DIRECTIONS

1. Create a marinade by combining the vinegar, bay leaves, soy sauce, garlic, black pepper, and tomatoes in a large glass bowl.

2. Submerge the chicken thighs in the marinade.

3. Cover the bowl and refrigerate for about eighteen (18:00) to twenty-four (24:00) hours.

4. Transfer the chicken thighs and the marinade to a heavy 4–quart pot.

5. Place the pot on the stove and bring to a gentle boil.

6. Cover the pot and allow the chicken to simmer in the marinade for about twenty-five (0:25) minutes.

7. Uncover the pot and use a pair of tongs to remove the chicken thighs from the marinade.

8. Set the chicken thighs aside on a plate.

9. Skim off any fat from the marinade in the pot, increase the heat and allow the liquid to reduce to about half.

10. While the liquid is reducing, heat some olive oil in a large sauté pan.

11. Lay the chicken thighs skin side down first in the sauté pan and brown.

12. Flip the chicken pieces to brown on the next side.

13. Add the onions to the same pan as the chicken and sauté them.

14. When the chicken and onions become browned, transfer them to a large serving dish.

15. Pour the reduced marinade over the chicken thighs.

16. Garnish the Adobo with sliced scallions and serve with steamed rice.

NOTES

_____
_____
_____
_____
_____
_____
_____
_____
_____
_____

SINGAPORE – HAINANESE CHICKEN RICE

Hainanese Chicken Rice is considered to be one of Singapore's national dishes. This dish originated in Hainan, China but became popular only when immigrants brought it to Singapore. Hainanese Chicken Rice consists of a separate dish of fragrant rice which is served with the chicken, along with sauces made of chili peppers and ginger.

SERVES 4

INGREDIENTS

For the Rice

white rice (rinsed)	2 cups
piece ginger (thinly sliced)	1 (2cm)
clove garlic (crushed)	1
vegetable oil	1 tbsp.
chicken stock	3 cups

For the Chicken

whole chicken	1 (1.2kg)
pandan leaves	4
salt	3 tsp.
piece ginger (thinly sliced)	1 (5cm)
spring onions	3
sesame oil	2 tsp.
cucumber (peeled and sliced)	1
Water	
Coriander sprigs	

DIRECTIONS

For the Rice

1. Heat the vegetable oil in a large pot.

2. Sauté the garlic and ginger in the oil, then add the rice and cook for two (0:02) minutes.

3. Add three cups of chicken stock and stir to combine.

4. Reduce heat to a simmer and place a lid on the pot.

5. Cook for fifteen (0:15) minutes until the liquid has absorbed.

6. Turn off the heat and let it stand for ten (0:10) minutes with the lid.

For the Chicken

1. Bring 8 cups of water to a boil.

2. Flavor the water by adding a teaspoon of salt and the pandan leaves.

3. Rub the rest of the salt over the chicken and place the ginger and green onions into the body cavity.

4. Place the chicken, breast side down, into the pot of boiling water and cover with a tight-fitting lid.

5. Cook the chicken for forty-five (0:45) minutes.

6. Turn off the heat and let stand for one (1:00) hour to allow the meat to continue cooking in the residual heat.

7. Uncover the pot, remove the chicken, and place it in a large container of iced water for five (0:05) minutes.

8. Remove the chicken and drain well, then pat dry with paper towels.

9. Remove the ginger and green onions from the chicken.

10. Lightly brush the chicken with sesame oil.

11. Use a knife to cut the chicken into pieces and then place on a serving platter.

12. Garnish with cucumber slices and sprigs of coriander.

13. Serve the chicken with the rice, along with an assortment of spicy sauces.

SOUTH KOREA – BIBIMBAP

Bibimbap is a favorite meal in South Korea. It is a bowl of cooked rice topped with an assortment of sautéed vegetables and sliced meat or sometimes a fried egg. Traditionally, it was eaten on the eve of the Lunar New Year and was thought to have been first prepared by Korean farmers.

SERVES 4

INGREDIENTS

medium grain rice	2 cups
large cucumber (sliced thinly into strips)	1
carrots (julienned)	2
parboiled bean sprouts	1 ½ cups
shiitake mushrooms (sliced)	4
zucchini (sliced thinly into strips)	1
sesame oil	2 tbsp.
spinach (parboiled)	1 ½ cups
cooked sliced beef/pork	½ lb.
fried eggs (topping)	4
Sesame seeds	
Salt	

DIRECTIONS

1. Cook the rice, then set aside.

2. Soak the cucumber strips in salted water for twenty (0:20) minutes, then drain and set aside.

3. Season the parboiled spinach with sesame seeds, one teaspoon of salt and two teaspoons of sesame oil, then set aside.

4. Season the parboiled bean sprouts with sesame seeds, one teaspoon of salt and two teaspoons of sesame oil, then set aside.

5. In a skillet, sauté the carrots with a dash of salt until tender.

6. Remove the carrots from the pan and set aside.

7. Sauté the mushrooms in the skillet with a dash of salt until tender.

8. Remove the mushrooms from the pan and set aside.

9. Next, sauté the zucchini strips with a dash of salt until tender.

10. Remove the strips from the pan and set aside.

11. Put the bibimbap together by first dividing the cooked rice into serving bowls.

12. Arrange the vegetables around the rice in each bowl.

13. Top with the cooked meat and place the fried egg in the center.

14. Serve with sesame oil and red pepper paste (kochujang) for additional flavor.

NOTES

_____
_____
_____
_____
_____
_____
_____
_____
_____
_____
_____
_____
_____
_____
_____
_____

SRI LANKA – RICE AND CURRY

Rice is the main staple in Sri Lankan cuisine. It is eaten either boiled or steamed. Rice is typically eaten with vegetable, meat or fish curries. Sri Lankan curries are spicy and infused with the characteristic flavors of turmeric and coconut milk.

SERVES 4–5

INGREDIENTS

rice (rinsed)	2 cups
vegetable oil	2 tbsp.
turmeric powder	¼ tsp.
cloves garlic (minced)	4
fresh curry leaves	5
cinnamon stick	1
runner beans (strings removed)	300 g
garam masala	1 tsp.
whole dried chili pepper	1
cloves	4
can (400g) coconut milk	1
curry powder	1 tbsp.
black mustard seeds	2 tsp.
small onion (peeled and chopped)	1
finger ginger root (peeled and roughly chopped)	1
lime (halved and juiced)	1
chopped coriander leaves	1 tbsp.
Salt	

DIRECTIONS

1. Boil the rice in a saucepan of salted water until tender.

2. Drain and set the cooked rice aside.

3. Make a seasoning paste by blending the onion, ginger, turmeric, garlic, and salt with a teaspoon of oil.

4. Heat the remaining vegetable oil in a pan.

5. Sauté the curry leaves and mustard seeds in the oil until they begin to crackle.

6. Add the seasoning paste to the pan, mix well, and cook until it becomes sticky.

7. Stir in the curry powder, then add the coconut milk to the pan.

8. Add the cloves, chili pepper, and the cinnamon stick, then allow to simmer for a few minutes.

9. Slice the runner beans and add them to the pan.

10. Cook for fifteen (0:15) minutes until the beans are tender.

11. Add the lime juice to the bean curry.

12. Add the garam masala and stir well, then turn off the heat.

13. Add the coriander leaves to the bean curry and stir lightly.

14. Serve with the boiled.

NOTES

_____
_____
_____
_____
_____
_____
_____
_____
_____
_____
_____
_____
_____

TAIWAN – BEEF NOODLE SOUP

The national dish of Taiwan is Beef Noodle Soup. This flavorful and savory dish is found in almost every restaurant in the country. Every year a competition is held in Taipei to see who can cook the best Beef Noodle Soup. Although there are many variations of this dish due to different vegetables and seasonings, the method of preparation remains the same where the broth and noodles are cooked separately but are served together.

SERVES 6–8

INGREDIENTS

boneless beef shank (cut into 1–inch cubes)	2 lbs.
Asian wheat flour noodles	2 lbs.
quarts water	2 ½
light soy sauce	½ cup
dark soy sauce	¼ cup
whole star anise cloves	2
whole Sichuan peppercorns	1 tbsp.
Chinese rice wine	1 cup
Sichuan chili bean sauce	1 tbsp.
sugar	2 tbsp.
large plum tomato (roughly chopped)	1
small red chili peppers (roughly chopped)	2–3
cloves garlic (peeled and smashed)	6
slices fresh ginger root	6
canola/peanut oil	3 tbsp.
Fresh greens (baby bok choy / spinach leaves)	

DIRECTIONS

1. Heat 2 tablespoons of oil in a large Dutch oven pot.
2. Add the beef to the pot and cook until brown on all sides.
3. Transfer the cooked beef to a bowl and set aside.
4. Add the remaining oil to the pot.
5. When the oil is hot and shimmering, add the ginger, garlic, cloves, and chili peppers.
6. Stir and cook until fragrant, then add the tomato.
7. Cook for one (0:01) minute, then stir in the sugar and allow it to dissolve.
8. Add the chili bean sauce and cook until the mixture begins to bubble.
9. Return the browned beef to the pot and mix to coat the meat with the spices.
10. Add the rice wine and cook for one (0:01) minute.
11. Add the star anise cloves, peppercorns, both types of soy sauce and the water.
12. Bring to a boil, then reduce to a simmer and cover the pot.
13. Cook for two hours (2:00) and thirty (0:30) minutes until the beef is tender.
14. Use a pair of tongs to remove the beef from the broth and set it aside in a separate container.
15. Strain the broth through a colander or mesh strainer and discard the solids.
16. Return the broth to the pot and add the beef.
17. Add spinach, or baby bok choy leaves to the hot broth and allow them to wilt.
18. Boil the noodles according to package instructions.
19. Divide the cooked noodles into serving bowls.
20. Ladle the broth, greens and beef chunks over the noodles.
21. Serve immediately.

TAJIKISTAN – OSH

Tajikistan's national dish is Osh. Sometimes referred to as Plov. This meal is flavorful rice and meat pilaf. There are different variations to this dish. Locals tend to use the vegetables which are in season. Lamb is usually the meat used to make Osh, but beef used occasionally. Typically, Osh is shared with relatives and friends when the Muslim fast, Ramadan, ends.

SERVES 5–6

INGREDIENTS

lamb/beef (cubed)	1 kg
basmati rice (rinsed)	1 kg
carrots (peeled and julienned)	7–8
onions (peeled and sliced thinly)	2
cumin	1 tbsp.
head of garlic	1
vegetable oil	7 tbsp.
Salt	
Black pepper	
Water/meat stock	

DIRECTIONS

1. Heat the vegetable oil in a large pan.

2. Add the cubes of meat to the pan and fry them on all sides until brown.

3. Add all of the cooked batches back to the pan and add the onions.

4. Add the carrots and stir well.

5. Allow the meat and vegetables to cook together for about seven (0:07) minutes.

6. Season the meat and vegetables with salt, cumin, and black pepper.

7. Add enough water or meat stock to the pan so that the meat and vegetables are submerged.

8. Cover the pan and allow to simmer for forty (0:40) minutes over medium heat.

9. Add the rinsed rice to the pan.

10. Submerge the rice in 2cm of hot water.

11. Add salt to taste and stir.

12. Cook until the rice has absorbed the water and the grains are tender.

13. Press the whole garlic into the rice.

14. Use a wooden stick to make a few holes in the pilaf, then cover and allow to steam for twenty (0:20) minutes over low heat.

15. Serve hot.

NOTES

_____
_____
_____
_____
_____
_____
_____
_____
_____
_____
_____
_____
_____
_____
_____
_____
_____
_____
_____

THAILAND – PAD THAI

Pad Thai is a stir fry noodle dish which is iconic in Thai cuisine. The dish originated during World War II when a rice shortage forced the government to promote noodles as a substitute. Today, rice noodles are used in the dish. Originally, pork was not used in Pad Thai because it was considered to be a Chinese meat.

SERVES 6

INGREDIENTS

dried rice noodles	12 oz.
eggs (beaten)	4
distilled white vinegar	½ cup
fish sauce	¼ cup
salt	1 ½ tsp.
peanuts (coarsely ground)	1 cup
bean sprouts	2 cups
tamarind paste	2 tbsp.
vegetable oil	1 tbsp.
chives (chopped)	½ cup
paprika	1 tbsp.
boneless, skinless chicken breasts (sliced into strips)	2
lime (cut into wedges)	1
minced garlic	1 ½ tsp.
White sugar	

DIRECTIONS

1. Soak the rice noodles in a bowl of water for about one (1:00) hour.

2. Drain and set aside.

3. Add ½ a cup of white sugar to a saucepan.

4. Add the fish sauce, vinegar and tamarind paste to the sugar, then whisk them all together over medium heat.

5. Bring to a simmer, then remove from the heat and set aside.

6. Heat one tablespoon of oil in a clean wok, then add the chicken strips and cook for about seven (0:07) minutes.

7. Remove the chicken from the heat when cooked and set aside.

8. Heat another tablespoon of oil in the wok and sauté the minced garlic in the oil.

9. Add the eggs and scramble them.

10. Add the cooked eggs to the chicken strips and rice noodles.

11. Toss to combine.

12. Add the tamarind sauce mixture and 1 ½ tablespoon of white sugar.

13. Season the Pad Thai with salt and toss to combine once more.

14. Cook for about five (0:05) minutes until the noodles are tender.

15. Stir in the peanuts and cook for an additional two (0:02) minutes.

16. Transfer the Pad Thai to a serving dish.

17. Garnish with bean sprouts, chives, lime wedges, and paprika.

18. Serve immediately.

NOTES

_____
_____
_____
_____
_____
_____
_____
_____
_____

TURKMENISTAN – PALAW

Palaw is a Turkmen rice pilaf which traditionnally contains lamb meat since sheep farming is popular. Modern Palaw is made with turkey or chicken. It is a simple dish that is normally served at dinner time, along with bread and vegetables. Palaw is typically eaten with the hands. Palaw is very popular in Turkmenistan and it is considered to be the national dish of the country.

SERVES 8

INGREDIENTS

lamb / chicken / turkey (cut into bite sized pieces)	1 kg.
salt	2 tbsp.
basmati rice	4 ½ cups
water	5 ½ cups
large carrots (julienned)	5
large onion (peeled and sliced)	1
vegetable oil/cotton oil	1 1/5 cups
Fresh herbs for garnish	

DIRECTIONS

1. Season the meat with a tablespoon of salt by mixing them in a large bowl.

2. Heat the oil in a large pot over medium-high heat.

3. Fry the meat in batches until golden brown on all sides.

4. Return all of the batches to the pot and add the sliced onions.

5. When the onions are soft, add the carrots to the pot and stir well.

6. Cook the meat and vegetables for five (0:05) minutes.

7. Add the water to the pot and cook for another five (0:05) minutes.

8. Add the salt to the pot and bring to a boil.

9. Add the basmati rice to the pot and stir well.

10. When the rice begins to absorb the liquid, reduce the heat, and cover the pot.

11. Allow the Palaw to simmer for thirty (0:30) minutes, stirring occasionally.

12. Turn off the heat and transfer the Palaw to a serving dish.

13. Garnish with fresh herbs if desired, then serve.

NOTES

UZBEKISTAN – OSH

Osh is an iconic rice pilaf dish in Uzbekistan. It has been around for centuries. In fact, Osh dates back to the 10th and 11th centuries where it was served on special occasions, especially weddings. It was traditionally served on top of round flatbreads. Osh is cooked in a qozon which is a special Uzbek cauldron used to cook pilaf. In Uzbekistan, men are the ones who typically cook Osh. It is served with vegetable salad and green tea.

SERVES 4

INGREDIENTS

fresh lamb leg steaks (cut into bite-sized cubes)	2 lbs.
medium onions (peeled and thinly sliced)	2
medium carrots (julienned)	5
basmati rice	3 ½ cups
head of garlic (unpeeled)	1
pitted dates (chopped)	1 cup
grapeseed oil	1 cup
boiling water	8 cups
pitted Kalamata olives	1 cup
ground cumin	2 tsp.
salt	3 tsp.
pinch black pepper	1
Chopped cilantro leaves (for garnish)	

DIRECTIONS

1. Toss the lamb meat with a generous amount of salt and pepper, then set aside.
2. Heat the oil in a large, non−stick pot, then fry the lamb in batches until brown on all sides.
3. Return all of the browned lambs to the pot, then add the onions.
4. Sprinkle in a pinch of the cumin, half of the salt and the black pepper.
5. Mix the Ingredients and cook until the onions turn golden brown.
6. Add the carrots to the pot.
7. Sprinkle in the rest of the salt and cumin.
8. Stir occasionally while the vegetables cook.
9. When the carrots have softened, reduce the heat and pour in 8 cups of boiling water.
10. Allow the Osh to simmer but do not bring to a boil.
11. Place the whole head of garlic into the pot and let it simmer for one (1:00) hour.
12. Remove the head of garlic and set it aside.
13. Rinse and drain the rice about four times to remove some of the starch.
14. Mix the chopped dates into the rice and add it to the pot.
15. Spread the rice evenly over the meat and vegetables, adding water only if the liquid is less than an inch below the rice.
16. Tuck the head of garlic back into the rice but do not stir.
17. When the rice has absorbed most of the liquid, use a slotted spoon to transfer the rice to a serving platter.
18. Place the head of garlic on top of the rice.
19. Increase the heat and allow the meat and vegetables to continue cooking.
20. When the broth has thickened, transfer the meat and vegetables to the platter of rice.
21. Sprinkle the olives over the Osh.
22. Garnish with chopped cilantro leaves.
23. Serve the Osh with warm flatbreads and a salad.

VIETNAM – PHO

Vietnamese beef noodle soup is called Pho. Pho has both French and Chinese origins. Authentic pho is simmered for hours to maximize the flavors. In Vietnam, Pho is typically a breakfast dish.

SERVES 4

INGREDIENTS

beef soup bones	4 lbs.
beef top sirloin (thinly sliced)	1 ½ lb.
package dried rice noodles	1 (8 oz.)
onion (unpeeled, halved)	1
slices fresh ginger	5
chopped cilantro leaves	½ cup
chopped green onions	1 tbsp.
pods star anise	2
bean sprouts	1 ½ cups
fish sauce	2 ½ tbsp.
hoisin sauce	¼ cup
chili–garlic sauce	¼ cup
bunch Thai basil	1
lime (quartered)	1
quarts water	4
salt	1 tbsp.

DIRECTIONS

1. Preheat the oven to 425 degrees F°.
2. Place the beef bones on a baking sheet, then roast for one (1:00) hour in the oven until brown.
3. Place the onion in a separate baking sheet and bake for forty-five (0:45) minutes until soft and black.
4. Transfer the onion and roasted beef bones to a large stockpot.
5. Add the fish sauce, salt, star anise, and ginger slices to the pot.
6. Pour in the water.
7. Bring the soup to a boil, then reduce the heat.
8. Let the soup simmer for six (6:00) to ten (10:00) hours over low heat.
9. Use a colander or strainer to strain the broth into a saucepan, then set aside.
10. Soak the rice noodles in a bowl of water for about one (1:00) hour.
11. Transfer the soaked noodles to a pot of boiling water for one (0:01) minute.
12. Divide the noodles into four portions and place into serving bowls.
13. Top the noodles with the beef sirloin slices, cilantro leaves, and green onions.
14. Bring the strained broth to a simmer, then pour it over each serving of noodles.
15. Stir and allow the bowls of Pho to rest for two (0:02) minutes until the beef slices are partially cooked and no longer pink.
16. Serve the Pho immediately with hoisin sauce, chili–garlic sauce, lime chunks, and Thai basil.

NOTES

_____
_____
_____
_____
_____
_____
_____
_____
_____
_____
_____
_____
_____
_____

Afghanistan – Quaboli Palaw

Quaboli Palaw is a favorite meal in Afghanistan. It is a mixed rice dish containing flavorful lamb or chicken chunks, carrot strips, raisins, and eastern spices. Afghans traditionally topped Quaboli Palaw with chopped almonds or pistachios.

SERVES 4

INGREDIENTS

long grained rice	2 cups
medium onion (diced)	1
of vegetable oil	4oz
of water	2 cups
of saffron powder	¼ tsp.
large carrots (sliced into thin strips)	2
chicken or 1 ½ lamb meat (sliced into bite-sized pieces)	1
ounces raisins or sultanas	4
of cumin	1 tsp.
of cinnamon	1 tsp.
brown sugar	1 tsp.
of ground cardamom	1 tsp.
almonds/pistachios (finely chopped)	¼ cup
Salt	

DIRECTIONS

1. Sauté the diced onion in vegetable oil until it begins to caramelize.

2. Add the chicken or lamb pieces and stir fry until lightly browned.

3. Add two cups of water to the pot and add a tsp — each of salt, cumin, ground cardamom, cinnamon and ¼ tsp. of saffron powder.

4. Cover the pot and allow the meat to simmer in this broth for about an hour or until the meat becomes tender.

5. Remove the meat from the pot and set aside separately.

6. Add two cups of rice to the broth and cook until the rice grains are tender.

7. Sauté the carrot strips in a mixture of ¼ cup vegetable oil and one tsp. of sugar until the carrots become lightly browned.

8. Remove the carrot pieces and cook the sultanas or raisins in the oil until they become swollen.

9. Mix the cooked rice, carrot strips, raisins, and meat and place into a greased casserole dish.

10. Cover the dish with foil and bake at 300°F° for approximately 45 minutes.

11. After plating, sprinkle chopped almonds or pistachios on the top and enjoy Quaboli Palaw.

NOTES

_____
_____
_____
_____
_____
_____
_____
_____
_____
_____
_____
_____

Algeria –Saffron & Raisin Couscous

Couscous originated in Northern Africa is considered to be the national dish of Algeria. These tiny balls of semolina are cooked in a variety of traditional ways as it is a staple food in this country. One couscous dish which is widely popular in Algeria is couscous with saffron, raisins and fresh mint.

SERVES 6

INGREDIENTS

couscous	1 ½ cups
fresh mint leaves	2 ¼ tbsp.
extra virgin olive oil	¾ tsp.
A dash of saffron powder or a few saffron threads	
Raisins	
A dash of salt	
water	1 ½ cups

DIRECTIONS

1. Pour 1 ½ cups of water into a saucepan and bring to a boil.

2. Add a dash of saffron powder or a few threads of saffron to the water.

3. Turn off the heat, place a lid over the saucepan and let the saffron infused hot water stand for about thirty minutes. The water will turn yellow.

4. Turn the heat back on under the saucepan and bring to a boil.

5. Add the 1 ½ cups of couscous, olive oil, salt and the desired amount of raisins.

6. Stir the mixture and then turn off the heat. Place a lid over the saucepan and let the mixture stand for another thirty minutes.

7. Use a fork to separate the grains of couscous as some may stick to each other. (This process is called 'fluffing' and helps the couscous mixture to attain a very light consistency.)

8. Taste the couscous and add more seasonings if desired.

9. Sprinkle in the finely chopped mint leaves to the couscous and stir well.

10. Serve warm or at room temperature. Couscous prepared in this way can be eaten with roasted vegetables, Mediterranean meats, or yogurt. It can also be served with bread and roasted fish.

NOTES

_____
_____
_____
_____
_____
_____
_____
_____
_____
_____
_____
_____
_____
_____
_____
_____
_____
_____
_____
_____

Azerbaijan –Yapaq Dolmasi

Yapaq Dolmasi literally means 'stuffed vine leaves.' This national dish of Azerbaijan is prepared by stuffing grape leaves with minced meat, fresh seasonings and rice. It is traditionally eaten with garlic yogurt.

SERVES 10

INGREDIENTS

lamb meat (minced)	2 lbs.
grape leaves	16 Oz.
cloves garlic (minced)	2
butter	½ cup
uncooked basmati rice	2 cups
onions (minced)	2
fresh dill (finely chopped)	½ cup
fresh cilantro (finely chopped)	½ cup
fresh parsley (finely chopped)	½ cup
plain yogurt	½ cup
Salt	
Pepper	

DIRECTIONS

1. Rinse the uncooked basmati rice with water. Drain.

2. Parboil the rice and set aside to cool in a large bowl.

3. Spoon ½ cup of butter into a hot pan, add the minced onions and sauté until soft. Add the cooked onions to the rice, then add the ground meat, dill, cilantro, and parsley. Add the salt and pepper.

4. Then mix using the hands. Set aside.

5. Fill a large pot with water and blanch the grape leaves for about three minutes to make them more pliable.

6. Cut and remove hard stems or veins.

7. Place a large grape leaf on a board, its vein side up and shiny side down. Place an adequate amount of filling on the stem end of the leaf. Roll the leaf and meat package tightly (stuffed leaves).

8. Arrange the dolmas at the base of a non–stick pan or Dutch oven pot which has been greased. Be sure to set them seam side down to prevent it from coming loose during cooking.

9. Fill the pot with water, and boil on low heat for about 45 minutes to an hour.

10. Mix ½ a cup of yogurt and 2 cloves of minced garlic.

11. Serve the warm Yapaq Dolmasi with the garlic yogurt.

NOTES

_____
_____
_____
_____
_____
_____
_____
_____
_____
_____
_____
_____
_____
_____
_____
_____
_____
_____
_____
_____
_____
_____
_____

Bahrain– Machboos

Machboos is a lunch meal that is considered to be Bahrain's national dish. It is a chicken and rice dish that is fragrant and spicy. Two distinct Ingredients of this dish is baharat and loomi. Baharat is a powdered blend of spices that is popular in Arab cuisine. Loomi are limes from Oman that have been boiled and sundried.

SERVES 4

INGREDIENTS

chicken (a mix of thigh, breast, legs, and wings)	3 lbs.
large tomatoes (diced)	2
basmati rice	2 cups
large onions (diced)	2
ghee / unsalted butter	3 tbsp.
Baharat spices	1 tbsp.
saffron powder	1 tsp.
green chili pepper (deseeded and diced)	1
vegetable oil	2 tbsp.
ginger (grated)	1 tbsp.
cloves garlic (sliced)	5
dried Oman limes (Loomi)	2–3
green cardamom pods	5
stick cinnamon (2 inches)	1
ground clove	1/8 tsp.
chicken stock	2 ½ cups
salt	2 ½ tsp.
cilantro (chopped)	3 tbsp.
parsley (finely chopped)	2 tbsp.
Rosewater (optional)	

DIRECTIONS

1. Pour the oil in a large Dutch oven pot and heat to medium-high. Fry the chicken until the skin becomes golden brown and crispy. Remove the chicken from the pot and set aside.

2. Add the ghee to the same pot and reduce the heat. Sauté the onions until they caramelize. Add the diced chili pepper, garlic, and ginger and after two minutes, add the Baharat spice blend and saffron powder. Stir in the chicken after a minute. Add the tomatoes, cardamom pods, cinnamon, ground cloves, and salt. Pierce the tough exterior of the limes with a fork and add them to the pot. Pour in the chicken stock, stir and bring to a boil. Cover the pot, reduce the heat and simmer for an hour.

3. Soak the basmati rice for fifteen minutes in water. Drain and rinse. Add the rice to the pot together with the parsley and cilantro. Stir well. Cover and simmer for an additional fifteen to twenty minutes till the rice is tender.

4. After plating the dish, sprinkle a few drops of rosewater over it. Serve Machboos with creamy yogurt raita and a fresh green salad.

NOTES

_____
_____
_____
_____
_____
_____
_____
_____
_____
_____
_____
_____
_____
_____
_____

Egypt–Falafel

Egyptian falafel refers to fried croquettes made mainly of fava beans. This traditional Egyptian dish is prepared in homes and also sold as street food. It is a vegetarian dish that is versatile enough to be eaten alone or in pita bread sandwiches, usually accompanied by yogurt and tahini based sauces. Its true origin is unknown but it is widely speculated that falafel was first prepared in the times of the Pharaohs.

SERVES 4–6

INGREDIENTS

dried fava beans	250 g
cloves garlic (crushed)	3
spring onions (finely diced)	5
gram flour	1 tsp.
leek (finely chopped)	½
bicarbonate soda	½ tsp.
coriander leaves (chopped)	1 tbsp.
parsley (chopped)	1 tbsp.
cumin powder	1 tsp.
dash cayenne pepper	1
Salt	
Black pepper	
Sesame seeds	
Sunflower/rapeseed oil for frying	

DIRECTIONS

1. Soak the fava beans overnight in water.

2. Drain using a sieve or colander.

3. Put the beans into a food processor and add the garlic, onions, salt, flour, leek, bicarbonate soda, cumin, black pepper, cayenne pepper, coriander, and parsley leaves.

4. Mince into a rough paste and set it out onto a flat surface.

5. Separate the thick paste into 12 – 16 lumps.

6. Form each lump into small croquettes or balls.

7. Sprinkle sesame seeds over each falafel.

8. Refrigerate the falafel for ten (0:10) minutes.

9. Fill a pan with the sunflower or rapeseed oil to a depth of about 3 cm.

10. Heat the oil and fry the falafel for about three (0:03) minutes per side.

11. Flip the falafel with a slotted spoon or spatula and ensure all sides cooked evenly.

12. Remove the falafel from the oil and place on paper towels.

13. Serve the falafel with a minty yogurt sauce or wrap it in a pita pocket.

NOTES

_____
_____
_____
_____
_____
_____
_____
_____
_____
_____
_____
_____
_____
_____
_____
_____
_____

Iran – Chelo Kebab

Iran's national dish Chelo Kebab consists of mouthwatering skewered meat cubes and fragrant, buttery basmati rice.

SERVES 6

INGREDIENTS

For the Kebabs

boneless lamb (cut into 1–inch cubes)	1 ½ lb.
tiny cherry tomatoes	18
black pepper	¼ tsp.
salt	¼ tsp.
cloves garlic (chopped)	2
onions (peeled and coarsely chopped)	2
Fresh lemon juice	3 tbsps.
Olive oil	3 tbsps.
Cooking spray	

For the Rice

basmati rice	1 ½ cups
water	6 cups
Salt	2 tsps.
saffron threads (chopped)	¼ tsp.
olive oil	1 tbsp.
Green onions (finely chopped)	2 tbsps.
Fresh mint (finely chopped)	2 tbsps.
Cilantro leaves (finely chopped)	2 tbsps.
Unsalted butter	3 tbsps.
lemon wedges	6

DIRECTIONS

For the Kebabs

1. Puree the onions and garlic, then mix with lemon juice, salt, pepper and oil to form a marinade.

2. Mix the lamb cubes and marinade in a resealable plastic bag, chill for eight (8:00) hours in the refrigerator.

3. Preheat the grill or broiler.

4. Remove the meat from the marinade and fit onto metal or wooden skewers.

5. Skewer the tomatoes on separate kebab sticks.

6. Coat grill rack or broiler pan with cooking spray and lay the kebabs on top of it.

7. Cook the lamb kebabs for about twelve (0:12) minutes until done, flipping occasionally.

8. Cook the tomato kebabs for about five (0:05) minutes, flipping occasionally.

For the Rice

1. Rinse the rice under running water and drain.

2. Boil six cups of water in a saucepan and season with two teaspoons of salt.

3. Add the rice and let it boil for about seven (0: 07) minutes, stirring occasionally.

4. Drain the cooked rice and reserve the cooking liquid.

5. In a hot skillet, combine two tablespoons of the cooking liquid, two tablespoons butter, oil, and saffron.

6. Gradually add one-third of the rice and spread evenly on the base of the skillet.

7. Add the remaining rice, spread evenly but do not stir.

8. Top the rice with the remaining butter.

9. Place a dish towel over the pan and cover with the lid.

10. Cook on high heat for about three (0:03) minutes until rice is tender and a crisp, brown layer forms at the base of the pan.

11. Turn off the heat, remove lid and towel, then invert the pan onto a serving platter.

12. Arrange the lamb and tomato skewers on the platter and top with the lemon wedges, chopped green onions, cilantro, and thyme.

13. Serve hot.

Iraq – Samak Masgouf

The most popular fish dish in Iraq is Samak Masgouf, made with white fish. Usually, carp caught from the river Tigris. Masgouf refers to the method of cooking the fish; traditionally, the fish is butterflied and skewered over a fire, but oven baking is just as effective.

SERVES 1

INGREDIENTS

fresh white fish (weighing approx. 2 lbs.)	1
onions (peeled and thinly sliced)	2
tomatoes (finely diced)	2
cloves garlic (minced)	3
fresh lemon juice	½ cup
curry powder	1 tsp.
parsley (finely chopped)	½ cup
Vegetable oil	2 tbsps.
Tomato paste	3 tbsps.
dried limes	2
Salt	
Pepper	
Tamarind	

DIRECTIONS

1. Gut and clean the fish; remove the head if desired.

2. Rinse the fish thoroughly, then butterfly and spread open on a tray.

3. Rub the fish liberally with salt and lemon juice, then set aside.

4. Heat the oil in a skillet and sauté the onions until translucent.

5. Add the salt, black pepper, and the minced garlic.

6. Cook for two (0:02) minutes, then cut the dried limes in halves and add the pulp to the skillet.

7. Stir in the tomato paste, lemon juice, curry powder, and oil.

8. Cook for five (0:05) minutes until the sauce thickens and add tamarind for extra flavor.

9. Skewer and roast the fish on an open flame until cooked, then place on a platter and smother in the sauce (Traditional method).

10. Alternatively, half of the sauce can be poured onto the fish and baked in a greased pan for twenty (0:20) minutes, then the rest of the sauce can be added before broiling for an additional ten (0:10) minutes (Modern method).

11. After the fish is cooked and plated, garnish with the chopped tomatoes and parsley if desired.

12. Serve Samak Masgouf warm.

NOTES

_____
_____
_____
_____
_____
_____
_____
_____
_____
_____
_____
_____
_____
_____
_____
_____
_____

Israel – Falafel

Israel's national dish Falafel is essentially a fried tasty chickpea ball. It is the ideal filling for pita sandwiches. The origin of the dish is unknown but it has existed for a long time in Israel and can be bought as street food. It is a common dish which Muslim Israelis use to break their sunset fast.

YIELDS 20

INGREDIENTS

dried chickpeas	1 ¼ cups
chopped onion	½ cup
cloves garlic (peeled)	2
flour	1 ½ cups
Water	4 tbsps.
vegetable oil	3 cups
sesame seeds	½ cup
salt	1 tsp.
baking powder	½ tsp.
ground coriander	½ tsp
ground cumin	1 tsp.
chili flakes	¼ tsp.
black pepper	½ tsp.
Chopped parsley leaves	3 tbsps.

DIRECTIONS

1. Soak the dried chickpeas in a bowl of water overnight.

2. Transfer the soaked chickpeas into a food processor and combine with onion, garlic cloves, and parsley leaves.

3. Pulse together to form a thick paste.

4. Add the salt, baking powder, flour.

5. Add the dried chili flakes, black pepper, cumin, and coriander together with three tablespoons of water. Blend, add an extra tablespoon of water if needed.

6. Transfer the chickpea paste from the food processor into a large bowl.

7. Pour the oil into a heavy pan and heat until hot.

8. Dampen hands and make small, compact balls from the paste, each about the size of a whole walnut.

9. Fry the balls in batches until golden brown, turning occasionally.

10. Use a slotted spoon to remove them from the pan.

11. Place the sesame seeds onto a shallow dish and roll each ball onto it so that the seeds stick to it.

12. Place the falafel balls onto a paper towel so excess oil can be absorbed.

13. Serve on pita bread with vegetables and tahini sauce.

NOTES

_____
_____
_____
_____
_____
_____
_____
_____
_____
_____
_____
_____
_____
_____
_____
_____
_____

Jordan – Mansaf

Mansaf is a Bedouin meal consisting of meat flavored in spices and yogurt. Traditionally, it is eaten amongst large families and social groups in Jordan. Mansaf is served with steamed rice and khubz, a type of flatbread.

SERVES 6–8

INGREDIENTS

plain Greek yogurt	4 cups
lean lamb (cut into 1 ½ inch cubes)	2 lbs.
steamed Jasmine / Basmati rice	3 cups
clarified butter/ghee	½ cup
pepper	1 tsp.
medium onion (finely diced)	1
egg (yolk removed)	1
coriander	½ tsp.
cumin	1 ½ tsp.
paprika	½ tsp.
cardamom	¼ tsp
pine nuts	½ cup
whole almond nuts (blanched)	½ cup
loaves pita bread/khubz	4–6
Salt	
Black pepper	
Parsley leaves (chopped)	

DIRECTIONS

1. Rinse the lamb cubes in water, then soak in a covered container of water for about six (6:00) hours in the refrigerator.

2. Pat the meat dry after removing from the water.

3. In a heavy skillet, melt ¼ cup of the clarified butter, then add the meat and cook for twenty (0:20) minutes until brown on all sides.

4. Season the meat with black pepper and salt, then add water to cover the meat.

5. Reduce the heat and cook for one (1:00) hour.

6. Add the diced onions to the meat, stir well and let it cook together for thirty (0:30) minutes.

7. In a separate saucepan, whisk the yogurt on medium heat till it liquefies.

8. Add a ½ teaspoon of salt and whisk in the egg white.

9. Bring the mixture to a boil, stirring continuously, then reduce the heat and allow it to simmer uncovered for about ten (0:10) minutes.

10. Pour the yogurt mixture into the simmering meat and add the coriander, cumin, pepper, paprika, and cardamom.

11. Stir together and cook for an additional fifteen (0:15) minutes, then turn off the heat.

12. In a separate frying pan, melt two tablespoons of clarified butter and sauté the almonds for five (0:05) minutes, then add the pine nuts and cook for three (0:03) minutes.

13. Turn off the heat and set the nuts aside.

14. Melt the remaining clarified butter and brush over the khubz.

15. Top with steamed rice and the mansaf, then pour the buttery nuts over the meat.

16. Garnish with chopped parsley and serve.

NOTES

_____

_____

_____

_____

_____

_____

_____

Kuwait – Machboos

Machboos is a rice and meat dish first prepared by the Bedouin people. The dish is very popular in Kuwait. Lamb is the meat of choice in this dish.

SERVES 6

INGREDIENTS

lamb (cut into cubes)	1 kg
water	2 ½ L
small onion (quartered)	1
onions (peeled and diced)	2
stick cinnamon	1
peppercorns	1 tsp.
cloves	½ tsp.
pieces cardamom	5
bay leaves	2
salt	1 ½ tbsp.
ground cinnamon	¼ tsp.
saffron powder	¼ tsp.
pinch minced ginger	1
saffron threads	¼ tsp.
lemon juice	2 tbsp.
oil	2 tbsp.
ground cumin	¼ tsp.
Basmati rice	1 kg.
sugar	½ tsp.
raisins (soaked overnight)	75 g
yellow split peas	75 g
Ground Cloves	
Black pepper	

DIRECTIONS

1. Place the meat cubes in a pot of water, all whole spices, salt, and the onion.
2. Turn on the heat and let the water come to a boil, then remove the scum that forms on the surface of the water.
3. Cover the pot, reduce the heat, and let the meat boil for ninety (0:90) minutes.
4. In a separate saucepan, boil the split peas in salted water for about twenty (0:20) minutes until tender.
5. Drain the peas and set aside.
6. Sauté the diced onions in one tablespoon of oil until golden brown.
7. Reduce the heat and then add the soaked raisins, cinnamon, one tablespoon salt, cloves, black pepper, and sugar.
8. Mix well while cooking then turns off the heat after a few minutes and set aside.
9. When the lamb is finished boiling, drain in a colander, save the stock and discard the whole spices.
10. Preheat the oven to 200 degrees F°.
11. Mix the ground spices and rub over the meat cubes, then place the lamb in a baking dish.
12. In a small bowl, combine a little water, lemon juice, one tablespoon of oil, one tablespoon of the meat stock, and saffron threads.
13. Pour this over the meat, then cover the baking dish with aluminum foil and bake for fifteen (0:15) minutes.
14. Rinse the rice in water several times till the water runs clear; the last time, rinse the rice in water and one teaspoon of salt, then drain.
15. In a clean saucepan, add the meat stock to the cover the rice by two centimeters.
16. Cook the rice over medium-high heat for about twenty (0:20) minutes until the liquid has been absorbed, then turn off the heat and set aside.
17. Remove the meat from the oven and stir in the cooked raisin and split pea mixture.
18. Serve the meat with the cooked rice.

Lebanon – Kibbeh

Kibbeh is a popular dish in Lebanese cuisine. It is a stuffed meat croquette and usually made with minced lamb or beef and a specific type of cracked wheat. There are variations to the dish. Some kibbeh can be eaten raw.

SERVES 8

INGREDIENTS

ground lamb or beef	2 lbs.
bulghur cracked wheat	½ lb.
salt	1 ½ tsp.
pepper	1 ½ tsp.
allspice	1 tsp.
cumin	¼ tsp.
medium onions (one finely chopped, one roughly chopped)	2
toasted pine nuts	½ cup
olive oil	2 tbsp.
Vegetable oil	

DIRECTIONS

1. Place the cracked wheat into a bowl together with cold water, then soak for thirty (0:30) minutes.

2. Drain the water, then transfer to a cheesecloth and squeeze the excess water out of the wheat.

3. Put the wheat into a food processor and add half of the ground meat, the roughly chopped onion, one teaspoon of salt and one teaspoon of pepper.

4. Combine and add an ice cube if necessary.

5. When a dough-like consistency achieved, transfer the mixture to a bowl, cover it, and set aside.

6. Begin preparing the kibbeh stuffing by sautéing the pine nuts and finely chopped onion in olive oil.

7. Add the remaining half of the ground meat and the cumin, allspice, salt, and pepper.

8. Break up the minced meat with a spatula and mix well with the seasoning while cooking.

9. Turn off the heat when the meat is lightly browned and allow it to cool for ten (0:10) minutes.

10. Pick up an egg-sized amount of the cracked wheat dough and form into a ball with the fingers.

11. Make a hole in the middle of the ball and add some of the stuffing.

12. Seal the top by pinching the dough together and shape into a ball or football.

13. After stuffing the dough, fry them in vegetable oil on high heat for ten (0:10) minutes or until golden brown.

14. Transfer to paper towels, then place on a serving platter.

15. Serve kibbeh with tahini sauce.

NOTES

_____
_____
_____
_____
_____
_____
_____
_____
_____
_____
_____

Libya – Usban

Libya's national dish Usban is a type of traditional sausage. Usban is made of rice, herbs and lamb meat which are stuffed into sausage casings or sheep intestines. It is a side dish which is served with couscous or rice on special occasions.

YIELDS 5–6 sausages

INGREDIENTS

sheep intestine sausage casings (each approximately 30 cm long)	5–6
sheep liver and heart (finely diced)	500 g
ground lamb meat	250 g
short grain rice	1 ½ cup
tomato paste	2 tbsp.
olive oil	½ cup
medium tomatoes (finely chopped)	2
finely chopped chives	3 cups
finely chopped parsley leaves	4 cups
finely chopped coriander leaves	3 cups
finely chopped basil leaves	3 cups
finely chopped mint leaves	1 cup
chili peppers (finely diced)	2
black pepper	1 tbsp.
dried mint	1 tbsp.
ground ginger	1 tbsp.
cayenne pepper	1 tbsp.
salt	1 tbsp.
turmeric powder	1 tbsp.
Lemon juice	
Vegetable oil for frying	

DIRECTIONS

1. Wash the sausage casings thoroughly several times with water.

2. Place the casings in a bowl and sprinkle lemon juice over them, then let sit for ten (0:10) minutes).

3. Soak the rice in water for fifteen (0:15) minutes, then drain and set aside.

4. Prepare the sausage stuffing by first combining the ground lamb meat and finely chopped heart and liver with olive oil and tomato paste in a large bowl.

5. Mix well, then add salt, black pepper, cayenne pepper, dried mint, and turmeric powder.

6. Add the chopped basil, coriander, mint, parsley and chives to the seasoned meat.

7. Add the diced tomatoes, ground ginger, and chili peppers next.

8. Spoon the rice into the meat stuffing and mix.

9. Stuff the sausage casings with the meat and rice mixture but leave enough space for the rice to expand when cooking.

10. Tie both ends of the casing to secure the stuffing inside.

11. Use a needle to prick the sausages before cooking.

12. Place the sausages in a large pot of boiling water, ensuring they are completely submerged.

13. Add additional salt to the water as well as a dash of turmeric and cayenne pepper.

14. Boil the sausages for one (1:00) hour; during this time prick any sausage that floats.

15. After boiling, remove the Usban from the water and fry them in vegetable oil until golden brown.

16. Slice and serve with couscous or rice.

Morocco – Tagine

In Morocco, Tagine refers to two things; slow-cooked meat or vegetables and the traditional clay or ceramic cooking pot which the meal is cooked in. As a meal, Tagine is the national dish of Morocco, and it is usually a rich stew of chicken or lamb cooked together with fruit, spices, and vegetables. Eat the Tagine is with rice or pitta bread.

SERVES 6

INGREDIENTS

large boneless chicken breasts (diced)	6
flour / 2 tbsp. corn flour	1 tbsp.
large onions (sliced)	2
cloves garlic (finely chopped)	3–4
olive oil	1–2 tbsp.
inch fresh ginger root (finely chopped)	1
dried apricots	6 oz.
tomato paste	2 tbsp.
cans whole tomatoes (diced)	2 (14 oz.)
cans chickpeas	2 (14 oz.)
pint chicken stock	½
saffron powder	1 tsp.
ground coriander	1 tsp.
cumin powder	1 tsp.
ground cinnamon	1 tsp.
cayenne pepper	1 tsp.
honey	3 tbsp.
Salt	
Black Pepper	
Coriander leaves (roughly chopped)	

DIRECTIONS

1. Heat the olive oil in a large skillet and sauté the onions and garlic for eight (0:08) minutes.

2. Add the chicken stock to the skillet and gradually stir in the flour, ensuring there are no lumps.

3. Add the honey and the tomato paste and mix well.

4. Stir in salt and black pepper along with the cumin, saffron, coriander, cinnamon, and cayenne pepper.

5. Add the chopped ginger root.

6. Gently stir in the canned tomatoes.

7. Pour this spicy mix into a traditional tagine or slow cooker.

8. Place the chicken cubes and the canned chickpeas into the tagine or slow cooker and mix well.

9. Mix in the dried apricots.

10. If using a traditional tagine, cook over a gas stove or barbeque grill for about two (2:00) hours and thirty (0:30) minutes.

11. If using a slow cooker, then cook on high for three (3:00) hours and thirty (0:30) minutes.

12. After cooking, garnish with chopped coriander leaves and serve with couscous, rice or flatbread.

NOTES

_____
_____
_____
_____
_____
_____
_____
_____
_____
_____

49

Oman – Shuwa

Shuwa is an Omani delicacy. It is prepared on special occasions such the Muslim festival of Eid. Shuwa is marinated lamb meat which is traditionally wrapped in banana leaves and baked in an underground sand oven for up to twenty four or forty eight hours in some villages. The succulent spiced meat is served with rice.

SERVES 5

INGREDIENTS

leg of lamb (1.5 –2.5 kg)	1
cloves garlic (crushed)	10
ground pepper	2 tsp.
cumin powder	1 ½ tsp
ground coriander seeds	2 tsp.
turmeric powder	1 ½ tsp.
ground clove	1 tsp.
vinegar	3 tbsp.
cooking oil	4 tbsp.
lemon (juiced)	1
Banana/palm leaves	
Red chili powder	

DIRECTIONS

1. Place the crushed garlic, pepper, cumin and coriander seeds into a bowl.

2. Add the turmeric powder, ground clove and the desired amount of red chili powder to the bowl.

3. Mix the dry Ingredients, then pour in the lemon juice, vinegar, and cooking oil.

4. Stir the mixture well so that the wet and dry Ingredients are thoroughly combined, then set aside.

5. Use a sharp knife to either slice into the leg of lamb or poke holes in the meat to allow the spices to penetrate.

6. Rub the spice mixture generously over the leg of lamb, adding more red chili powder if desired.

7. Wrap the seasoned leg of lamb in banana leaves or palm leaves.

8. Refrigerate the leg overnight and before baking, preheat the oven to 250 degrees F°.

9. Place the bundle (still wrapped) in a large roasting pan and cover with a lid.

10. Place the pan in the oven and roast for about four (4:00) hours, basting with pan juices every thirty (0:30) minutes and turning the leg over once or twice.

11. Uncover and roast for twenty (0:20) minutes at 320 degrees F°, turning once.

12. When the meat cooked through and is tender, remove from the oven and discard the leaves.

13. Slice and serve Shuwa with basmati rice.

NOTES

_____
_____
_____
_____
_____
_____
_____
_____
_____
_____
_____
_____
_____
_____
_____
_____

Pakistan – Biryani

Pakistan's national dish is called Biryani. It is a spicy meal of rice and meat, usually chicken or lamb.

SERVES 6

INGREDIENTS

trimmed lamb shoulder (cut into bite-sized pieces)	2 lb.
canola oil	1 cup
large yellow onions (sliced thinly)	3
garam masala	2 tbsp.
crushed red pepper flakes	1 tsp.
turmeric powder	½ tsp.
black peppercorns	18
pods green cardamom	9
pods black cardamom	3
(2 inches) sticks cinnamon	2
cloves garlic (minced)	6
tomatoes (cored and minced)	6
serrano chili peppers (stemmed and minced)	5
piece ginger (peeled and minced)	1
plain yogurt	½ cup
roughly chopped mint leaves	¾ cup
roughly chopped cilantro leaves	¼ cup
cumin seeds	½ tsp.
crushed saffron threads	½ tsp.
whole cloves	4
dried bay leaves	2
basmati rice (soaked in water for 30 minutes, drained)	2 ½ cups
Salt	
Rosewater	
Orange food coloring (optional)	

DIRECTIONS

1. Heat a ¼ cup of oil in a skillet and sauté the onions for about twenty (0:20) minutes until brown and crispy.
2. Set aside the onions and heat the remaining oil in a 5-quart pot.
3. Add the garam masala, pepper flakes, turmeric, ten peppercorns, five green cardamom pods, two black cardamom pods, and a cinnamon stick to the oil.
4. Sauté for one (0:01) minute until fragrant.
5. Add the ginger, garlic, tomatoes and serrano chili pepper.
6. Stir and cook for three (0:03) minutes.
7. Add the lamb and season with salt.
8. Cook the lamb for about five (0:05) minutes until browned, then cover the pot and reduce the heat.
9. Cook for one (1:00) hour until the meat is tender.
10. Uncover and stir in the fried onions, yogurt, ½ cup mint, and two tablespoons cilantro.
11. Cook for fifteen (0:15) minutes, then turn off the heat and set aside.
12. Combine a ½ cup of hot water, and the saffron threads then set aside.
13. Bring 4 cups of water to a boil in a large saucepan and add the rice, cumin, cloves and bay leaves.
14. Add the remaining peppercorns, cardamom pods, and cinnamon stick.
15. Sprinkle salt.
16. Cook for about ten (0:10) minutes until the rice is al–dente, then drain and set aside.
17. Transfer half of the lamb into a separate pot and then layer half of the rice over it.
18. Pour a few drops of rose water and coloring over the rice along with half of the saffron mixture.
19. Gently mix the rice to absorb the color and fragrances.
20. Layer the remaining lamb and rice; prepare as before with the saffron mix, rose water and coloring.
21. Place the lid on the pot and steam for ten (0:10) minutes over low heat.
22. Garnish with the remaining cilantro and mint leaves, then serve.

Qatar – Machboos

Qatari Machboos is an aromatic, spiced rice and meat dish. It is popularly cooked in almost every home in Qatar and is considered to be the country's national dish.

SERVES 4–6

INGREDIENTS

basmati rice	2 cups
seasoned chicken cubes/store bought chicken skewer chunks	2 1/3 lb.
large onion (peeled and diced)	1
chicken stock	2 ½ cups
ghee / clarified butter	3 tbsp.
Baharat spice mix	1 tbsp.
turmeric powder	1 tsp.
vegetable oil	3 tsp.
green chili pepper (seeded and diced)	1
freshly grated ginger	1 tbsp.
cloves garlic (minced)	5
tomatoes (diced)	3
dried limes / loomi	3
green cardamom pods	5
pinch powdered clove	1
stick cinnamon	1
salt	2 ½ tsp.
rosewater (for sprinkling at the end)	1–2 tbsp.

DIRECTIONS

1. Heat the oil in a large Dutch oven pot to medium-high heat.

2. Fry the chicken cubes in the hot oil and brown all sides.

3. Use a slotted spoon to remove the cooked chicken and set aside.

4. Add the ghee to the remaining oil in the pot and add the onions.

5. Sauté the onions for about twelve (0:12) minutes or until brown.

6. Add the garlic, ginger and green chili pepper to the onions.

7. Sauté together for two (0:02) minutes, then add the turmeric powder and the Baharat spice mix, and cook for one (0:01) minute.

8. Return the chicken to the pot and mix well with the spices.

9. Add the tomatoes, cardamom pods, the cinnamon stick, and the powdered clove.

10. Punch a few holes in the dried limes and add them whole to the pot.

11. Pour in the chicken stock and stir well.

12. Bring to a boil, reduce the heat, cover and allow to simmer for about one (1:00) hour.

13. Add the rice and stir to combine.

14. Bring to a boil, reduce the heat, cover and allow to simmer for fifteen (0:15) to twenty (0:20) minutes or until the rice is tender and has absorbed the liquid.

15. Stir frequently during this time and add more boiling water if necessary.

16. Turn off the heat and transfer the Machboos to a serving dish.

17. Sprinkle with rosewater and serve.

Saudi Arabia – Saleeg

One of Saudi Arabia's most prominent dishes is Saleeg. It is a milky rice dish topped with chicken. Although it is a favorite dish, it is rarely served in restaurants; it is traditionally a home-cooked meal. A chili and tomato sauce called duggus typically served with Saleeg.

SERVES 4

INGREDIENTS

chicken (cleaned and quartered)	1
ghee / butter	1 tbsp.
white rice	1 cup
pods cardamom	3
milk	2 cups
lemon	½
white pepper	1 tsp.
black pepper	½ tsp.
water	8 cups
small mastic tears (resin used in Arabic cuisine)	4
Vinegar	
Salt	

DIRECTIONS

1. Rinse the rice in clean water, drain, and set aside.

2. Rub the chicken parts in a mixture of salt and vinegar, then rinse and set aside.

3. Heat eight cups of the water in a large saucepan and add the cardamom pods, two mastic tears, and the white pepper.

4. Add the chicken to the flavored water, partially cover the saucepan and allow to cook over medium heat until the chicken is tender.

5. Remove the pieces of chicken from the broth and season it with the juice of half a lemon, half teaspoon of salt and the black pepper.

6. Preheat an oven to 200 degrees F°, then bake the chicken until brown and crispy.

7. Set the baked chicken aside.

8. Strain the broth that the chicken was first cooked in and discard the cardamom pods.

9. Return the strained broth to the saucepan and bring to a boil.

10. Add the rice to the broth and cook until tender.

11. Strain the rice but allow a little broth to remain in the pan, then add the milk.

12. Stir the rice and milk over low heat, then season with salt.

13. In a separate pan, heat the ghee with the remaining mastic tears until it melts.

14. Pour this mixture over the Saleeg and then turn off the heat.

15. Place the baked chicken pieces on top of the Saleeg.

16. Serve immediately.

NOTES

_____
_____
_____
_____
_____
_____
_____
_____
_____
_____

Somalia – Lahoh

Lahoh is a popular savory flatbread. It is a popular dish that complements stews and soups in Somalia. Some Somalians eat Lahoh with honey and butter. Lahoh has a spongy consistency, similar to a pancake. One of the main features of Lahoh is that it is cooked only on one side and has a solid frothy appearance.

YIELDS 8

INGREDIENTS

For Starter

water	1 cup
white flour	1/3 cup
whole wheat flour	1/3 cup
yeast	1 tsp.

For Dough

cornmeal	1 cup
white flour	1 ¼ cup
salt	1 tsp.
dry yeast	1 tsp.
water	¾ cup

DIRECTIONS

For Starter

1. In a large bowl, combine the white flour, whole wheat flour, and yeast

2. Gradually add the water to prevent lumps.

3. Cover the bowl and let sit for thirty-six (36:00) hours.

For Dough

1. Mix the starter with cornmeal, one cup of white flour, salt and yeast.

2. Knead into a soft, pliable ball of dough.

3. Allow the dough to rise for forty (0:40) minutes.

4. Combine the water and the remaining flour in a pan and heat over low heat.

5. Whisk until a thick paste is formed, then turn off the heat.

6. After the dough has risen, add the water and flour paste to it, mix with water to create a thin batter.

7. Cover and let sit for thirty (0:30) minutes until it appears frothy.

8. Preheat a skillet and lightly grease it.

9. Spoon some of the batters into the skillet, making a spiral, circular shape.

10. Cook on one side until the batter is dry at the top and the edges can peel away from the pan, then set aside to cool.

11. Repeat until the batter finished.

12. Serve Lahoh with a savory stew or enjoy with honey and butter.

NOTES

_____
_____
_____
_____
_____
_____
_____
_____
_____
_____
_____
_____
_____
_____
_____
_____
_____
_____

Syria –Kibbeh

The national dish of Syria is Kibbeh, a meat filled croquette. Kibbeh dough is made from bulgur wheat and typically filled with ground lamb. There are many variations of this dish, including one that is eaten raw. Fried kibbeh is the most popular and it is served as a snack or appetizer.

YIELDS 15 kibbeh

INGREDIENTS

For the Dough

bulgur wheat	1 ½ cups
ground lamb	1 lb.
medium yellow onion (peeled and cut into wedges)	1
Bharat seasoning (Middle Eastern spice mix)	1 ½ tsp.
canola oil (for frying)	6 cups

For the Filling

ground lamb	1 lb.
pine nuts	½ cup
Bharat seasoning	1 ½ tsp.
sprigs parsley (chopped)	6
Salt	

DIRECTIONS

For the Dough

1. Lay a cheesecloth or kitchen towel over a medium-sized bowl.

2. Place the bulgur wheat in the cloth and cover with cold water.

3. Sct asidc and allow the wheat to soak for twenty (0:20) minutes.

4. Use a food processor to pulse the ground lamb, then transfer this to a bowl.

5. Add the onion wedges to the food processor and pulse until minced, then set aside.

6. Drain and squeeze the excess liquid from the bulgur wheat and add it to the bowl of lamb meat.

7. Add the Bharat seasoning and minced onion to the lamb and wheat.

8. Mix all of these Ingredients until it forms a thick paste.

9. Add a teaspoon of cold water if the mixture is too dry.

10. Roll the mixture into balls the size of golf balls, then place onto a cookie sheet and refrigerate until they are ready to be stuffed.

For the Filling

1. Toast the pine nuts in a pan, then set aside to cool.

2. Brown the second pound of ground lamb in a pan.

3. Add the pine nuts, chopped parsley and a teaspoon of Bharat seasoning to the lamb meat.

4. Season with adequate salt, then turn off the heat and set aside.

5. Remove the Kibbeh dough from the refrigerator.

6. Press a hole into the center of each ball and thin the edges with the fingers until a cup-shaped pocket forms.

7. Stuff each with a tablespoon of lamb meat filling and shape into a torpedo or football.

8. Heat the canola oil in a large Dutch oven pot and fry the Kibbeh until golden brown, flipping as necessary.

9. Place the Kibbeh on a rack to cool.

10. Serve Kibbeh with labneh, cucumber slices and sprigs of mint.

United Arab Emirates – Biryani

Biryani is a very popular dish in the United Arab Emirates. It is a spicy rice and meat dish which usually includes cashew nuts.

SERVES 8–10

INGREDIENTS

chicken breasts (cut into ½ inch cubes and fried)	2 lbs.
basmati rice	3 cups
freshly grated ginger	1 tbsp.
turmeric powder	1 tsp.
chili powder	¼ tsp.
cinnamon	¼ tsp.
ground cloves	¼ tsp.
ground cardamom	¼ tsp.
medium onions (thinly sliced and deep fried)	2
yogurt	1 cup
lemon juice	2 tbsp.
chopped mint leaves	4 tbsp.
chopped coriander leaves	4 tbsp.
vegetable oil	4 tbsp.
small chili pepper (finely chopped)	1
toasted cashew nuts	4 tbsp.
saffron	1/8 tsp.
salt	2 ½ tsp.
water	10 cups

DIRECTIONS

1. Place the fried chicken cubes in a large bowl and season it with 1 ½ teaspoon of salt.

2. Add the turmeric, ginger, chili powder, cinnamon, cloves and cardamom to the chicken.

3. Mix these Ingredients well and set aside for ten (0:10) minutes.

4. Add the onions to the chicken, together with the yogurt, lemon juice, mint leaves, coriander, chili pepper and two tablespoons of oil.

5. Mix well and allow to marinate for one (1:00) hour.

6. Meanwhile, boil the rice in 10 cups of water over medium heat for ten (0:10) minutes.

7. Drain the rice but reserve 3 cups of rice stock.

8. Place half of the rice at the base of a casserole dish and top with the marinated chicken mixture.

9. Place the next half of the rice over the chicken mixture and pour the remaining oil over the top.

10. Mix the rice stock with the saffron and a teaspoon of salt, then pour this evenly over the top.

11. Cover the dish with aluminum foil and preheat the oven to 350 degrees F°.

12. Bake the Biryani for one (1:00) hour.

13. Garnish with toasted cashews and serve immediately.

NOTES

_____
_____
_____
_____
_____
_____
_____
_____
_____
_____
_____
_____

Tunisia– Tunisian Couscous

In Tunisia, couscous is cooked and served with meat, beans, vegetables and an assortment of spices. Couscous has been a staple of the Tunisian diet for many years and it is considered the country's national dish.

SERVES 6

INGREDIENTS

medium couscous	500 g
chicken thighs	4–6
medium potatoes (peeled and quartered)	3
can chickpeas (drained)	1
peas	1 cup
medium onions (peeled and sliced)	2
cloves garlic (peeled and crushed)	2
tomato puree	1 tbsp.
harissa paste	2 tsp.
cayenne pepper	1 tsp.
ground black pepper	½ tsp.
salt	½ tsp.
turmeric	1 tsp.
cumin	1 tsp.
coriander	1 tsp.
water	1 L
chicken stock cube	1
passata	300 ml
Olive oil	

DIRECTIONS

1. Add a tablespoon of water to the dried couscous and separate any clumps by working through the grains with the hands.

2. Repeat with a small spoon of olive oil.

3. Place the couscous into a colander or steamer which can fit tightly atop a saucepan.

4. Set aside the couscous until it is ready to be cooked.

5. Heat some olive oil in a saucepan.

6. Sauté the onions and garlic in the olive oil for two (0:02) minutes until soft.

7. Add the tomato puree, spices, and harissa to the onions.

8. Stir to coat the onions in the spice mixture, then add the chicken thighs.

9. Stir to coat the chicken thighs in the spicy mixture, adding a little water if necessary.

10. Add the potatoes, passata, chicken stock cube and one liter of water, then mix well.

11. Add the drained chickpeas and peas, then stir and allow to simmer.

12. Clamp the colander of couscous over the saucepan, so that the steam from the simmering stew cooks the couscous.

13. After fifteen (0:15) minutes, dismantle the cooking set up, stir the stew and mix the couscous with a fork.

14. Replace the colander atop the saucepan.

15. Allow the stew and couscous to cook for thirty (0:30) minutes or until the chicken is cooked.

16. Place the couscous in a serving bowl and strain the stew over it, ensuring the rich gravy cover the couscous.

17. Set aside the chicken and vegetables from the stew.

18. Fold the gravy into the couscous with a spoon and allow it to rest for five (0:05) minutes.

19. Place the chicken and vegetables on top of the couscous.

20. Serve.

Turkey –Doner Kebab

Doner Kebab is a traditional Turkish delicacy. Made of seasoned meat cooked on a vertical rotisserie. The outer layers of the flesh are shaved off while it roasts. The meat is used in flatbread sandwiches. Invented in the 19th century Ottoman Empire. Doner Kebab is commonly sold in Turkish eateries and street stalls.

SERVES 4

INGREDIENTS

plain flour	1 tsp.
dried oregano	1 tsp.
dried Italian herbs	½ tsp.
garlic powder	½ tsp.
onion powder	½ tsp.
cayenne pepper	¼ tsp.
salt	½ tsp.
ground black pepper	¼ tsp.
minced lamb	500 g

DIRECTIONS

1. Preheat the oven to 180 degrees C.

2. In a large bowl, combine the flour, oregano, Italian herbs, garlic powder, onion powder, cayenne pepper, salt, and black pepper.

3. Add the minced meat to the flour and spices.

4. Use a kneading technique and mix the Ingredients for about three (0:03) minutes.

5. When the minced lamb is smooth, and all of the dry Ingredients are evenly combined, shape it into a thin cake.

6. Place the meat in a greased baking tray.

7. Bake for one (1:20) hour and twenty minutes.

8. Flip the meat halfway during baking time to ensure it browns on the other side.

9. After cooking the meat, wrap it in foil and allow it to rest for ten (0:10) minutes.

10. Use a sharp knife to slice the Doner Kebab very thinly.

11. Place the meat slices in toasted pita pockets, along with a green salad.

12. Drizzle the pita sandwiches with spicy sauces and serve.

NOTES

_____
_____
_____
_____
_____
_____
_____
_____
_____
_____
_____
_____
_____
_____

Yemen – Saltah

Saltah is a Yemeni soup which is primarily made using vegetables and ground meat such as lamb or beef. Some versions of this dish contain rice or eggs. Saltah originated during the Ottoman Empire. Leftover food donated to charitable homes was mixed and cooked together in stone pots called haradhas. This soup or Saltah became popular among the poor. Saltah is typically eaten with flatbread, the most traditional one being malooga.

SERVES 8

INGREDIENTS

ground lamb meat/beef	1 lb.
onions (peeled and finely chopped)	2
cloves garlic (minced)	3
tomatoes (finely diced)	2
vegetable oil	¼ cup
small potatoes (peeled and diced into ½–inch cubes)	4
beef stock	5 cups
large eggs (beaten)	2
zhug (Israeli pesto)	2 tbsp.
Huldah (fenugreek paste)	2 tbsp.
freshly ground black pepper	½ tsp.
cumin seeds	½ tsp.
chopped cilantro leaves	2 tbsp.
salt	1 tsp.

DIRECTIONS

1. Heat the vegetable oil in a large saucepan over medium-high heat.

2. Add the onions to the pan, then add the ground meat.

3. Use a spoon to break up the clumps of meat and mix with the onions and cook for about ten (0:10) minutes.

4. Add the garlic, tomatoes, and potatoes to the pan.

5. Season with salt, cumin seeds, and black pepper.

6. Pour in the beef stock.

7. Increase the heat and bring to a boil, then reduce to a simmer.

8. Cook for one (1:00) hour until the meat and potatoes are tender, adding water if necessary.

9. Stir in the eggs.

10. Add the chopped cilantro to the soup and cook for two (0:02) minutes.

11. Turn off the heat and pour the zhug and hulbah onto the surface of the soup.

12. Serve the Saltah hot, along with traditional malooga flatbread.

NOTES

_____
_____
_____
_____
_____
_____
_____
_____
_____
_____
_____
_____
_____
_____
_____
_____
_____
_____
_____
_____

Albania – Qofte Ferguara

Qofte Ferguara or fried meatballs is considered to be the national dish of Alb..ania. The country's cuisine is influenced by Greek, Italian, and Turkish cooking.

YIELDS 24 meatballs

INGREDIENTS

ground meat (chicken, lamb, beef)	1 lb.
feta cheese (crumbled)	2–3 tbsp.
Ground black pepper or ½ tsp. black peppercorns	1tsp.
salt	1tsp.
slice of stale bread	1
onion (finely grated)	1
crushed garlic	1tsp.
crushed dried mint leaves	1–2 tsp.
flour	½ cup
olive oil	1 cup
Water	

DIRECTIONS

1   Cut off the edges of the slice of bread and break up the slice. Soak the pieces of bread in water for a few seconds until it becomes very soft. Then squeeze the bread to remove the water.

2   In a bowl, add the ground meat and season it with salt, peppercorns or black pepper, grated onion, mint leaves, and garlic. Add the crumbled feta cheese, and bread bits. Work the seasonings, bread bits, and crumbled feta cheese into the meat and mix thoroughly. Leave the meat to marinate for about fifteen minutes.

3   Take a tbsp of the meat mixture in hand and shape the Qofte into ½ inch thick patties that resemble sausages. Place a ½ cup of flour onto a shallow dish or plate. Roll each Qofte in the dry flour.

4   Pour olive oil into a frying pan or skillet and heat to approximately 350° – 365° before frying the Qofte. It is a good idea to fry a few Qofte at a time instead of filling the pan. When the Qofte turns golden brown, use a slotted spoon to take them out of the pan. Place them on absorbent paper to remove any excess oil.

5   Qofte Ferguara is traditionally served hot with potato or rice dishes.

NOTES

_____
_____
_____
_____
_____
_____
_____
_____
_____
_____
_____
_____
_____
_____
_____
_____

Andalusia – Gazpacho

The region of Andalusia is famous for its cold soups, notably Gazpacho, a delicious summer soup made from fresh vegetables and bread. Andalusia is located in Southern Spain where fresh olives, tomatoes and citrus fruit are plentiful. The dish was first made for laborers who worked on these plantations.

SERVES 4–5

INGREDIENTS

large, ripe tomatoes (cored and chopped into 1-inch chunks)	4
small cucumber (peeled, seeded and cut into 1-inch chunks)	1
small red onion (peeled and cut into 1-inch chunks)	1
bell pepper (chopped into 1-inch chunks)	1 med
slices white sandwich bread	2
minced chives	2 tbsp.
cloves garlic (crushed)	2
extra virgin olive oil	1 cup
kosher salt	1 ½ tsp.
sherry vinegar	2 tbsp.
Freshly ground black pepper	

DIRECTIONS

1. Add the tomatoes to a large bowl together with the onion, garlic, and cucumber.

2. Season the vegetables with black pepper and salt.

3. Mix well and set aside for thirty (0:30) minutes.

4. Drain the liquid from the bowl into a separate container.

5. Remove the crust from the bread, tear into small pieces, and add to the container of vegetable liquid.

6. Place the drained vegetables onto a baking sheet and freeze for thirty (0:30) minutes.

7. Allow the vegetables to thaw for thirty (0:30) minutes, then transfer to the container of soaked bread.

8. Mix thoroughly, then transfer everything to a blender. Blend at high speed, then drizzle in the olive oil and sherry vinegar as it blends.

9. Strain the gazpacho using a fine mesh strainer.

10. Season the gazpacho with additional salt and black pepper.

11. Ladle the soup into serving bowls.

12. Drizzle each serving with additional olive oil, black pepper, and sherry vinegar.

13. Top each serving with minced chives.

14. Serve fresh or store in the refrigerator and consume within three days.

NOTES

_____
_____
_____
_____
_____
_____
_____
_____
_____
_____
_____
_____
_____
_____
_____
_____

Andorra – Escudella De Pages

Escudella De Pages is a hearty winter stew consisting of vegetables, meat and pasta. It is a dish that has its roots in Spanish, French and Catalonian cuisine. This simple and traditional Andorran dish is a country stew that utilizes three kinds of meat and vegetables grown in rural Andorra.

SERVES 6

INGREDIENTS

ham bone	1
veal bones	4
ounces salted pork	4 oz.
chicken (sliced into bite-sized pieces)	½
veal (sliced into bite-sized pieces)	½ lb.
potatoes (peeled and diced)	½ lb.
quarts of water	2 ¼
Pinch of saffron threads	
finely chopped onions	4 oz.
olive oil	3 tbsp.
medium leek (chopped)	1
carrot (finely diced)	5 oz.
green cabbage (finely chopped)	4 oz.
rice	4 oz.
elb..ow/ciocchetti pasta	3 oz.
Great Northern beans (cooked)	4 oz.

DIRECTIONS

1. Blanch the salted pork in hot water to remove excess salt and then dice the pork into small pieces.

2. In a large skillet, heat the olive oil and sauté the chopped onions. As soon as the onion begins to brown, add the salted pork pieces, chopped chicken and veal.

3. Add the chopped potatoes, carrots and leek to the skillet. Add the chopped green cabbage. Stir to allow the meat and vegetable flavors to marry.

4. In a large saucepan, create a broth by adding the ham and veal bones to water. Simmer on low heat and when it is almost ready, add the saffron and salt.

5. Remove the bones from the broth and discard.

6. Empty the vegetable and meat mixture from the skillet into the broth.

7. Add the beans, rice, and pasta to this.

8. Cook for about fifteen minutes until the pasta and rice become tender.

9. Use a spoon to dish out the stew into bowls and serve piping hot with a chunk of homemade bread.

NOTES

_____
_____
_____
_____
_____
_____
_____
_____
_____
_____
_____
_____
_____
_____
_____
_____

Armenia – Khash or Pacha

Khash, also called pacha is a meat stew made from animal tongues, hooves and stomach. It is popularly cooked in Armenia during the cold season and eaten with lavash bread.

SERVES 6

INGREDIENTS

calf tripe/stomach	2 lbs.
hooves (from calf)	4
lamb tongues	6
garlic cloves	2
Salt	
Paprika	
Pepper	

DIRECTIONS

1. Each of the meat products must be cooked separately before adding it to the stew.

2. Preparing the hooves

3. Clean the hooves by first soaking them in boiling water. The hot water will loosen the hard hoof from the flesh and makes it easy to remove.

4. Prepare an open flame and singe the hair from the skin of the feet. Scrape off any extra hairs with a sharp knife.

5. Wash thoroughly before soaking the feet overnight in water.

6. Preparing the tripe/calf stomach

7. Soak the calf stomach overnight in water. The next day, remove from the water and dice the stomach into 1-inch pieces.

8. Boil the pieces in water for ten minutes, then drain. Return the meat to the pot and add fresh water, cook for fifteen minutes.

9. Preparing the lamb tongues

10. Place the whole lamb tongues in a pot of hot water and cook until the skins peel off easily. Dice the cooked lamb tongues.

11. Making the khash

12. Place the hooves in a large pot and begin cooking them in water and garlic.

13. Add the calf stomach to the pot and cook for two hours. The meat will begin to fall off the bones in the calf feet. Remove the bones and any scum which forms. When the stomach and feet are halfway done, add the lamb tongues. Sprinkle adequate salt and pepper.

14. When the khash is finished cooking, remove some of the fat and let it melt in a separate frying pan.

15. Sprinkle paprika and cook for a few minutes until it dissolves. Pour the paprika infused fat back into the stew.

16. Serve khash with vinegar and lemon juice.

NOTES

_____
_____
_____
_____
_____
_____
_____
_____
_____
_____
_____
_____
_____
_____
_____
_____
_____

Asturias – Fabada Asturiana

The signature dish of Asturias is Fabada Asturiana, a type of rich stew. The main Ingredients of the dish are white beans and sausage. It was thought to have originated at the end of the 19th century. The dish is usually eaten for lunch in Northern Spain, especially during the colder months. It is traditionally served with bread and Asturian cider.

SERVES 6

INGREDIENTS

dry lima beans	1 lb.
pork loin (cut into 2-inch squares)	1 ½ lb.
yellow onion (chopped into ¼ inch pieces)	1
cloves garlic	4
bay leaf	1
chorizo sausage (sliced)	6–7 oz.
sweet paprika	1 tbsp.
pinch saffron powder	1
Salt	
Olive oil	
Water	

DIRECTIONS

1. Place the beans in a large pot of cold water.
2. Turn on the heat and boil the beans for one (0:01) minute, then turn off the heat, cover the pot and set aside for one (1:00) hour.
3. In a separate pot, add olive oil and heat.
4. Sauté together the chopped onions, whole garlic cloves and the pork in the hot olive oil.
5. When the onions are tender and transparent, turn off the heat.
6. Drain the beans and add them to the pot of sautéed pork, onions and garlic.
7. Pour adequate water into the pot to cover the beans and pork.
8. Place the bay leaf into the pot.
9. Add the pinch of saffron powder.
10. Add the sliced chorizo to the pot along with the sweet paprika.
11. Turn the heat back on and bring the stew to a boil.
12. Reduce the heat then let the stew simmer for one hour and thirty (1:30) minutes or until the meat becomes tender.
13. Add salt to taste, then turn off the heat.
14. Serve Fabada Asturiana with crusty bread and cider.

NOTES

_____
_____
_____
_____
_____
_____
_____
_____
_____
_____
_____
_____
_____
_____
_____
_____
_____
_____
_____
_____
_____
_____
_____
_____

Austria – Weiner Schnitzel Mit Beilagen

Cows and pigs were abundantly farmed in Austria and veal and pork were commonly eaten. The most common dish is Weiner Schnitzel mit beilagen which is a thin, fried veal or pork cutlet served with sides. Years ago, pork cutlets was the preferred choice by Austrians but using veal cutlets in this dish was a sign of wealth.

SERVES 6

INGREDIENTS

pork/veal boneless cutlets (sliced ¼ inch thick)	12
eggs (beaten)	3
milk	2 tbsp.
flour	2 cups
breadcrumbs	2 cups
Vegetable oil	
Salt to taste	
Lemon wedges	
Sprigs of parsley	
Whole cranberry sauce	

DIRECTIONS

1. Use a meat pounder to pound each cutlet into a thin 1/8 inch piece of meat. Sprinkle salt onto the cutlets. Set aside.

2. Create an egg and milk mixture by whisking three eggs and 2 tbsps. Of milk together. Place two cups of flour in a large bowl. In another bowl, place 2 cups of breadcrumbs. First, coat each cutlet in flour, then coat it in the egg mixture and finally coat it in the breadcrumbs which will stick to the moist egg mixture.

3. Pour vegetable oil into a cast iron skillet to cover a ½ inch of the pan. Heat the vegetable oil to medium-high heat.

4. Delicately place the cutlets into the hot oil, only frying a few at a time depending on the size of the skillet and how many cutlets can comfortably fit into it.

5. When the cutlets become golden brown, remove from the oil with a slotted spoon. Place two cutlets onto a plate.

6. Arrange lemon wedges, whole cranberry sauce and a sprig of parsley over the meat as a garnish.

7. Schnitzel Mit Beilagen traditionally served with side dishes such as salads or rice. Within Austria, there are also many varieties of this dish featuring different sauces and sauteed vegetables.

NOTES

_____
_____
_____
_____
_____
_____
_____
_____
_____
_____
_____
_____
_____
_____
_____
_____
_____
_____
_____
_____
_____

Balearic Islands – Coca de Trempó

The cuisine of the Balearic Islands is typically Mediterranean. A traditional and popular summer dish in one of the islands is Coca de Trempó. It is a special type of flatbread which is topped with a vegetable salad; similar to a pizza. Olive oil and tomatoes are two of its main Ingredients.

YIELDS 1 Coca

INGREDIENTS

For the Coca

egg	1
warm water	1/3 cup
salt	½ tsp.
active dry yeast	2 tsp.
extra virgin olive oil	1/3 cup
flour	1 ½ cups
unsalted butter (at room temperature)	1 ½ cups

For the Trempó

ripe tomatoes (peeled and minced)	2 lbs.
green bell pepper (seeded and finely chopped)	1
small white onion (peeled and finely sliced)	1
salt	1 ½ tsp.
extra virgin olive oil	6 tbsp.

DIRECTIONS

For the Coca

1. Preheat the oven to 400 degrees F°.

2. Add the yeast to the warm water in a bowl and let it sit for five (0:05) minutes until dissolved.

3. Add the egg, salt and olive oil to the bowl of dissolved yeast.

4. Add half a cup of the flour and begin to knead into a dough.

5. Add the rest of the flour one handful at a time during kneading.

6. Add the butter to the dough and knead until smooth and elastic.

7. Place a paper towel over the bowl of dough and let it rest for thirty (0:30) minutes.

8. Grease a 10x15-inch baking tray with 1-inch sides with a bit of unsalted butter.

9. When the dough has risen, evenly spread the dough along the base and sides of the baking tray.

10. Use a fork to perforate the dough in multiple places to avoid bubbles from forming, then set aside.

For the Trempó

11. Pat the vegetables with a paper towel to remove extra moisture.

12. Combine the tomatoes, green pepper and onion in a bowl and season with the salt and olive oil.

13. Spread the vegetable mixture over the Coca dough, then place in the preheated oven.

14. Bake for thirty (0:30) minutes until edges are firm and lightly browned, then slice.

15. Serve warm.

NOTES

_____
_____
_____
_____
_____
_____
_____
_____
_____

Basque Country & Navarre – Marmitako

Marmitako is a humble stew made of fresh tuna and potatoes that is eaten in Basque Country and Navarre. The name literally means "from the pot." The dish originated on fishing vessels that went out in search of tuna during the summer months. Today, Marmitako is made with either tuna or bonito fish and is a classic meal in Basque kitchens and restaurants.

SERVES 2

INGREDIENTS

fresh tuna (cubed)	½ lb.
small onion (peeled and sliced)	1
green pepper (sliced)	1
large potatoes (peeled and cut/broken into chunks)	2
clove garlic (crushed)	1
dried pimiento choricero pepper/s (soaked in water, then peeled and sliced)	1–2
small tomato (grated into a salsa)	1
Txakoli (white wine)	1 cup
Chopped parsley	
Water	
Salt	
Olive oil	

DIRECTIONS

1. Place a little olive oil into a stew pot, turn on the heat and then lightly sauté the onion slices until translucent.

2. Add the green pepper slices to the onions and let cook for a few minutes.

3. Add the garlic and the potato chunks to the pot.

4. Pour in a cup of white wine or txakoli.

5. Stir the Ingredients together and then add the pimientos Choriceros.

6. Pour in water to cover the vegetables.

7. Add the salt to the stew.

8. Place the lid on the pot and allow the stew to simmer, stirring occasionally and adding more water if necessary.

9. Once the potatoes are nearly done, add the tomato salsa.

10. When the potatoes are tender, add the cubes of tuna and cook for about four (0:04) minutes or until properly cooked.

11. Turn off the heat.

12. Sprinkle fresh parsley over the Marmitako.

13. Serve this delicious tuna and potato stew with glasses of white wine.

NOTES

_____
_____
_____
_____
_____
_____
_____
_____
_____
_____
_____
_____
_____
_____
_____
_____
_____
_____
_____

Belarus – Draniki

Draniki is a type of pancake that is made from potatoes. This nourishing breakfast dish has been prepared in Belarus since the 19th century when potatoes were the main agricultural crop. In the past, draniki was prepared using only three Ingredients; potatoes, onion and salt but as time passed, more modern recipes have been developed.

SERVES 4

INGREDIENTS

large potatoes	5
medium onion	1
egg	1
flour	1–2 tbsp.
black pepper	½ tsp.
Salt to taste	
vegetable or sunflower oil	8 tbsps.

DIRECTIONS

1. Peel the skins off each of the potatoes and rinse in cold water. Remove the skin of the onion and grate on the fine side of the grater. Grate the peeled potatoes using the same side of the grater.

2. Place the grated potato into a strainer and drain off any excess liquid.

3. Combine the grated onion and potatoes in a bowl. Beat the egg separately before adding it to the onion and potato mixture. Sprinkle adequate salt and black pepper. If the mixture contains excess liquid and appears to be runny, add a couple of tbsps of flour.

4. Heat four tbsps of oil in a wide shallow skillet. Spoon some of the pancake mixtures into the skillet, forming it into a circular shape. Pancakes should be about a ¼ inch thick. Fry on high heat. After two minutes, flip the pancake and allow the other side to cook.

5. Place the cooked Draniki on absorbent paper after frying so the excess oil can be absorbed. Plate and serve with a large dollop of sour cream.

NOTES

_____
_____
_____
_____
_____
_____
_____
_____
_____
_____
_____
_____
_____
_____
_____
_____
_____
_____
_____
_____
_____
_____
_____

Belgium – Carbonnades Flamandes

More than 1000 varieties of beer is produced in Belgium and as it is a plentiful commodity, it is used in Belgian cuisine such as Carbonnades Flamandes which is a famous Belgian beef and beer stew.

SERVES 6

INGREDIENTS

beef (diced)	3 lbs.
slices bacon (diced)	4
pint beer	1
medium onions (sliced)	3
cloves garlic (crushed)	3
flour	3 tbsps.
bay leaves	2
olive oil	2 tbsps.
beef broth	1 ½ cups
sprigs thyme	4
parsley (chopped)	1 cup
whole grain mustard	1 tbsp.
brown sugar	1 tbsp.
Salt	
Pepper	

DIRECTIONS

1. Create a marinade for the beef by combining the beer, garlic, bay leaves, and a pinch of salt in a large bowl. Marinate the beef for at least two hours.

2. Remove the meat from the liquid and pat dry with paper towels. Keep the marinade to add to the stew.

3. Add the olive oil to a large Dutch oven pot and turn on the heat. When the oil is hot, add the beef. Cook until the meat is golden brown.

4. Remove the meat from the pot with a slotted spoon and set aside.

5. Retain the oil in the Dutch oven pot and fry the bacon until crisp. Remove the cooked bacon and set aside.

6. In the same pot, add the sliced onions and a pinch of salt. Allow the onions to caramelize then add the flour. Stir to coat the onions with the flour. When the flour cooked, pour in the beef broth.

7. Add the beef marinade to the pot and stir in the fried bacon and the sprigs of thyme. Add the beef to the stew and stir it.

8. Place the lid on the pot, reduce the heat, and let the stew simmer for about an hour and thirty minutes.

9. Add the brown sugar, mustard, and pepper to the stew and cook for an additional thirty minutes. Turn off the heat when the meat is tender.

10. Sprinkle the chopped parsley over the stew. Plate and serve with fries, mashed potato, or buttered vegetables.

NOTES

_____
_____
_____
_____
_____
_____
_____
_____
_____
_____
_____
_____

Bosnia & Herzegovina – Cevapi

Cevapi is a type of skinless sausage which originated in the Balkan Peninsula during the Ottoman period. Although it is a local delicacy in Serbia, Slovenia and Croatia, it is considered the national dish of Bosnia and Herzegovina. The sausages are traditionally eaten in a flatbread sandwich accompanied by chopped onions and shopska salata; a cold salad.

SERVES 4–6

INGREDIENTS

ground beef (80/20 meat–fat ratio)	3 lbs.
vegetable seasoning blend	2 tbsps.
cloves garlic (minced)	3
sparkling water	½ cup
hot beef broth	1 cup
salt	1 tsp.
pepper	½ tsp.
Ciabatta bread / Naan	

DIRECTIONS

1. Create a vegetable seasoning blend by mincing an assortment of seasonings together such as chives, cilantro, and parsley.

2. Mix the minced garlic and water in a bowl for fifteen minutes. Drain the water and retain the garlic. To this, add the ground beef, vegetable seasoning blend, beef broth, salt, pepper, and the sparkling water. Mix thoroughly with the hands. Add additional sparkling water if required.

3. Roll the meat dough into two-inch balls, then begin forming each ball into small meat logs about the size of a thumb. Place the finished cevapi on a cookie sheet and cover with plastic wrap. Refrigerate for thirty minutes.

4. Lay the sausages on a very hot grill. Do not overcrowd; cook in batches. Reduce the heat to medium-high and cook the cevapi on all sides until cooked through five to seven (0:05-0:07) minutes to medium well. Please note that when the cevapi is ready to be flipped, it will not stick to the grill. Set aside.

5. Slice the ciabatta bread and smear about two tbsps of hot beef broth over the inside of the slices.

6. Place face down on the grill and smear beef broth on the top. If using Naan bread, sprinkle the hot beef broth over both sides of it and grill it. After about two minutes, remove the bread from the grill and serve with the cevapi, chopped onions, and cold salad.

NOTES

Bulgaria – Banitsa

Bulgarian banitsa is a pastry dish that is eaten for breakfast or as a savory snack. Although the dish is widely made throughout the year and sold at bakeries and snack shops, it is traditional to hide a coin in homemade banitsa at Christmas time as it is believed that whoever finds it when eating will have a prosperous year ahead.

SERVES 4–6

INGREDIENTS

yogurt (Bulgarian sheep's milk yogurt is best)	¾ lb.
sheets phyllo dough	12
sirene (Bulgarian feta cheese)	½ lb.
eggs	5
butter	8 tbsps.
Salt	
Pepper	

DIRECTIONS

1. Crack four eggs (whites and yolks) into a medium-sized bowl. Add the yogurt. Use a whisk to combine the eggs and yogurt. Add the salt and pepper. Crumble the feta cheese and then add this to the bowl. Mix well. Divide into four portions and set aside.

2. Melt the butter in the microwave. Brush melted butter on a sheet of phyllo dough. Lay another sheet of phyllo dough onto the buttered sheet. The sheets will stick together. Turn it over and apply melted butter to the dry side. Paste this phyllo sheet with a portion of the egg, cheese and yogurt mixture previously set aside. Roll the sheet on its longest side to form a long cylinder. Repeat this till you have four rolls of dough.

3. Line a 10-inch spring form baking pan with parchment paper. Place one of the rolls of phyllo dough against the circular wall of the baking pan. Add another roll inside of this and keep going until the dough rolls reach the center of the pan. The completed arrangement should resemble the spiral pattern on a snail's shell.

4. Crack the last egg and separate the white from the yolk. Whisk the egg yolk with the remaining melted butter. Use this as a wash and brush on top of the entire banitsa. Bake at 400° F° for 25 minutes or until it is golden. Slice and serve hot or cold.

NOTES

_____
_____
_____
_____
_____
_____
_____
_____
_____
_____
_____
_____
_____
_____
_____
_____
_____

Canary Islands – Papas Arrugadas

Papas Arrugadas or Wrinkly Potatoes are a very popular potato dish in the Canary Islands. It is served alongside any other main course dish, usually with two types of traditional sauces; Mojo Picon and Mojo Verde. Originally, the potatoes were cooked in sea water until the skins became wrinkled but today, tap water and a generous helping of salt is used.

SERVES 2

INGREDIENTS

For the Potatoes

small salad potatoes	1 lb. 2 oz.
sea salt	1 oz.
water	1 L

For the Mojo Picon

large red bell pepper (chopped)	1
groundnut oil	6 tbsp.
cloves garlic	4
sea salt	½ tsp.
sugar	½ tsp.
white wine	2 tbsp.
smoked paprika	¼ tsp.

For the Mojo Verde

large green bell pepper (chopped)	1
groundnut oil	6 tbsp.
cloves garlic	4
sea salt	½ tsp.
sugar	½ tsp.
white wine	2 tbsp.
fresh coriander	2 oz.

DIRECTIONS

For the Potatoes

1. Preheat the oven to 150 degrees F°.
2. Place the potatoes in a large saucepan with the water.
3. Add the salt to the saucepan and turn on the heat.
4. Bring to a boil, then reduce the heat and let simmer for thirty (0:30) minutes or until the potatoes are soft.
5. Remove any excess water.
6. Place the potatoes on a baking tray and bake in the preheated oven for fifteen (0:15) minutes until the skins are wrinkled and covered with the salt residue.
7. Remove from the oven and set aside.

For the Mojo Picon

1. Place all the Ingredients into a food processor and blend until a sauce forms.

For the Mojo Verde

1. Place all the Ingredients into a food processor and blend until a sauce forms.
2. Serve the Papas Arrugadas warm with separate servings of each type of sauce.

NOTES

_____
_____
_____
_____
_____
_____
_____
_____
_____
_____

Castile & León – Castilian Garlic Soup

One of the most traditional dishes of the region is Sopa de Ajo or Castilian Garlic Soup. It originated as a peasant dish by shepherds; garlic and leftover bread were used to make a hot meal on cold nights. Eggs were sometimes added to the soup. It is also said to be a known hangover cure in Castile and León.

SERVES 4

INGREDIENTS

large cloves garlic	8
extra virgin olive oil	¼ cup
sweet paprika	1 tbsp.
cayenne pepper	½ tsp.
chicken stock	6 cups
oloroso sherry	¼ cup
ground cumin	¼ tsp.
pieces crusty bread (½ inch thick slices)	4
pinch saffron threads	1
large eggs	4
Freshly grated Parmesan cheese	
Salt	

DIRECTIONS

1. Heat the olive oil in a large soup pot and gently sauté the cloves of garlic for about four (0:04) minutes until golden brown.

2. Remove the garlic from the pot and set aside.

3. Take the pot off the heat and add the sweet paprika and cayenne to flavor the oil.

4. Stir in the chicken stock and sherry, then return the pot to the stove.

5. Add the saffron threads and cumin.

6. Use a fork to crush the previously sautéed cloves of garlic, then add it to the soup.

7. Season the soup with adequate salt.

8. Place the lid on the pot and let it simmer for about fifteen (0:15) minutes.

9. While the soup simmers, toast the slices of bread on both sides, then set aside.

10. Break the eggs one at a time in the soup, and poach each egg for about two (0:02) minutes until the white firms and seals the yolk inside.

11. Ladle the soup into serving bowls, then add a poached egg into each bowl.

12. Place a slice of toasted bread over the egg and sprinkle grated cheese over the top.

13. Place the bowls of soup, eggs, and bread onto a tray, and placed in the hot oven.

14. Broil until the cheese melts, then remove from the oven.

15. Serve hot.

NOTES

_____
_____
_____
_____
_____
_____
_____
_____
_____
_____
_____

Catalonia – Crema Catalana

Crema Catalana is a classic dessert dish in Catalan cuisine. This creamy dessert is flavored with hints of citrus and cinnamon and topped with a caramelized sugar layer. It is also known as Crema de Sant Josep or St. Joseph's cream and traditionally made on March 19th which is celebrated as Father's Day in the region.

SERVES 10

INGREDIENTS

creamy milk	5 cups
strips orange zest	4
white sugar and extra for the caramelized crust	1 cup
cornstarch	1 tbsp.
large egg yolks	8
vanilla extract	2 tsp.
cinnamon sticks	2
water	½ cup
pinch of salt	1

DIRECTIONS

1. In a medium saucepan, add the orange zest, milk, and salt.

2. Turn on the heat and add the cinnamon sticks.

3. Bring to a boil.

4. Reduce the heat and let simmer for about three (0:03) minutes to allow the flavors to marry.

5. In a mixing bowl, whisk the egg yolks with one cup of white sugar until a pale, fluffy mixture forms.

6. Set the whisked egg and sugar aside.

7. Add the cornstarch and water to a separate bowl and whisk together until adequately mixed, then set aside.

8. Take out the cinnamon sticks and orange zest from the saucepan and discard.

9. Gradually pour the flavored milk from the saucepan into the bowl of egg yolk and sugar, whisking continuously to incorporate the Ingredients into a smooth liquid.

10. Return this liquid to the saucepan and bring to a simmer.

11. Whisk the liquid continuously for about four (0:04) minutes.

12. Pour the liquid through a strainer and into a clean bowl.

13. Add the vanilla extract and give it a quick whisk.

14. Pour the liquid into ten separate 5-ounce ramekins.

15. Allow the custard to cool at room temperature, then refrigerate for at least eight (8:00) hours.

16. Evenly sprinkle two tsp.s of sugar over each serving, then use a kitchen torch to caramelize the sugar into a hard, brown layer.

17. Serve immediately.

NOTES

_____
_____
_____
_____
_____
_____
_____
_____
_____
_____

Cornwall – Cornish Pasty

Cornwall in Britain is famous for its pasties which are short crust pastries containing a hearty meat and vegetable filling. Locally, they are called oggies and became a popular lunch meal for tin miners and farm laborers. In 2011, the Cornish pasty was given protected status by the European Commission to preserve the quality and reputation of the dish as well as the regional food heritage.

YIELDS 4 pasties

INGREDIENTS

For the Pastry

all-purpose flour	1 cup
butter (cubed)	1 oz.
lard (cubed)	1 oz.
cold water	2–3 tbsp.
pinch salt	1

For the Filling

rump steak (cut into small cubes)	½ cup
Swede (cut into ¼ inch cubes)	½ cup
potato (peeled and cut into ¼ inch cubes)	¼ cup
onion (finely diced)	¼ cup
Egg wash (1 egg and 1 tsp. water combined)	
Salt	
Pepper	

DIRECTIONS

1. Begin making the pastry by putting the salt, flour, and butter into a mixing bowl.

2. Use the fingers to combine the butter, flour, and salt until it resembles fine breadcrumbs.

3. Add the cold water to the mixture.

4. Use a cold utensil to stir the Ingredients until the dough begins to bind.

5. Add a little cold water if the mixture appears too dry and combine into a ball of dough.

6. Wrap the ball of dough in plastic wrap and refrigerate for thirty (0:30) minutes.

7. Divide the pastry into four and roll out each portion into a flat circle measuring approximately seven inches in diameter.

8. Brush the edge of the circle with egg wash, then set aside.

9. Prepare the pasty filling by combining the swede, potato, onion, and meat in a large bowl.

10. Season the filling with salt and pepper, then mix thoroughly with a spoon.

11. Divide the filling into four portions.

12. Spoon each portion onto each of the pasty circles, ensuring the filling is placed on half of the circle.

13. Fold the circle in half to cover the filling.

14. Use a fork to crimp the side edges of each pasty, so the filling is sealed inside.

15. Brush each pasty with the remaining egg wash.

16. Preheat the oven to 425 degrees F°.

17. Place the pasties onto a greased baking dish and bake them for forty-five (0:45) minutes until golden brown.

18. Serve the Cornish Pasties either hot or cold.

Croatia – Istrian Yota

Istrian Yota is a famous stew eaten in Istria and other parts of northwestern Croatia. The stew is made from dried beans and smoked meats like pancetta and spare ribs. It is seasoned with a lot of garlic. The main ingredient of Istrian Yota is Sauerkrau, which hints at the Austrian and Hungarian origins of this dish.

SERVES 4

INGREDIENTS

Borlotti or pinto beans	5 oz.
sauerkraut	10 oz.
potatoes	7 oz.
smoked spare ribs	18 oz.
smoked bacon / local pancetta	4 oz.
garlic	2/3 oz.
bay leaves	2
peppercorns	2–3
Salt	
Parsley	

DIRECTIONS

1. Fill a bowl with water and add the beans, then allow it to soak for 24 hours.

2. Rinse the beans and set aside.

3. Rinse the sauerkraut in water and drain.

4. Peel and mince the garlic cloves.

5. Chop the bacon/pancetta into very tiny pieces.

6. Finely chop the parsley.

7. Combine the garlic, bacon, and parsley by mixing it all into a thick paste.

8. Peel the potatoes and cut into cubes.

9. Place the sauerkraut and spare ribs in a pot of water and bring to a boil.

10. Fill another saucepan with water and boil the soaked beans.

11. When the beans are half cooked, combine with the sauerkraut and spare ribs.

12. Allow the beans, ribs, and sauerkraut to cook together.

13. Add the bay leaves, peppercorns and the paste of garlic, bacon, and parsley to the pot.

14. A few minutes before the stew cook, add the potatoes.

15. Stir well and sprinkle salt to taste.

16. Turn off the heat when the potatoes become tender, and the stew has thickened.

17. Use a slotted spoon to remove the spare ribs.

18. Serve the spare ribs separately from the stew.

NOTES

_____
_____
_____
_____
_____
_____
_____
_____
_____
_____
_____
_____
_____

Cyprus – Fasolada

Fasolada is considered to be the national dish of Cyprus. It is a bean and vegetable soup, cooked and served with plenty of olive oil. Fasolada is a dish that has its origins in Ancient Greece; it was a traditional soup dedicated to the Greek God Apollo and was cooked especially for the Pyanopsia Festival.

SERVES 6–8

INGREDIENTS

dried white beans (navy beans/haricot beans)	2 cups
virgin olive oil	7 tbsps.
tomato paste	2 tbsps.
water	10 cups
carrots (sliced into coins)	3
spring onions (finely diced)	3
cloves garlic (crushed)	2
ripe tomatoes (seeded and sliced)	3
bay leaf	1
bunch parsley (finely chopped)	½
celery stalk (chopped)	1
Salt	
Juice of 1 lemon	
Pepper	

DIRECTIONS

1. Soak the white beans in cold water for twelve hours (12:00).

2. Rinse the beans.

3. Fill a saucepan of water, turn on the heat, and add the soaked beans.

4. Place the lid on the saucepan and boil the beans for fifteen minutes (0:15).

5. Drain, discard the water and set the beans aside.

6. Heat the olive oil in a non–stick soup pot.

7. Sauté the finely chopped onions and crushed garlic in the olive oil until soft.

8. Add the ripe tomatoes, carrots, and celery.

9. Stir together and add the tomato paste.

10. Add the beans to the pot.

11. Add the bay leaf.

12. Pour in the lemon juice.

13. Pour in water to cover the Ingredients.

14. Season with salt and pepper.

15. Bring to a boil and cook on high heat for five (0:05) minutes.

16. Reduce the heat, cover the pot, and let the soup simmer for two (2:00) hours.

17. Stir occasionally and add more water if necessary.

18. Adjust the cooking time if needed and turn off the heat when the beans are tender.

19. Ladle into serving bowls.

20. Drizzle with lemon juice and olive oil, then top with chopped parsley before serving.

Czech Republic –Vepro Knedlo Zelo

A classic Czech dish, Vepro Knedlo Zelo is the shortened form of Veprova Knedliky Zeli which translates to roast pork, dumpling, and sauerkraut. These three delicacies are prepared separately but served together.

SERVES 4–5

INGREDIENTS

Roast Pork

pork roast	2 lbs.
vegetable oil	1 tbsp.
mustard	1 tbsp.
Caraway seeds	2 tbsps.
medium onion (chopped)	1
Butter	2 tbsps.
cornstarch	1 tbsp.
salt	1 tbsp.
ground black pepper	1 tsp.
beer/water	½ cup
garlic powder	1 tbsp.

Dumplings

sachet dry yeast	½
flour	4 cups
egg	1
warm water	2 cups
sugar	1 tsp.
Salt	2 tbsps.
stale bread roll (cubed)	1

Sauerkraut

slices bacon (cut into small strips)	4
sauerkraut with juice	1 lb.
medium onion (chopped)	1
caraway seeds	1 tsp.
cornstarch	1 tsp.
cold water	2 tsp.
Salt	
Pepper	
Sugar to taste	
Vinegar to taste	

DIRECTIONS

Roast Pork

1. Combine the caraway seeds, vegetable oil, mustard, salt, pepper, and garlic powder into a paste.
2. Rub this paste onto the pork and let it marinate for forty-five minutes (0:45).
3. Preheat the oven to 325 degrees.
4. Place the chopped onions into a roasting pan and pour the beer or water over it.
5. Place the marinated pork on top of the onions.
6. Cover with foil and bake for about one and a half hours (1:30), basting the pork with its natural juices occasionally.
7. Turn the pork over while baking, so all sides of the meat is cooked evenly.
8. Create a gravy by combining the remaining pork juice, cornstarch, and butter into a saucepan and allowing it to simmer until thick.

Dumplings

1. Combine flour, salt, egg and cubed bread roll in a bowl.
2. Mix the yeast with warm water and sugar, allow it to rise, then add this to the bowl.
3. Knead together for ten minutes (0:10).
4. Create four dumpling logs and set on a floured sheet.
5. Cover the logs and let it rise.
6. Boil the logs in salted water in a covered pot for about twenty minutes (0:20).
7. Remove dumplings from the pot and slice.

Sauerkraut

8. Fry the bacon until golden brown and set aside.
9. Sauté the chopped onion in butter until soft.
10. Add the sauerkraut to the onions and cook until tender.
11. Toss in the fried bacon and season with salt and pepper.
12. Sprinkle in the caraway seeds.
13. Combine the cornstarch and water separately, then stir it into the sauerkraut.
14. Allow it to simmer for a few minutes before turning off the heat.
15. Add sugar and vinegar to taste.
16. Lay slices of roast pork with a few dumplings and a portion of sauerkraut on a serving dish. Drizzle the gravy over all of it and serve.

Denmark– Frikadeller

Danish meatballs are known as Frikadeller in Denmark. This dish can be traced back to 1648 but did not become popular until the 18th century. It is now eaten regularly by the Danish people and considered to be the national dish of Denmark. Ground pork is traditionally used in the preparation of frikadeller. The Frikadeller can be served with boiled red potatoes or homemade rye bread.

SERVES 6

INGREDIENTS

ground pork	½ lb.
ground veal	½ lb.
whole milk	¼ cup
egg (beaten)	1
minced onion	¼ cup
breadcrumbs	¼ cup
seltzer water	¼ cup
margarine or butter	¼ cup
all-purpose flour	¼ cup
Salt	
Pepper	
Chopped dill weed (garnish)	

DIRECTIONS

1. In a large bowl, combine the ground veal and pork, minced onion and egg.

2. Pour in the milk and add the breadcrumbs.

3. Knead the flour into the meat mixture.

4. Add enough salt and pepper to the mixture to season it well.

5. Gradually add the seltzer water to form a thick moist meat paste.

6. Refrigerate the meat paste for an hour (1:00), so It will be easier to shape the meatballs.

7. Scoop up two tbsps. And half of the meat paste for each meatball and work into flattened ovals the size of an egg.

8. Heat a large skillet and melt the margarine or butter.

9. Place a few meatballs at a time in the melted margarine, flipping after fifteen (0:15) minutes.

10. When the meatballs are cooked evenly and are no longer pink in the center, remove them from the skillet.

11. Place the frikadeller onto a serving plate and sprinkle freshly chopped dill weed over them.

12. Serve the frikadeller hot or cold with a side of boiled red potatoes or slices of homemade rye bread.

NOTES

_____
_____
_____
_____
_____
_____
_____
_____
_____
_____
_____
_____
_____
_____
_____
_____
_____

79

Estonia – Verivorst with Mulgikapsad

In Estonia, blood sausages or Verivorst is especially made at Christmas time. It is eaten with Mulgikapsad, a type of sauerkraut and a red berry jam.

YIELDS 12 sausages
SERVES 4

INGREDIENTS

For Verivorst

salt pork	1 lb.
pig's blood	1 qt.
fresh pork belly	½ lb.
salt	1 tbsp.
Dried marjoram	3 tbsps.
pearl barley	1 ½ lb.
chopped onions	2 cups
hog casings, each cut into 18 inch long pieces	12

For Mulgikapsad

fresh lean pork (cut into bite-sized pieces)	2 ½ lbs.
sauerkraut	4 ½ cups
barley	¾ cup
bay leaf	1
Water	
Salt	
Pepper	

DIRECTIONS

For Verivorst

1. Boil the pearl barley in salted water for about forty-five (0:45) minutes.
2. Drain and place in a large bowl.
3. Add the marjoram and salt to the barley, mix well, and set aside.
4. Cut the salt and fresh pork into half inch chunks.
5. Put the pork into a heated saucepan with a little water to get it cooking.
6. Increase the heat and brown the pork.
7. When the pork begins sizzling, add the chopped onions and cook for thirty (0:30) minutes until they are tender and brown.
8. Add the cooked pork and onion to the barley.
9. Stir well and season to taste.
10. Allow the mixture to cool properly.
11. Pour the blood into the mixture and stir gently to avoid foaming.
12. Prepare the hog casings by rinsing them twice and soaking them in water.
13. Fit a funnel into one end of the casing and begin stuffing the sausage mixture into it.
14. Do not overstuff the sausage, fill it less than three–quarters full and ensure there is empty casing on both ends.
15. Tie both ends of the casing together with twine.
16. Poach the sausages in hot water for about fifteen (0:15) minutes.
17. If any sausage floats, prick any air pockets with a knife and let it continue to poach.
18. Lay the poached sausages on a tray to dry.
19. Place them in a greased baking tray and bake for one (1:00) hour at 350 degrees F° or until the sausages become crispy.

For Mulgikapsad

1. Place the meat in a saucepan.
2. Lay the sauerkraut over the meat.
3. Rinse the uncooked barley in water, then drain and add to the pan.
4. Add the salt, pepper, and bay leaf.
5. Pour enough water to cover the Ingredients.
6. Bring to a boil, then cover the pan, reduce the heat, and allow to simmer undisturbed for about 2–3 hours.
7. When cooked, stir and adjust the seasonings to taste.
8. Serve the crisp Verivorst with Mulgikapsad and lingonberry jam.

Finland – Karelian Pasties

A Karelian Pasty is an open pastry shell filled with rice porridge. It is also called karjalanpiirakka and Karelian Pie. The dish originated in Karelia, a historical territory that lay between Finland and Russia. In modern times, it is considered Finland's national dish. Karelian Pasties are usually eaten with a side dish called munavoi.

YIELDS 16

INGREDIENTS

For Rice Porridge Filling

rice	1 cup
milk	2 cups
water	2 cups
Salt	

For Rye Crust Pastry Shell

rye flour	1 cup
all-purpose flour	¼ cup
water	½ cup
salt	1 tsp.

DIRECTIONS

For Rice Porridge Filling

1. Pour the water into a saucepan and then add the cup of rice.
2. Turn on the heat and bring to a boil.
3. Stir occasionally.
4. Place the lid on the saucepan and cook for twenty (0:20) minutes.
5. Pour in the milk.
6. Replace the lid and cook until the milk is absorbed and the rice is tender and creamy.
7. Set aside.

For Rye Crust Pastry Shell

1. Place both types of flour in a large bowl together with the salt.
2. Gradually add the water and knead into a stiff dough.
3. Form the dough into a log.
4. Divide the dough into sixteen equal pieces.
5. Shape each piece into a ball.
6. Lightly sprinkle flour on a board and roll out each ball into a six-inch circle.
7. Place three tbsps. of the rice porridge onto the center of each circle.
8. Fold the two opposite sides of each circle of dough, partly over the porridge filling, about half inch away from the middle, leaving the center of the filling exposed.
9. Crimp the folded edges by pinching the dough together with the fingers so that the pasty resembles a cowrie seashell.
10. Preheat the oven to 450 degrees F°
11. Line a baking tray with parchment paper.
12. Set the Karelian Pasties onto the parchment paper and bake for about fifteen (0:15) minutes until golden, brushing once with a wash made of hot milk and butter.
13. Take the pasties out of the oven and while hot, brush again with the wash.
14. Allow the pasties to cool.
15. Serve the Karelian Pasties with munavoi, a boiled egg, and butter side dish.

NOTES

_____
_____
_____
_____
_____
_____
_____
_____

France – Pot au Feu

Pot au Feu is a savory beef stew that originated in France and graced the tables of both the poor and rich alike. Traditionally, the dish is prepared with vegetables, spices and meat in a large iron pot. It is served with bread.

SERVES 6–8

INGREDIENTS

beef cheek	1
beef shoulder (cut into quarters)	1 kg
beef bones with marrow	2
leeks	6
cloves	8
celery roots (peeled)	2
potatoes (peeled and halved)	4
baby carrots	5
bay leaves	2
sprig thyme	1
stalks parsley	4
black peppercorns	5
head cabbage (cut into chunks)	½
onions (peeled and halved)	2
cold water	6 L
small turnips	8
sea salt	1 tbsp.

DIRECTIONS

1. Fill a saucepan with water and add the beef cheek and shoulder pieces.

2. Turn the heat on high and bring to a boil.

3. While the meat is cooking, use a spoon to skim the surface of the water and remove any scum.

4. After about fifteen (0:15) minutes, drain and discard the water, clean the pan and return the meat to the pan to be cooked further.

5. Stick the cloves into the onion, then add to the saucepan.

6. Place the beef bones the pan and add the leeks and celery and Season with the bay leaves, thyme, and parsley.

7. Sprinkle salt and pepper, then pour in the cold water so that the vegetables and meat are covered.

8. Bring to a boil, occasionally skimming the surface of the water to remove any scum.

9. Reduce the heat and allow the stew to simmer uncovered for approximately two and a half (2:30) hours.

10. Add the cabbage, carrots, potatoes, and turnips to the pot.

11. Stir and simmer for thirty (0:30) minutes or until the vegetables are tender.

12. Turn off the heat, ladle into serving bowls and sprinkle chopped parsley to garnish.

13. Serve with cornichons, bread and a dash of sea salt.

NOTES

_____
_____
_____
_____
_____
_____
_____
_____
_____
_____
_____
_____
_____
_____

Galicia – Pulpo Gallego

Pulpo Gallego (alternatively known as pulpo estilo feira, Polbo á feira and pulpo a la gallega) is a Galician style octopus dish. Fresh octopus is used to prepare this popular dish and it is served in bars, restaurants and street stalls in Galicia. Boiled potatoes or crusty bread traditionally accompany the Pulpo Gallego.

SERVES 6

INGREDIENTS

octopus	2-3 lbs.
green onions (sliced thinly)	2-3
paprika	1 tbsp.
cayenne pepper	¼ tsp.
cloves garlic (minced)	4
smoked paprika	1 tsp.
bay leaves	2
sprig oregano	1
bunch parsley	1
extra virgin olive oil	½ cup
Fennel bulb tops	
Salt	
Pepper	
Lemon wedges (to serve)	

DIRECTIONS

1. Tenderize the octopus by boiling it in a large pot of salted water for two (0:02) minutes.

2. Remove the octopus from the boiling water and set aside to cool, then trim off fatty bits and clean the head.

3. Line the base of a heavy pot with parsley, fennel tops, oregano, bay leaves, and green onions.

4. Use a sharp knife to slice the octopi into large pieces.

5. Place the sliced octopi into the bot of herbs.

6. Cover the pot with a heavy lid and turn on the heat.

7. Cook for approximately ninety (0:90) minutes to four (4:00) hours, depending on the size and toughness of the meat.

8. Once the octopi are soft, remove it from the pot and cut it into smaller pieces.

9. Drizzle the tender octopi with a generous dash of olive oil.

10. Place the pieces on the grill and cook for an additional eight (0:08) minutes until grill marks appear.

11. The octopi can also be cooked in an oven at 225 degrees F°.

12. Place the grilled or broiled octopi into a bowl and toss with the remaining olive oil, garlic, the two types of paprika and the cayenne pepper.

13. Add salt and black pepper to taste.

14. Serve Pulpo Gallego with lemon wedges, bread or boiled potatoes.

NOTES

_____
_____
_____
_____
_____
_____
_____
_____
_____
_____
_____
_____
_____

Georgia – Khachapuri

Khachapuri is a stuffed buttery bread that is topped with egg and cheese. It is considered a staple food in Georgia and the cooks there have prepared it in a variety of tasty ways. It is served with Georgian orange wine and traditionally eaten by tearing off the sides and dipping it in the gooey topping of egg and cheese.

SERVES 8

INGREDIENTS

flour	3 ½ cups
water	1 cup
milk	½ cup
yeast	1 tsp.
salt	1 tsp.
sugar	1 tbsp.
oil	1 tbsp.
Farmers cheese	1 ½ cups
shredded mozzarella cheese	1 ½ cups
crumbled Feta cheese	1 ½ cup
eggs	5
Butter	
Olive oil	

DIRECTIONS

1. In a bowl or stand mixer, combine the flour, salt, sugar, and yeast.

2. Combine the water and milk in a saucepan and heat at 115 degrees F°.

3. Add the hot liquid to the dry Ingredients and begin kneading the dough.

4. Add the oil and knead into a soft, round dough.

5. Grease a deep glass bowl with olive oil and set the dough into it.

6. Cover the bowl with a sheet of plastic wrap and let it sit in a warm place for about one (1:00) hour.

7. Take off the plastic wrap and press into it a few times with the hands.

8. Cover with plastic wrap once more and let the dough sit for an additional thirty (0:30) minutes.

9. Set the risen dough on a floured board.

10. Use a knife to separate the dough into four equal pieces.

11. Form each piece into a 9-inch circle.

12. Roll opposite ends of the circle towards the center, leaving a space in the middle.

13. Pinch the edges together so that the dough resembles a boat.

14. Place the khachapuri dough onto a baking tray lined with greased parchment paper.

15. Combine the crumbled feta cheese, Farmers cheese, and mozzarella in a bowl.

16. Spoon the cheese mixture into the khachapuri boats.

17. Crack one egg into a small bowl and combine with one teaspoon of water to form an egg wash.

18. Brush the dough with the egg wash, and bake in a preheated oven at 450 degrees F° for fifteen (0:15) minutes until golden brown.

19. Remove from the oven and add small bits of butter to the cheese mixture.

20. Use a spoon to create a well in the middle of the cheese filling.

21. Crack one egg onto each khachapuri, so that the yolk sits in the well.

22. Place the khachapuri back into the oven and bake for about six (0:06) minutes until the eggs are cooked but still runny.

23. Serve immediately.

Germany – Sauerbraten

A famous German dish is Sauerbraten and is considered one of the country's national dishes. It is essentially a German pot roast made with beef, veal or venison as the main meat. Traditional sauerbraten was prepared using horse meat.

SERVES 6

INGREDIENTS

beef rump	3 lbs.
whole cloves	10
large onions (diced)	2
red wine vinegar	1 cup
bay leaves	2–3
white sugar	1 tbsp.
water	1 cup
gingersnap cookies (crumbled)	10
Vegetable oil	2 tbsps.
All-purpose flour	2 tbsps.
salt	1 tbsp.
black pepper	1 tbsp.

DIRECTIONS

1. Create a marinade for the meat by combining the red wine vinegar, black pepper, white sugar, onions, salt, cloves, and bay leaves.

2. Marinate the beef rump in a covered container for 2–3 days in the refrigerator, turning it daily.

3. Remove the meat from the container and pat dry with paper towels.

4. Reserve the marinade.

5. Combine the flour with a little salt and black pepper, then coat the beef rump with the flour mixture.

6. Heat the vegetable oil in a large Dutch oven pot.

7. Place the beef in the pot and fry for about ten (0:10) minutes or until all sides are brown.

8. Pour in the previously reserved marinade so that it coats the meat.

9. Cover the pot and reduce the heat to medium-low.

10. Allow the beef to cook for about four (4:00) hours or until it is tender and thoroughly cooked.

11. Transfer the cooked beef rump to a serving platter and use a sharp knife to slice the beef.

12. Strain the cooking liquid to remove any solids, then return the liquid to the pot.

13. Add the crumbled gingersnap cookies and simmer for ten (0:10) minutes till the gravy thickens.

14. Pour the gravy over the sliced beef.

15. Serve hot with potato dumplings.

NOTES

_____
_____
_____
_____
_____
_____
_____
_____
_____
_____
_____
_____
_____

Gibraltar – Profiteroles

The cuisine of Gibraltar can be described as a blend between Mediterranean and British due to the inhabitants who settled there from Malta, Genoa and Portugal and the country's ties with Britain. Profiteroles is the country's national dish and it is a decadent sweet pastry that is served at celebrations and festivals.

SERVES 4

INGREDIENTS

For the Pastry

Butter	3 tbsps.
flour	1/3 cup
(whisked)	2 eggs
water	1/3 cup

For the Filling

milk	1 ¼ cups
Cocoa powder	2 tbsps.
caster sugar	1/3 cup
egg yolks	3
Flour	1 ½ tbsps.

For the Sauce

dark chocolate chips	1 cup
freshly brewed coffee	¼ cup
thin cream	1/3 cup

DIRECTIONS

For the Pastry

1. Heat the water and butter in a saucepan.
2. Stir continuously for three (0:03) minutes until the butter melts, and the liquid comes to a boil.
3. Add the flour and mix well with a wooden spoon.
4. Reduce the heat and cook for about two (0:02) minutes, stirring until the mixtures leave the sides of the pan.
5. Allow the mixture to cool for five (0:05) minutes.
6. Gradually add the whisked eggs, mixing continuously until a thick paste forms.
7. Use a teaspoon to place blobs of the paste onto a baking sheet and smear the tops with any leftover egg.
8. Preheat the oven to 200 degrees F° and bake the pastries for twenty (0:20) minutes or until they are golden.
9. Remove from the oven and pierce the base of each profiterole with a knife to allow steam to escape.
10. Return to the oven and bake for an additional ten (0:10) minutes.

For the Filling

1. Heat the milk in a saucepan.
2. Combine the caster sugar, egg yolks, cocoa powder and flour using a whisk.
3. Gradually whisk the hot milk into the mixture.
4. Pour the mixture into a clean saucepan, stir it continuously and let it cook for five (0:05) minutes until the custard thickens.
5. Remove from the stove, cover with baking paper, and allow it to cool.

For the Sauce

1. Pour some water into a saucepan and let simmer.
2. Set a heatproof bowl over the simmering water.
3. Add the chocolate chips, coffee, and cream to the bowl and use a spoon to stir it as the chocolate melts.
4. Cook for five (0:05) minutes until the mixture is creamy and smooth.
5. Slice each profiterole, fill it with the custard, and drizzle the sauce over it before serving.

Greece – Moussaka

Moussaka is a staple dish in Greece. It is layered meat and eggplant casserole baked with a Béchamel sauce. Lamb meat is popularly used in this dish. In urban households, Moussaka is prepared for special occasions.

SERVES 6

INGREDIENTS

eggplants (cut into 1 cm slices)	2
minced lamb	1.6 lbs.
onion (peeled and chopped)	1
bay leaves	2
flour	1 tbsp.
Tomato puree	2 tbsps.
cinnamon stick	1
garlic cloves (crushed)	2
dried oregano	1 tsp.
dried mint	1 ½ tsp.
flaked sea salt	½ tsp.
fine sea salt	1 tbsp.
can diced tomatoes (14 oz. Can)	1
red wine	7 fl. oz.
Olive oil	7 tbsps.
potato slices (cut 1 cm thick)	1 lb. 2 oz.
Black pepper	

For the Béchamel Sauce

egg (beaten)	1
grated parmesan	1 oz.
grated nutmeg	1 tsp.
milk	14 fl. Oz.
butter	2 oz.
flour	2 oz.

DIRECTIONS

1. Season the eggplant slices with a sprinkle of salt and set aside.
2. Sauté the garlic and onions in a pot over medium-high heat, then add the lamb meat together with the oregano, mint, bay leaves and cinnamon.
3. Mix well and cook for ten (0:10) minutes.
4. Pour in the wine, add the salt and plenty black pepper.
5. Add the flour, tomatoes and tomato puree, then allow to simmer for thirty (0:30) minutes, occasionally stirring until the sauce thickens and the meat is tender.
6. Season with additional salt and black pepper if needed.
7. Rinse the eggplant slices in cold water, pat dry, and fry in oil, then set aside.
8. Boil the potato slices for five (0:05) minutes, then rinse in cold water.

For the Béchamel Sauce

1. Melt the butter in a saucepan and add the flour.
2. Cook for a few minutes, then stir in the milk gradually.
3. Add parmesan and grated nutmeg, then leave to simmer for five (0:05) minutes.
4. Season with salt and black pepper.
5. Turn off the heat and add the beaten egg.
6. Cover with plastic wrap and set aside.
7. Spoon a third of the meat a large casserole dish.
8. Add one layer of the eggplant slices as well as one layer of the potato slices.
9. Repeat to form two more layers and finish with the rest of the eggplant slices.
10. Pour the béchamel sauce evenly over the dish then top with a little grated parmesan.
11. Preheat the oven for 356 degrees F°, then bake the moussaka for forty-five (0:45) minutes until golden.
12. Serve hot.

Hungary– Goulash

Hungarian Goulash is a simple soup or stew made from meat and vegetables seasoned with paprika. Goulash can be dated back to medieval Hungary when shepherds cooked thick stews from dried meats and fresh vegetables. Today, the dish is considered the country's national dish.

SERVES 4

INGREDIENTS

beef (cut into 1–inch pieces)	1 ½ lb.
yellow onions (peeled and diced)	1 ½ lb.
sweet Hungarian paprika	¼ cup
cloves garlic (minced)	5
carrots (diced)	2
bay leaf	1
red bell peppers (seeded and sliced into ½ inch chunks)	2
yellow bell pepper (seeded and sliced into ½ inch chunks)	1
tomatoes (diced)	2
Pork lard / butter	3 tbsps.
beef broth	5 cups
salt	1 tsp.
freshly ground black pepper	½ tsp.
medium potatoes (peeled and cut into ½ inch chunks)	2

DIRECTIONS

1. Brown the beef chunks in a large pot and reserve.
2. Add the lard or butter to a Dutch oven pot and heat over medium-high heat until melted.
3. Sauté the onions in the melted lard or butter for about eight (0:08) minutes or until brown.
4. Remove the pot from the heat and stir in the Hungarian paprika and minced garlic.
5. Add the reserved beef and return the pot to the stove, and cook for about fifteen (0:15) minutes.
6. Add the red and yellow bell pepper chunks to the pot, stir and cook for seven (0:07) minutes.
7. Add the carrots, tomatoes, and potatoes.
8. Season the goulash with salt, black pepper, and the bay leaf.
9. Pour in all of the beef broth.
10. Bring to a boil, cover the pot with the lid, and reduce the heat slightly.
11. Simmer for forty (0:40) minutes.
12. Remove the lid and add additional salt if needed.
13. Serve with slices of rye bread and a dollop of sour cream.

NOTES

_____
_____
_____
_____
_____
_____
_____
_____
_____
_____
_____
_____
_____
_____
_____

Iceland–Mjolkursodinn

Mjolkursodinn is a bird and milk dish. The bird used in this dish is the puffin which is native to Iceland. There are many recipes with puffin meat as the main course but the most popular is Mjolkursodinn. The meat of the puffin is cooked in milk and eaten with a separate sauce along with vegetables and potatoes on the side.

SERVES 4

INGREDIENTS

For the puffins

freshly caught puffins	4
large slices of bacon (approx. 50 g)	2
Butter	3 ¼ tbsp.
whole milk	1 ¼ cup
water	1 ¼ cup
Salt to taste	
String for trussing	

For the Sauce

Butter	2 tbsps.
Flour	4 tbsps.
cooking liquid (reserved from the cooked puffin)	1–2 cups
Caramel sauce for color	
Redcurrant jelly as desired	
Whipped cream as desired	

DIRECTIONS

For the puffins

1. Skin the puffins or pluck and singe the skin.
2. Use a sharp knife to cut and gut each bird.
3. Remove the breasts or use the entire bird in the dish.
4. Wash the meat in cold water and rub liberally with salt.
5. Truss the birds if using whole.
6. Cook the bacon in a pan; remove the cooked bacon, and leave the fat in the pan.
7. Add the puffins to the bacon fat and cook until all sides are brown.
8. Turn off the heat and transfer the Puffins to a larger cooking pot, securing them tightly against each other.
9. In a separate saucepan, heat the milk and water together.
10. Pour this over the puffins and bring to a boil.
11. Cook for about two (2:00) hours until tender, turning the birds occasionally during this time.
12. Remove the birds from the liquid and keep warm, reserve 1 or 2 cups of the broth for the sauce.

For the Sauce

1. Melt the butter in a saucepan and add the flour.
2. Stir continuously until smooth.
3. Strain the cooking liquid and gradually incorporate it into the butter and flour mixture.
4. Add the caramel sauce, redcurrant jelly, and whipped cream if desired.
5. Serve this sauce with the puffins, along with caramelized potatoes and lightly boiled peas and carrots.

Ireland – Colcannon

Colcannon is an Irish potato dish that originated in the 1700s. It is a side dish, similar to American mashed potato but it incorporates butter and vegetables such as cabbage, kale, and leeks. It is a tradition to hid charms in bowls of colcannon at Halloween, and unmarried girls who found them believed they were a sign for a future marriage proposal.

SERVES 4

INGREDIENTS

medium Yukon Gold potatoes (approx. 1 ¾ lb.)	5
Unsalted butter	6 tbsps.
leeks (white and pale green parts)	2
cloves garlic (thinly sliced)	2
shredded Savoy cabbage	2 cups
milk	1 ¼ cups
heavy cream	½ cup
scallion (thinly sliced)	1
Freshly ground black pepper	
Water for boiling	
Kosher salt	

DIRECTIONS

1. Fill a saucepan with water and bring to a boil over medium-high heat.

2. Add a little salt and then put the potatoes in.

3. Simmer for about forty (0:40) minutes until the potatoes are tender.

4. Allow the potatoes to cool, then peel and set aside.

5. Slice the leeks lengthwise in half, then slice thinly crosswise.

6. Sauté the leeks in four tablespoons of melted butter for about ten (0:10) minutes until soft.

7. Add the garlic and toss together for about three (0:03) minutes until the leeks are beginning to brown.

8. Add one cup of the shredded savoy cabbage to the garlic and leeks.

9. Stir constantly while cooking, until the cabbage wilts.

10. Stir in the milk and heavy cream and let simmer.

11. Add the boiled potatoes to the pot, together with the second cup of shredded savoy cabbage.

12. Use a potato masher to mash the potatoes.

13. Season with salt and pepper.

14. Give everything a thorough mix and turn off the heat.

15. Spoon the colcannon into a big serving bowl.

16. Top with the remaining butter and chopped scallions.

17. Serve with boiled ham.

NOTES

_____

_____

_____

_____

_____

_____

_____

_____

_____

_____

_____

_____

Isle of Man – Bonnag

Bonnag is a type of baked sweet bread, either made plain or flavored with dried fruit and spices. It originated in the Isle of Man and is considered a traditional Manx staple for hundreds of years. Bonnag slices are usually served at tea time.

SERVES 8

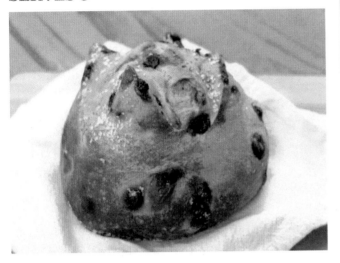

INGREDIENTS

baking soda	1 tsp.
all-purpose flour plus extra as needed	3 cups
sugar	1 cup
skim milk	1 cup
lemon juice/vinegar	2 tsp.
unsalted butter	2 tbsp.
dried berries (sultanas, dried cranberries)	¾ cup
vanilla	½ tsp.
mixed spice/pumpkin pie spice	1 ½ tsp.
milk (for wash)	1 tsp.

DIRECTIONS

1. Preheat the oven to 350 degrees F°.
2. Pour the lemon juice into a measuring cup then add milk to take the mixture up to the 1 cup mark.
3. Set aside the milk and lemon juice mixture for ten (0:10) minutes.
4. In a large bowl, combine the dry Ingredients; sugar, flour, baking soda, and mixed spice.
5. Use the fingers to rub in the butter and dry Ingredients until it is properly incorporated, then mix in the dried berries and vanilla.
6. Mix the dough with the milk and lemon juice mixture, ensuring there are no dry patches and the dough is not overmixed.
7. Add additional flour if the dough is very wet.
8. Knead briefly on a clean surface and shape into a wet, soft ball.
9. Grease an 8 inch round cake tin and place the ball of dough onto it.
10. Use a sharp knife to cut an X into the top surface of the dough.
11. Brush the top of the Bonnag loaf with milk.
12. Place the tin into the preheated oven and bake for about fifty-five (0:55) minutes until the loaf has risen and a toothpick comes out clean.
13. Slice and serve with tea.

NOTES

_____
_____
_____
_____
_____
_____
_____
_____
_____
_____
_____
_____
_____
_____
_____
_____
_____
_____

Italy – Pizza

Pizza is considered the national dish of Italy. However, it is popular in many other countries especially in the West. It is essentially a large flat open–faced sandwich topped with cheese and tomato sauce as well as meat and vegetables.

SERVES 4–8

INGREDIENTS

Olive oil	6 tsps.
grated Mozzarella cheese	1 1/3 cup
grated Parmesan cheese	¼ cup
Roma tomatoes (cut into ¼ inch thick slices)	2
clove garlic (minced)	1
yellow cornmeal	1 tbsp.
salt	½ tsp.
fresh basil leaves	6–8
Tomato sauce	
Pepperoni slices (optional)	

For the Dough

warm water	½ cup
Olive oil	3 tbsps.
salt	1 tsp.
all-purpose flour	2 cups
Dry yeast	2 tsps.

DIRECTIONS

1. Mix the yeast and warm water in a bowl, then let it sit for five (0:05) minutes.
2. Mix the flour, salt, and oil in a food processor, then add the yeast and water.
3. Mix to form a dough, then place it on a lightly floured surface and knead into a smooth ball.
4. Coat the ball of dough in a little oil, then place into a bowl and cover with plastic wrap.
5. Let the dough sit for one (1:00) hour until it has doubled in size.
6. Punch down the dough and divide into halves, then set aside.
7. Preheat the oven to 450 degrees F°.
8. Place two baking sheets onto a flat metal baking dish and sprinkle with cornmeal.
9. Roll out each piece of the pizza dough into a circle measuring about ten inches in diameter and place each onto a baking sheet.
10. Smear two teaspoons of oil and minced garlic over each pizza base, then drizzle tomato sauce over each.
11. Sprinkle the Mozzarella cheese over each pizza, then arrange the tomatoes and pepperoni slices over the top.
12. Top with the Parmesan cheese.
13. Arrange the basil leaves over the cheese.
14. Drizzle the pizzas with the remaining olive oil and then bake for about fifteen (0:15) minutes until the cheese melts and the dough cooked.
15. Garnish with fresh basil and a sprinkle of salt.
16. Cut into wedges and serve hot.

NOTES

_____
_____
_____
_____
_____
_____
_____
_____
_____

Latvia – Janu Siers

One of the largest festivals in Latvia is Janu. To commemorate this occasion, a special type of cheese is made. It is called Janu Siers and is considered to be the national dish of Latvia. Traditionally, visitors to Latvian homes on the night of the festival are given the homemade cheeses as gifts.

YIELDS 1 parcel of cheese

INGREDIENTS

full cream milk	3 L
cottage cheese	1 kg
butter	100 g
salt	2 tsp.
eggs (lightly whisked)	2
caraway seeds	2 tsp.
turmeric / yellow food dye (optional)	1 tsp.

DIRECTIONS

1. Pour the milk into a large saucepan and turn on the heat.

2. Add the cottage cheese to the saucepan and begin stirring the milk and cheese together for about twenty (0:20) minutes until whey begins to form.

3. Place a sieve over a bowl and pour in the milk and cheese mixture to remove the solids.

4. Melt the butter in a separate saucepan.

5. Add the liquid cheese mixture to the saucepan containing the melted butter.

6. Reduce the heat and use a wooden spoon to mix the butter and cheese mixture thoroughly.

7. Add the salt.

8. Add the whisked eggs and the caraway seeds.

9. Add the turmeric or food dye if desired for yellow colored cheese.

10. Cook for about four (0:04) minutes, continually stirring until it thickens and curds begin to form.

11. Place a piece of cheesecloth in the sieve and pour in the mixture.

12. Allow the liquid to strain, then pull the corners of the cheesecloth together and spin them until a parcel of cheese forms.

13. Put the parcel of cheese into a bowl.

14. Cover the bowl with a plate.

15. Let the bowl cool to room temperature, then place in the refrigerator.

16. Serve the cheese after twenty four (24:00) hours.

NOTES

_____
_____
_____
_____
_____
_____
_____
_____
_____
_____
_____
_____
_____
_____
_____

Liechtenstein – Kasknopfle

Kasknopfle is a cooked noodle and cheese dish that is popular in Liechtenstein. The noodles are homemade. It is a hearty, classic dish that is served hot. In Liechtenstein, this dish is topped with caramelized onions and served with a salad or applesauce.

SERVES 4–6

INGREDIENTS

milk	1 cup
eggs	4
salt	1 tsp.
pepper	1 tsp.
all-purpose flour	3 cups
shredded Gruyere cheese	1/3 cup
shredded Emmenthaler cheese	1/3 cup
(shredded) Fontina cheese	1/3 cup
onions (peeled and cut into thin slices)	2
butter	2 tbsp.
Water	6-8 cups

DIRECTIONS

1. Create a sticky noodle batter by whisking together the milk, eggs, salt, pepper, and flour in a bowl.

2. Allow the batter to rest undisturbed for thirty (0:30) minutes until the lumps dissolve.

3. Put the water in a saucepan or pot and bring to a boil.

4. Sprinkle a generous dash of salt into the boiling water.

5. Make the noodles by placing the batter on a Spaetzle Maker or the flat side of a cheese grater, and press the batter through the holes with a scraper (or any flat square object), letting the squiggly noodles fall directly into the saucepan/pot of boiling water.

6. Cook for two (0:02) minutes or until the noodles float to the surface.

7. Remove them in batches with a slotted spoon when cooked.

8. Set the cooked noodles aside.

9. Melt the butter in a skillet and add the onion slices.

10. Sauté the onions in the butter until it caramelized.

11. Set aside a small amount of caramelized onions for the topping.

12. Add the Gruyere cheese, Emmenthaler cheese, and shredded Fontina cheese to the remaining caramelized onion slices in the skillet.

13. Mix the cheese and onions until the cheese melts.

14. Transfer the cooked noodles into the pan with the cheese and onions.

15. Fold the noodles into the cheese and onion mixture, then turn off the heat.

16. Top the Kasknopfle with the caramelized onions previously set aside.

17. Serve hot with applesauce on the side.

NOTES

_____

_____

_____

_____

_____

_____

_____

_____

Lithuania – Cepelinai

Cepelinai is a zeppelin shaped potato dumpling. It is stuffed with minced meat and smothered in a creamy bacon gravy. This delicious delicacy is considered to be Lithuania's national dish.

SERVES 4

INGREDIENTS

russet potatoes (peeled)	7 lbs.
Vitamin–C pill (crushed)	1
salt	4 tsp.
minced pork	6 oz.
ground beef	6 oz.
medium onion (peeled and chopped)	1
large onions (peeled and chopped)	2
country bacon (diced)	6 oz.
sour cream	1 cup
Vegetable oil for frying	
Pepper	

DIRECTIONS

1. Boil 1/6 of the potatoes in salted water for thirty (0:30) minutes, then drain, mash and set aside to cool.

2. Place the crushed vitamin C pill into a bowl, then grate the remaining potatoes in the bowl, occasionally mixing as the vitamin C will prevent the potatoes from becoming discolored.

3. Wrap the grated potatoes in a cheesecloth, then squeeze out as much liquid as possible into a container.

4. Let the potato liquid rest for a few minutes until the starch settles at the bottom of the container.

5. Gently pour away the liquid and collect the potato starch that settles.

6. Place the starch in a bowl, then add the mashed potatoes, the grated potatoes and two teaspoons of salt.

7. Knead these Ingredients together and set aside.

8. Create the dumpling filling by combining the minced pork and beef, chopped medium onion, salt, and pepper.

9. Take a lump of potato dough in the hands, flatten it and add a small dollop of meat filling.

10. Fold the dough over the filling, seal the edges and shape into a zeppelin/football dumpling.

11. Repeat until the potato dough, and meat filling finish.

12. Fill a large stockpot with salted water, then bring to a boil on the stove.

13. Add the Cepelinai to the pot and reduce the heat to medium-high.

14. Boil the dumplings for fifteen (0:15) minutes until cooked through, then remove from the pot and set aside.

15. Prepare the gravy by first sautéing together the bacon and the two large chopped onions in vegetable oil.

16. When the bacon cook and the onions are translucent, mix in some salt, pepper, sour cream and a little hot water if desired.

17. Generously top the dumplings with the bacon gravy.

18. Serve hot.

NOTES

_____

_____

_____

_____

_____

Luxembourg – Judd mat Gaardebounen

Judd mat Gaardebounen is a smoked pork and bean dish that is iconic in Luxembourg. Smoked pork collar is the choice of cut for this dish. It originated in the village of Gostingen, located in the south eastern part of the country which is famous for its excellent broad beans.

SERVES 5–6

INGREDIENTS

smoked pork collar	1.5 kg
fresh broad beans (shelled and blanched in salted water)	1 kg
waxy potatoes (peeled and quartered)	1 kg
sunflower oil	2 tbsp.
cloves garlic (crushed)	4
sprigs parsley (chopped)	6
leek (chopped)	1
stalks celery (chopped)	4
butter	3 ½ tbsp.
flour	1/3 cup
cubed carrots	1 cup
large whole onion (studded with 4 cloves)	1
dry white wine	½ cup
bay leaves	2
dried summer savory	2 tbsp.
Salt	
Pepper	

DIRECTIONS

1. Boil the potatoes in water for about five (0:05) minutes, then drain and set aside.

2. Place the smoked collar, carrots, leeks, onion, celery, and bay leaves in a pot.

3. Pour in enough water to cover the meat and vegetables, then bring to a simmer.

4. Cover the pot and allow it to simmer for two (2:00) hours.

5. In a separate pan, create a roux with the flour and butter by first melting the butter and then gradually whisking in the flour.

6. Add a cup of the stock liquid from the meat and vegetables to the roux and whisk to remove any lumps.

7. Simmer for five (0:05) minutes until the sauce thickens.

8. Add the wine and savory to the sauce and let it simmer for ten (0:10) minutes.

9. Season the sauce with salt and pepper.

10. Stir in the blanched beans to the sauce, turn off the heat after a few minutes and set aside.

11. Heat the sunflower oil in a frying pan and add the boiled potatoes.

12. Sauté the potatoes until golden, then add the crushed garlic and a cup of the meat and vegetable stock.

13. Increase the heat and cook until the liquid evaporates, then set aside.

14. Remove the smoked pork from the cooking stock, let stand for two (0:02) minutes and then slice thickly.

15. Serve the pork slices with the beans, sauce and sautéed potatoes.

NOTES

_____
_____
_____
_____
_____
_____
_____
_____
_____
_____

Macedonia – Tavce Gravce

The national dish of Macedonia is Tavce Gravce. This is a Macedonian styled baked bean stew. This dish is traditionally prepared with fresh beans and served in earthenware. It is usually eaten with bread and popularly eaten at dinnertime. Recipes for this dish are usually transferred from generation to generation and there are many variations.

SERVES 8

INGREDIENTS

white beans (rehydrated)	2 cups
medium onions (diced)	2
sundried tomatoes (halved and seeded)	1 cup
salt	1 tsp.
black pepper	1 tsp.
sunflower/peanut oil	¼ cup
paprika	1 tsp.
ground cumin	1 tsp.
red pepper flakes	1 tbsp.
cloves garlic (finely chopped)	3
dried mint	1 tbsp.
bay leaf	1

DIRECTIONS

1. Place the rehydrated beans into a large pot and pour in enough water to cover the beans by an inch.

2. Add the bay leaf and the diced onions to the pot.

3. Set the heat to medium-high and cook for two (2:00) hours until the beans are tender, stirring occasionally and adding water if necessary.

4. Turn off the heat when it resembles a creamy stew and set aside.

5. Preheat the oven to 400 degrees F°.

6. Heat the oil in a sauté pan, then add the garlic, mint, red pepper flakes, paprika, black pepper, salt, and cumin.

7. Sauté the spices for one (0:01) minute or until a fragrant aroma arises and the spices flavor the oil.

8. Pour the spicy oil in the pot of beans and stir well until the beans glisten.

9. Mix in the sundried tomatoes to the bean stew.

10. Transfer the bean stew into a clay pot, Dutch oven or traditional tagine.

11. Bake the beans in the oven for about thirty (0:30) minutes until the stew thickens.

12. Serve Tavce Gravce with pita bread or slices of dense sourdough.

NOTES

_____
_____
_____
_____
_____
_____
_____
_____
_____
_____
_____
_____
_____
_____

Madrid – Cocido Madrileno

Cocido Madrileno originated in Madrid, Spain. It is a two course dish with a noodle soup and a meat, sausage and garbanzo bean stew. This dish is eaten on May 15th, the feast day of Saint Isidore who is revered as Madrid's patron saint.

SERVES 6

INGREDIENTS

ham bone	1
fresh pig's foot (halved)	1
beef stew meat	1 lb.
bacon (sliced thickly)	¼ lb.
fresh ham meat	¼ lb.
chicken	½
dry garbanzo beans	2 cups
carrot (cut into three pieces)	1
small turnip (halved)	1
small yellow onion (peeled and quartered)	1
potatoes (peeled and halved)	6–8
large savoy cabbage (cut into eighths)	1
chorizo sausage	1
angel hair pasta (broken into four portions)	1 ½ cup
water	13 cups
morcilla (black pudding)	1
Salt	

DIRECTIONS

1. Soak the garbanzo beans in a large bowl of cold water for twelve (12:00) hours, then drain and set aside.

2. Place the beef, ham bone, pig's foot, bacon, and ham meat into a large pot together with thirteen cups of water and bring to a boil.

3. Remove any fat or scum that comes to the surface of the water as it boils.

4. Add the chicken, soaked garbanzo beans, carrot, turnip and onion to the pot.

5. Let the meat and vegetables simmer for two (2:00) hours.

6. Add the chopped potatoes to the pot.

7. Season the meat and vegetables with adequate salt and add more water if necessary.

8. Allow to simmer for about thirty (0:30) minutes more, then set aside.

9. Transfer two cups of the meat and vegetable stock to a separate pot and add two additional cups of water.

10. Cook the savoy cabbage, morcilla and chorizo in the stock and water until the cabbage is tender, then set aside.

11. Transfer equal amounts of the meat stock and cabbage stock to another pot and bring to a boil.

12. Add the pasta and cook till tender.

13. Serve the pasta and broth as a soup.

14. Then serve the meat, vegetables, beans, cabbage, and sausage together as a second course to the meal.

NOTES

_____
_____
_____
_____
_____

Malta – Stuffat al Fenek

Stuffat al fenek is a hearty rabbit stew that is popular in Malta. It is prepared at celebrations and festivals. This rich stew is eaten with Maltese baked potatoes and crusty bread.

SERVES 4–6

INGREDIENTS

rabbits (skinned, jointed and portioned for stew)	2
bottle of rich red wine	¾
onions (peeled and chopped)	2
cloves garlic (peeled and minced)	4
bay leaves	8–10
can (400g) whole tomatoes	1
tomato puree	3 tbsp.
carrots (peeled and sliced)	2
medium potatoes (peeled and cut into chunks)	6–8
Olive oil	3 tbsp.
Salt	
Water	
Pepper	

DIRECTIONS

1. Create a marinade by combining half the crushed garlic, salt, pepper, four bay leaves, and the red wine in a large bowl.

2. Add the rabbit meat to the marinade, mix well and refrigerate for two (2:00) hours.

3. Heat the olive oil in a pot, remove the meat from the marinade and sear the meat in the pot until brown on all sides.

4. Set aside the marinade and the seared rabbit meat.

5. In the same pot, sauté the onions and remaining bay leaves over low heat.

6. After five (0:05) minutes, add the remaining garlic to the pot and allow it to fry lightly.

7. Add the can of tomatoes to the pot and gently squash the whole tomatoes with the spoon so that they can absorb the flavors.

8. Increase the heat and cook for five (0:05) minutes, stirring occasionally.

9. Pour in the rest of the marinade, and bring to a boil, then add the seared rabbit meat to the pot.

10. Stir everything together, then add enough water to cover the meat.

11. Cover the pot and reduce to a simmer.

12. After thirty (0:30) minutes add the carrots, tomato puree, and potatoes to the pot.

13. Stir and let simmer for another thirty (0:30) minutes.

14. Set the lid to cover half of the pot and allow the sauce to thicken.

15. Adjust the salt and pepper to taste.

16. After fifteen (0:15) minutes, stir the stew and turn off the heat when the meat and vegetables are tender.

17. Serve Stuffat al Fenek with crusty bread.

NOTES

_____
_____
_____
_____
_____
_____
_____
_____
_____
_____

Moldova – Sarmale

Sarmale is a traditional Moldovan dish and considered to be the national dish of Moldova. Essentially, Sarmale are cabbage leaf rolls. They are stuffed with a mixture of meat, rice and vegetables. Grape leaves can also be used instead of cabbage. Sarmale is eaten with sour cream. This dish is usually prepared for celebrations like Christmas and Easter.

SERVES 5

INGREDIENTS

medium head of cabbage	1
sunflower seed oil	¼ cup
tomato paste	3 tbsp.
long grain rice	3 ¼ cup
pork loin roast (diced)	2 lb.
chopped onions	1 lb.
chopped carrots	1 lb.
dried dill weed	½ tsp.
diced parsley / turnip root	6 oz.
1 pinch salt	
Freshly ground black pepper	
Water	

DIRECTIONS

1. Rinse the rice in cold water, then drain.
2. Submerge the rinsed rice in boiling water and let it soak for fifteen (0:15) minutes.
3. Drain the rice and set aside.
4. Heat two tablespoons of oil in a pan and add the carrots, onions and parsley root.
5. Add the tomato paste and sauté together.
6. Allow the vegetables to cook for five (0:05 minutes) or until tender.
7. Transfer the vegetables to the bowl of rice and set aside.
8. Add two tablespoons of oil to the pan and heat.
9. Add the pork and cook for two (0:02) minutes until brown on all sides.
10. Transfer the pork to the bowl of rice and vegetables, season with the dill weed and black pepper, mix and set aside to cool.
11. Separate the leaves from the head of cabbage.
12. Place the leaves in a shallow pot of water and bring to a boil.
13. Cook the leaves for ten (0:10) minutes until tender and flexible.
14. Leave a layer of leaves at the base of the pot and remove the rest.
15. Place two tablespoons of the rice, pork and vegetable mix onto the middle of each leaf and roll tightly.
16. Place the cabbage rolls back into the pot, top with a few flat boiled leaves and pour in adequate boiling water to cover the rolls.
17. Cover the pot and let the Sarmale simmer for thirty (0:30) minutes until the rice cooked.
18. Serve with a dollop of sour cream.

NOTES

_____
_____
_____
_____
_____
_____
_____
_____
_____
_____
_____
_____
_____

Monaco – Barbagiuan

Barbagiuan is a savory cheese and spinach pastry. It is traditionally eaten on November 19th, the principality's national day and for the Fete du Barbagiuan, a festival held to promote national cuisine with special focus on Barbagiuan pastries.

YIELDS 20

INGREDIENTS

For the Pastry

plain flour	210g
salt	½ tsp.
olive oil	¼ cup
egg (beaten)	1

For the Filling

fresh spinach (chopped)	50g
Swiss chard leaves (shredded)	2–3
olive oil	1½ tsp.
medium onion (finely chopped)	½
leek (white part only, chopped)	1
dried oregano	½ tsp.
ricotta cheese	2½ tbsp.
grated Parmesan cheese	1 tbsp.
egg white (beaten)	1
Salt	
Pepper	
Vegetable oil for frying	

DIRECTIONS

For the Pastry

1. Sift the flour and salt into a bowl.
2. Add the beaten egg and the olive oil to the flour, then mix with a fork.
3. Add a little water and form a firm ball of dough.
4. Knead the dough for about five (0:05) minutes and reshape into a ball.
5. Wrap the dough in plastic wrap and refrigerate for thirty (0:30) minutes.
6. Roll out the dough on a lightly floured surface until about 2 mm thick.
7. Use a 6 cm cutter to cut as many circles in the dough.

For the Filling

1. Sauté the onions and leek for about five (0:05) minutes in the olive oil.
2. Add the spinach, Swiss chard, and oregano to the pan.
3. Cook for ten (0:10) minutes until the chard is tender.
4. Transfer the vegetables to a bowl and mix in the ricotta and parmesan cheese.
5. Season with pepper and salt, then set aside to cool.
6. Place a teaspoon of filling onto the center of each pastry circle, brush edges with egg white and fold over the circle to form a semi-circle.
7. Crimp the edges shut with a fork.
8. Heat the vegetable oil to 190 degrees C and fry the pastries until brown and crisp.
9. Transfer the pastries to a plate lined with paper towels.
10. Serve warm.

NOTES

_____
_____
_____
_____

Montenegro – Kacamak

Kacamak is Montenegro's national dish. It is a hearty dish similar to polenta. It is made with just a few Ingredients but has many variations depending on the sub region of the country. Kacamak originated as a peasant's meal; when potatoes were introduced to the highland regions, the people there mixed potatoes with corn flour and cheese to yield a high energy meal which sustained them throughout the day. In the present day, Kacamak can be found in almost all restaurants in Montenegro and is usually served with yogurt or buttermilk.

SERVES 8

INGREDIENTS

large potatoes	2
yellow cornmeal	1 ¼ cups
feta cheese	½ cup
oil	¼ cup
pinches salt	2
Water	

DIRECTIONS

1. Fill a saucepan of water and bring to a boil.
2. Add the potatoes and sprinkle in a pinch of salt.
3. Boil the potatoes until cooked, then peel and dice into large cubes.
4. Fill a clean saucepan with three cups of water, then add the potato cubes and a pinch of salt.
5. Bring to a boil and cook until the potato cubes begin to break apart.
6. Reduce the heat to a simmer.
7. Without draining the boiling water, insert a potato masher, and smash the potato cubes into a liquid paste.
8. Gradually add the yellow cornmeal to the pot and mix it well to incorporate it into the mashed potatoes.
9. Stir the mixture continuously with a spoon to remove any lumps.
10. Remove from the heat when the mixture resembles cream of wheat porridge.
11. Add the oil to the Kacamak and stir well while it is still hot.
12. Crumble the feta cheese and add it to the Kacamak.
13. Stir until the cheese melts.
14. Serve immediately with creamy yogurt or buttermilk.

NOTES

_____
_____
_____
_____
_____
_____
_____
_____
_____
_____
_____
_____
_____
_____
_____
_____
_____
_____

Netherlands – Stamppot

Stamppot, also known as hutspot is a hearty dish made of mashed potato, vegetables and smoked sausages such as Dutch Rookworst, Spanish Chorizo or Polish Kielbasa. There are different versions of this dish depending on whether kale, sauerkraut or endives are used. Stamppot is traditionally made on October 3rd in the Dutch city of Leiden to celebrate its liberation from the Spanish.

SERVES 4–5

INGREDIENTS

large russet potatoes (peeled and cut into 1-inch cubes)	5
unsalted butter	2 tbsp.
milk	½ cup
medium onion (peeled and chopped)	1
cloves garlic (minced)	2
bunch kale (de-stemmed and chopped into ½ inch pieces)	1
white wine vinegar	½ tsp.
olive oil	3 tbsp.
green onions (chopped)	4
cooked, smoked pork sausage (sliced)	1 lb.
water	¼ cup
salt	2 tsp.
black pepper	¼ tsp.

DIRECTIONS

1. Boil the potatoes in salted water for about fifteen (0:15) minutes until soft.

2. Drain the cooking water and return the potatoes to the pot.

3. Add the butter, salt, and black pepper to the potatoes.

4. Mash the potatoes with a potato masher until the desired texture is achieved, then set aside.

5. Heat a tablespoon of oil in a skillet, add the onions and sauté for six (0:06) minutes until soft

6. Add the garlic to the onions along with the chopped kale.

7. Add the white wine vinegar and water to the kale, then place the lid on the skillet.

8. Cook the kale for about three (0:03) minutes until wilted.

9. Remove the lid, stir the Ingredients, and allow the kale to cook for an additional three (0:03) minutes until tender.

10. Season the kale with a pinch of salt and black pepper if desired, then transfer it to the mashed potatoes.

11. Fold in the kale to the mashed potatoes until thoroughly combined, then set aside.

12. Heat a tablespoon of olive oil in the same skillet and add the sliced sausages.

13. Brown the sausages and set aside.

NOTES

_____

_____

_____

_____

_____

_____

_____

_____

_____

_____

_____

Northern Ireland – Ulster Fry

Ulster Fry is the traditional dish of Northern Ireland. It is typically a breakfast dish consisting of soda and potato farls, tomatoes, eggs and pork sausages. In Northern Ireland, the meal is served in pubs and restaurants for both breakfast and lunch. It has a reputation of being a good cure for a hangover.

SERVES 1

INGREDIENTS

small, ripe tomatoes (halved)	2
soda farl (a flat version of soda bread)	1
potato farls (Irish potato bread)	2
large eggs	2
mushrooms (sliced)	4
vegetable roll (sausage meat mixed with scallions)	1
sausages	2
thick slices bacon	2
pinch salt	1
pinch black pepper	1
Canola oil (for frying)	

DIRECTIONS

1. Heat a little canola oil in a shallow skillet.
2. Add the tomatoes and sauté in the oil for a few minutes.
3. Add the vegetable roll and sausages to the skillet and sauté together with the tomatoes over low heat.
4. Add the mushrooms to the skillet.
5. Stir together and cook for a few minutes until browned, then set aside.
6. Heat the grill to medium-high and place the bacon beneath it.
7. Transfer the tomatoes from the skillet to the dish with the bacon and grill until the cooked.
8. Slice the soda and potato farls, then set aside.
9. Heat a little oil in a frying pan
10. Crack the eggs into the pan.
11. Season the eggs with a pinch of salt and black pepper and cook until yolks have set but insides are still runny.
12. Remove the eggs when cooked and add a little more oil to the pan.
13. Increase the heat and when the oil is hot, place the slices of soda and potato farls into the pan.
14. Flip the farls constantly to prevent burning. Once golden brown, turn off the heat.
15. Place the farls on a serving plate with the bacon, tomatoes, mushrooms, and sausages, then top with the fried eggs.
16. Serve Ulster Fry with a cup of hot tea.

NOTES

_____
_____
_____
_____
_____
_____
_____
_____
_____
_____
_____
_____

Norway – Farikal

Farikal is Norway's national dish. It originated in western Norway but it is now popular throughout the country. The word Farikal means "sheep in cabbage." It is a simple casserole made of cabbage, mutton and whole peppercorns. Lamb can also be used in place of mutton for a milder tasting Farikal. The dish itself has a distinct umami flavor. It is traditionally eaten on the 26th of September or the last Thursday of September in some parts of Norway. Farikal is served with potatoes, carrots, cowberry sauce and flatbread.

SERVES 6

INGREDIENTS

lamb breast/shoulder	3 lbs.
large head of cabbage	1
all-purpose flour	2 tbsp.
whole black peppercorns	1 tbsp.
Dash of salt	
Water	

DIRECTIONS

1. Cut the lamb meat into bite-size pieces, then wash and set aside.

2. Wash the head of cabbage and roughly chop into pieces.

3. Discard the root end of the cabbage and set aside the chopped leaves.

4. Line the base of a pot with half of the cabbage leaves.

5. Dredge the lamb meat in flour, then lay atop the cabbage leaves in the pot.

6. Fill a saucepan with water and bring to a boil, then pour the boiling water over the lamb and cabbage leaves so that half the meat submerged in the water.

7. Add a dash of salt to the pot.

8. Sprinkle in the whole peppercorns.

9. Place the pot on the stove over low heat.

10. Allow the Farikal to simmer for one (1:00) hour.

11. Add the remaining cabbage leaves.

12. Cover the pot with a tight-fitting lid and continue to simmer for one (1:00) hour or until the meat and cabbage leaves are tender.

13. Turn off the heat and transfer to serving bowls.

14. Serve Farikal with boiled potatoes, flatbread, and cowberry sauce.

NOTES

_____
_____
_____
_____
_____
_____
_____
_____
_____
_____
_____
_____
_____
_____
_____
_____
_____

Poland – Bigos

Poland's national dish is called Bigos or Hunter's Stew. It is a combination of game meat, poultry, pork, beef, sauerkraut and vegetables. Any combination of fresh and leftover meats are normally used. Traditionally, the dish is served for Christmas and Easter as well as at outdoor events such as hunts and carnival sleigh rides.

SERVES 6–8

INGREDIENTS

sauerkraut (rinsed and drained)	1 lb.
smoked Polish sausage (cut into 1–inch pieces)	½ lb.
fresh Polish sausage (precooked and chopped into 1–inch rounds)	½ lb.
leftover meat (any kind, cut into 1–inch pieces)	1 lb.
large tomatoes (peeled and diced)	3
salt	1 tsp.
dry red wine	1 cup
bay leaf	1
pepper	¼ tsp.
small head of cabbage (chopped)	1
medium onion (peeled and chopped)	1
bacon fat / vegetable oil	1 tbsp.
boiling water	2 cups
dried Polish Borowiki mushrooms / dried Italian porcini mushrooms	½ oz.
prunes (pitted)	1 cup

DIRECTIONS

1. Combine the prunes and dried mushrooms in a large glass bowl.

2. Pour the boiling water over them and let steep for thirty (0:30) minutes until the mushrooms are soft

3. Roughly chop the mushrooms and prunes and set aside with the soaking liquid.

4. Heat the bacon fat or vegetable oil in a large Dutch oven pot.

5. Add the onion and fresh cabbage.

6. Sauté until the cabbage wilts down by half, then stir in the sauerkraut.

7. Add the tomatoes, sausages, leftover meat, bay leaf, and the red wine.

8. Add the mushrooms and prunes together with the soaking liquid but not the sandy residue which may have accumulated at the bottom of the soaking bowl.

9. Mix the Ingredients well and bring to a boil over medium heat.

10. Add salt and pepper.

11. Reduce the heat, cover and allow the stew to simmer gently for about one and a half (1:30) hours, adding additional liquid as necessary to prevent burning.

12. Uncover and remove the bay leaf after cooking.

13. Top with greens and serve Bigos with boiled potatoes.

NOTES

_____
_____
_____
_____
_____
_____
_____
_____
_____
_____

Portugal – Bacalhau

Bacalhau or dried, salted codfish has been a staple in Portuguese cuisine for many years. Bacalhau is prepared with potatoes, olive oil and garlic as a base but in various parts of Portugal, other Ingredients are added. It is traditionally prepared as a Christmas Eve dinner.

SERVES 4

INGREDIENTS

Bacalhau / dried, salted codfish	1 ½ lb.
medium potatoes (peeled and cut into quarters)	4–6
olive oil	½ cup
cloves garlic (sliced)	4–6
sweet paprika	1 tbsp.
salt	¼ tsp.
pepper	½ tsp.
dried parsley	1 tbsp.
yellow bell pepper (sliced)	1
red bell pepper (sliced)	1
white wine	½ cup
Portuguese black olives	20
large onion (peeled and sliced)	1

DIRECTIONS

1. Soak the codfish in water overnight, changing the water about three to four times to remove some of the salt.

2. Place the potatoes in a pot of water and boil for five (0:05) minutes.

3. Drain the potatoes and set aside.

4. Preheat the oven to 375 degrees F°.

5. Heat half of the olive oil in a sauté pan.

6. Add the garlic and sauté for a few minutes, then add the potatoes, onions and the sliced bell peppers.

7. Mix the paprika, salt, pepper, and dried parsley and sprinkle one-quarter of the mixture over the sautéing vegetables.

8. Rub the codfish with the rest of the seasoning mix.

9. Stir the vegetables, then place the seasoned codfish in the middle of the sauté pan, surrounding it snugly with the vegetables.

10. Drizzle the codfish and vegetables with the rest of the olive oil and the white wine.

11. Put the pan into the preheated oven and bake for thirty (0:30) minutes, gently tossing the vegetables and fish once or twice during this time.

12. Increase the heat to 425 degrees F° and top with the olives.

13. Bake for an additional ten (0:10) minutes, then remove from the oven.

14. Serve hot.

NOTES

_____
_____
_____
_____
_____
_____
_____
_____
_____
_____
_____
_____
_____
_____
_____

Republic of Tatarstan – Echpochmak

Echpochmak is Tatarstan's iconic triangular pastry. It is traditionally made of unleavened dough and stuffed with finely chopped meat and potatoes. It is crunchy on the outside and juicy on the inside. Typically, meats with a high fat content are used to make the stuffing, such as goose meat, duck or mutton.

SERVES 6–8

INGREDIENTS

butter (melted)	7 tbsp.
kefir	½ cup
sour cream	½ cup
yolk	1 egg
salt	1 tsp.
flour (sifted)	2 cups
baking powder	1 tsp.
goose breast fillet (finely chopped)	1 (300g)
medium onions (peeled and finely diced)	3
finely diced potato	1 1/3 cup
Black pepper	
Egg wash	
Meat stock (chicken/beef stock)	

DIRECTIONS

1. Combine the baking powder, flour, a teaspoon of salt, egg yolk, kefir, sour cream and melted butter in a deep glass bowl.

2. Knead these Ingredients into a soft, elastic ball of dough.

3. Cover the bowl and set aside for one (1:00) hour.

4. In a separate bowl, combine the finely chopped onions, potatoes, and goose meat.

5. Season generously with salt and black pepper, then mix well and set aside.

6. Set the ball of dough onto a floured surface and roll out into a 3 mm thick flat layer.

7. Press an overturned plate or bowl onto the rolled out dough and cut out as many circles as possible, each measuring approximately 15 cm in diameter.

8. Spoon a generous helping of the goose stuffing in the center of each circle.

9. Fold the edges of each circle over the stuffing to form a triangular shaped pastry, leaving a small hole in the middle.

10. Pinch the raised seams of each pastry tightly together and place them side by side on a greased baking sheet.

11. Brush the pastries with egg wash.

12. Preheat the oven to 350 degrees F° before placing the pastries in the oven.

13. Bake them for twenty-five (0:25) minutes.

14. While the pastries are baking, heat the meat stock in a saucepan.

15. Remove the pastries from the oven.

16. Spoon two tablespoons of hot meat stock into the small hole on the top of each Echpochmak; the liquid will further cook the stuffing on the inside.

17. Place the pastries back into the oven and bake for an additional ten (0:10) minutes.

18. Turn off the oven and let them sit in the hot oven for about fifteen (0:15) minutes before serving.

Romania – Mici

Romanian skinless sausages are called Mici. They are made of ground meat and are baked, fried or grilled. Mici is traditionally served with bread, potatoes or salad and topped with mustard. This meal is served at picnics and for special occasions such as Labor Day. Mici is said to have been invented in Bucharest in the 20th century when an innkeeper ran out of sausage casings. He formed small oval sausages without the casings, then grilled them over charcoal and served them to customers.

SERVES 6

INGREDIENTS

ground pork	1 lb.
ground beef chuck	1 lb.
water	2 tbsp.
olive oil	2 tbsp.
thyme	2 tsp.
cloves garlic (minced)	3-9
hot red pepper flakes	1 tsp.
hot Hungarian paprika	1 tbsp.
caraway seeds	2 tsp.
salt	1 tsp.
freshly ground black pepper	1 tsp.
Oil for frying	

DIRECTIONS

1. In a large bowl, combine the ground pork and beef with the olive oil and water.

2. Add the minced garlic, thyme, red pepper flakes, and the Hungarian paprika.

3. Mix well and add salt, black pepper, and the caraway seeds.

4. Add a little water if the meat becomes too dry and thoroughly combine the seasonings with the meat.

5. Cover the bowl and place in the refrigerator for six (6:00) hours or allow it to chill overnight.

6. With damp hands, divide the meat mixture into eighteen equal portions.

7. Shape each portion into oval sausages about 3 inches long and 1 ½ inch thick.

8. Cook the sausages by frying them in a hot skillet until done or bake them at 350 degrees F° for fifteen (0:15) minutes.

9. Alternatively, grill or broil the sausages until cooked and crispy.

10. Serve the sausages hot or cold with bread, baked potatoes or salad.

NOTES

_____
_____
_____
_____
_____
_____
_____
_____
_____
_____
_____
_____
_____
_____
_____
_____
_____
_____

Russia – Shchi

One of the national dishes of Russia is Shchi. This is a savory cabbage soup. There are many variations to Shchi, some of which are made with fresh cabbage and others are made with sauerkraut (called sour shchi). Variations containing spinach and sorrel are called green shchi. This soup is eaten with sour cream and rye bread.

SERVES 6

INGREDIENTS

large head of cabbage (shredded)	1
large carrot (peeled and grated)	1
celery rib (chopped)	1
large onion (peeled and chopped)	1
large russet potatoes (peeled and chopped)	2
can (14 oz.) undrained, diced tomatoes	1
butter	3 tbsp.
vegetable stock/water	8 cups
bay leaf	1
Black peppercorns to taste	
Salt	
Pepper	
Fresh dill (garnish)	
Sour cream (garnish)	

DIRECTIONS

1. Melt the butter in a large Dutch oven or soup pot.

2. Add the chopped onions and sauté them in the melted butter until translucent.

3. Add the grated carrot, chopped celery, and shredded cabbage to the pot.

4. Sauté the vegetables together for about three (0:03) minutes.

5. Add the bay leaf and mix in the black peppercorns.

6. Pour in the vegetable stock or water and bring to a boil.

7. Reduce the heat and cover the pot, then let the soup simmer for about fifteen (0:15) minutes.

8. Add the chopped potatoes to the soup and bring to a boil.

9. Cover the pot, reduce the heat, and allow the soup to simmer again for about ten (0:10) minutes.

10. Add the canned tomatoes and bring to a boil, then let simmer uncovered for five (0:05) minutes.

11. Season the soup with salt and pepper.

12. Use a spoon to remove the bay leaf and peppercorns if desired.

13. Ladle the Shchi into serving bowls and top each with a dollop of sour cream.

14. Garnish with fresh dill.

15. Serve warm with slices of rye bread.

NOTES

_____
_____
_____
_____
_____
_____
_____
_____
_____
_____
_____
_____

Serbia – Cevapcici

Cevapcici are small hand–made meat sausages created without a casing. More than one type of minced meat is used and the sausages are usually grilled. It is similar to Turkish kofta kebabs. Cevapcici originated in the Balkans during the Ottoman period. It is served with flatbread, sour cream and ajvar which is a red pepper and aubergine relish.

SERVES 4

INGREDIENTS

ground pork	1 ½ lb.
ground beef	1 lb.
ground lamb	½ lb.
egg white	1
cloves garlic (minced)	4
paprika	½ tsp.
salt	1 tsp.
baking soda	1 tsp.
cayenne pepper	1 tsp.
ground black pepper	2 tsp.
onion (peeled and finely chopped)	1
bread rolls/pita bread pockets	4

DIRECTIONS

1. Combine the ground pork, beef, and lamb with the egg white in a large bowl.

2. Season the meat and egg mixture with garlic, salt, black pepper, cayenne pepper, baking soda, paprika, onions, and black pepper.

3. Mix well using the hands.

4. Form the meat mixture into finger–length sausages, each measuring about a ¾ inch thick.

5. Lay the sausages on a plate and cover with plastic wrap.

6. Refrigerate the sausages for one (1:00) hour or overnight, to allow the flavors to marry.

7. Preheat the grill and slice the bread rolls.

8. Grill the sausages for about thirty (0:30) minutes, turning them as necessary.

9. Serve the Cevapcici in the bread rolls or pita bread pockets together with ajvar or sour cream.

NOTES

111

Slovakia – Bryndzové Halušky

Slovakia's national dish is called Bryndzové Halušky. Bryndza is a type of soft cheese made from sheep's milk. It is paired with bacon and potato dumplings called Halušky. Since most of Slovakia's early inhabitants were farmers, they developed this dish from farmed potatoes and homemade cheeses. This dish can be found in households and Slovak restaurants. It is typically made for the Halušky Festival held in Turecká. Traditionally, a glass of sour milk or zincica is drunk with Bryndzové Halušky.

SERVES 6

INGREDIENTS

medium russet potatoes (peeled and grated finely)	5
all-purpose flour	2 cups
egg (beaten)	1
salt	1 tsp.
bacon (chopped)	7 oz.
bryndza / feta cheese / cream cheese / sour cream	9 oz.
Chives (chopped)	
Dill (chopped)	
Butter	
Water (for boiling the Halušky)	

DIRECTIONS

1. Make the Halušky dough by combining the grated potato with the flour, egg, and salt.

2. Bring to boil a large pot of salted water.

3. Run the dumpling dough through a spaetzle maker so that the dough drops into the boiling water.

4. Cook the dumplings in batches and use a slotted spoon to remove them from the pot when they float to the surface.

5. Set aside the cooked Halušky on a serving platter.

6. Fry the chopped bacon in a skillet, then set aside.

7. Combine the Bryndza with a little butter (if using feta, blend until smooth and creamy.)

8. Spoon the Bryndza or the blended feta the warm Halušky.

9. Sprinkle the fried bacon and drippings over the top.

10. Garnish the dish with chopped chives and dill, then serve.

NOTES

_____
_____
_____
_____
_____
_____
_____
_____
_____
_____
_____
_____
_____
_____
_____
_____
_____
_____
_____
_____

Slovenia – Belokranjska Povitica

One of Slovenia's most iconic dishes is Belokranjska Povitica. It is a cake similar to a strudel and it is traditionally made at family and village celebrations. This dish originated in southeastern Slovenia, in a village called Bela Krajina. There are sweet and savory versions of this dish.

SERVES 4–6

INGREDIENTS

For the Dough

white flour	½ kg
egg (beaten)	1
oil	2 tbsp.
pinch salt	1
apple cider vinegar	1 tsp.
lukewarm water	1/3-½ L

For the Filling

eggs (beaten)	2
Salt/ 2–3 Tsp. sugar (depending on the sweet/savory version)	2-3 tsp.
(500g) package ricotta cheese	1
milk	0.1 L
sour cream	0.2 L
butter	7/8 cup
Raisins (for sweet version)	
Pork cracklings (for savory version)	
Egg wash	

DIRECTIONS

For the Dough

1. Knead together the flour, egg, salt, apple cider vinegar and water for ten (0:10) minutes.

2. Divide the ball of dough into four pieces.

3. Shape into balls, brush them with oil, and allow to rest for thirty (0:30) minutes.

4. Roll out the balls of dough in four very thin rectangles.

5. Trim and discard any thick edges, then allow to rest for fifteen (0:15) minutes before spreading the filling.

For the Filling

1. In a large bowl, combine the ricotta cheese with butter, sour cream and milk.

2. Use a hand mixer to incorporate the eggs and either salt (for savory version) or sugar (for sweet version).

3. Mix until thick and creamy, then add raisins (for sweet version) or pork cracklings (for savory version).

4. Divide the filling and spread it evenly onto each of the stretched dough rectangles.

5. Roll each into long cylinders and tuck in the ends.

6. Grease a circular baking pan, then arrange the four rolls in a continuous spiral.

7. Brush the rolls with egg wash, then bake for thirty (0:30) minutes at 200 degrees F° until golden brown.

8. Slice and serve.

NOTES

_____
_____
_____
_____
_____
_____
_____

Spain – Paella

Paella is a popular Spanish rice dish that includes meat, vegetables and seafood. It is typically flavored with saffron. This exotic dish originated in the city of Valencia and is said to be a blend of Roman and Arabian cuisine which were the two prominent cultures of early Spain. Paella is traditionally cooked in a special pan over an open fire.

SERVES 4–6

INGREDIENTS

short grained rice (Bomba / Calasparra)	2 cups
chicken broth	4 cups
frozen peas (thawed)	1 cup
mussels (scrubbed and cleaned)	1 lb.
small clams (scrubbed)	1 lb.
jumbo shrimp (deveined with tails on)	1 lb.
Spanish chorizo sausage (sliced ½ inch thick)	1 lb.
saffron threads	½ tsp.
cloves garlic (minced)	3
yellow onion (peeled and diced)	1
red bell pepper (seeded and sliced)	1
olive oil	2 tbsp.
Kosher salt	
Black pepper	

DIRECTIONS

1. Warm the olive oil in a paella pan or sauté pan over medium-high heat.

2. Fry the sausages for three (0:03) minutes in the oil, flipping them occasionally until they become brown on all sides.

3. Add the onion, bell pepper slices and garlic to the sausages.

4. Sauté for another three (0:03) minutes until the vegetables are soft.

5. Season with salt and pepper.

6. Add the rice to the pan, then the saffron.

7. Mix well and cook for two (0:02) minutes until the rice becomes yellow.

8. Pour in the chicken broth and sprinkle 1 ½ teaspoon of salt.

9. Bring to a boil, then reduce the heat and cover the pan.

10. Allow the Paella to cook for twenty (0:20) minutes or until the rice has absorbed nearly all of the liquid.

11. Press the mussels and clams into the rice, hinge side down.

12. Arrange the shrimp over the rice.

13. Sprinkle the peas over the rice.

14. Cover the pan and cook for five (0:05) minutes until the shrimp is pink and the shellfish have opened.

15. Discard any unopened clams.

16. Serve immediately.

NOTES

_____
_____
_____
_____
_____
_____
_____
_____
_____
_____
_____
_____
_____
_____
_____
_____

Sweden – Ostkaka

Ostkaka is a Swedish cheesecake which is typically topped with strawberries or eaten with other berry jams or fruit compotes. It is a sweet dessert which has origins in two parts of Sweden; Smaland and Halsingland. Ostkaka is always eaten warm as it is not as flavorful when eaten hot or cold. November 14th has been named the Day of Ostkaka in Sweden.

SERVES 6

INGREDIENTS

milk	½ cup
heavy cream	½ cup
cottage cheese	1 ¼ cup
rice flour	3 tbsp.
Almond flour / 4 tbsp. ground almonds	¼ cup
sugar (divided)	¼ cup
eggs	2
fresh strawberries (sliced)	7 oz.
Black pepper	

DIRECTIONS

1. Preheat the oven to 350 degrees F° and grease an 8–inch cake tin.

2. In a large bowl, whisk the eggs and a ¼ cup of sugar together.

3. Add the almond flour or ground almonds to the eggs and sugar.

4. Add the milk, rice flour, cottage cheese, and heavy cream.

5. Whisk these Ingredients together until smooth.

6. Pour the batter into the greased cake tin and bake in the oven for about one (1:00) hour or until the cake rises and is slightly brown at the top.

7. Prepare the strawberry topping by tossing the sliced berries with one tablespoon of sugar and a dash of black pepper.

8. When the cake cooled slightly, top with the strawberries.

9. Slice and serve the Ostkaka warm.

NOTES

Switzerland – Fondue

Fondue is a Swiss delicacy. It is a gooey blend of melted cheeses, spices and wine. This interesting dish was made famous by the Swiss Cheese Union as a way of increasing cheese consumption in the 1930's. After World War II ended, this organization sent Fondue sets to military regiments and event organizers in the country. Fondue became so popular that it is now considered a symbol of Swiss unity. Traditionally, fondue is eaten with bread. Cubes of bread is dipped into the hot fondue using long stemmed forks.

SERVES 6–8

INGREDIENTS

shredded gruyere cheese	1 ½ cups
shredded Emmental cheese	1 ½ cups
shredded Appenzeller cheese	½ cup
all-purpose flour	2–3 tbsp.
clove garlic (halved)	1
dry white wine	1 cup
fresh lemon juice	1 tsp.
dash kirsch (Swiss liquor)	1
pinch nutmeg	1
Freshly ground black pepper	
Crusty slices of bread (cubed)	

DIRECTIONS

1. In a large bowl, mix the three types of shredded cheese with the flour and set aside.

2. Rub the garlic halves on the insides of a Fondue Pot.

3. Pour the wine into the pot and set it over medium-low heat.

4. Allow the wine to become hot but do not allow it to boil.

5. Stir in the lemon juice and add the kirsch to the hot wine.

6. Gradually add handfuls of the cheese mixture to the wine, continually stirring until it all melts.

7. When fondue begins to bubble gently, season it with black pepper and nutmeg.

8. Transfer the Fondue pot to a tabletop alcohol safety burner so that it keeps hot.

9. Serve the hot Fondue with cubes of crusty bread.

NOTES

_____
_____
_____
_____
_____
_____
_____
_____
_____
_____
_____
_____
_____
_____
_____
_____
_____
_____
_____
_____
_____
_____

Ukraine – Borscht

Borscht is a hearty Ukrainian soup which is characteristically ruby red in color. This color is achieved from the inclusion of beetroot in the soup. Each region of Ukraine prepares the soup differently but the traditional version always includes beetroot. Some variations of this soup also includes meat. Sour cream is typically added to hot Borsht when it is being served to guests.

SERVES 10–12

INGREDIENTS

medium beets (washed)	3
large potatoes (peeled and chopped into bite sized pieces)	2
cooking oil	4 tbsp.
medium onion (finely diced)	1
carrots (grated)	2
head of cabbage (thinly sliced)	½
bay leaves	2
cups water	10
cups chicken broth	6
ketchup	5 tbsp.
can kidney beans	1
lemon juice	4 tbsp.
chopped dill	1 tbsp.
freshly ground black pepper	¼ tsp.
Salt	

DIRECTIONS

1. Fill a saucepan with ten cups of water.
2. Add the beets, cover the pan and boil for one (1:00) hour until soft.
3. Remove the beets from the pan and set aside.
4. Add the potato chunks to the saucepan containing the beet broth.
5. Boil the potatoes for about ten (0:10) minutes, then add the sliced cabbage and boil for an additional ten (0:10) minutes.
6. While the potatoes are boiling, add the oil to a clean skillet and heat over medium-high heat.
7. Add the grated carrots and diced onion to the skillet and sauté for about ten (0:10) minutes.
8. When the vegetables are almost finished cooking, stir in the ketchup, then turn off the heat and set aside.
9. Peel the beets and slice them into matchsticks.
10. Return the beets to the pot containing the potatoes, cabbage, and beet broth.
11. Add the chicken broth, kidney beans, and lemon juice to the pot.
12. Add the black pepper and the bay leaves.
13. Add the sautéed carrots and onions to the pot.
14. Sprinkle in the chopped dill.
15. Cook the soup for ten (0:10) minutes until the cabbage softens.
16. Adjust the salt and pepper, then turn off the heat.
17. Serve each bowl of Borscht with a dollop of sour cream.

NOTES

_____
_____
_____
_____
_____
_____
_____

U.K / Britain – Fish & Chips

Fish and chips gained popularity as early as the eighteenth century in Britain. It is so popular now, this is considered to be Britain's national dish. Fish and chips is traditionally eaten hot, with salt and vinegar.

SERVES 6

INGREDIENTS

large russet potatoes	12
all-purpose flour	5 cups
paprika	3 tbsp.
black pepper	1 tbsp.
skinless, boneless Alaskan cod fillets	3 lbs.
12–oz. bottle fizzy lager beer	1
Kosher salt	
Water	
Canola oil for frying	
Malt vinegar	

DIRECTIONS

1. Begin by peeling the skin off the potatoes.

2. Set the potatoes on a cutting board and use a sharp knife to slice them into long chips about 5/8 inch thick.

3. After cutting, store the chips in a bowl of water to prevent them from browning.

4. Pour enough canola oil into a frying pan or deep fryer.

5. Right before frying, drain the water and add the chips to the pan or deep fryer when the oil becomes hot.

6. Fry the chips until they cooked; soft on the inside and crisp on the outside. Fry in batches to avoid overcrowding.

7. Use a slotted spoon to remove the cooked chips and set them on absorbent paper. Toss the chips with kosher salt. Set aside.

8. Create a batter for the fish by combining three cups of flour, paprika, and a bottle of lager beer. Whisk the batter to remove lumps and add a little water if required.

9. Place the remaining two cups of flour in another dish with three teaspoons of kosher salt and a tablespoon of black pepper.

10. In a large frying pan or deep fryer, pour in enough canola oil for frying and heat to 375°F°.

11. Coat each fish filet in the dry flour mixture first, then dip it into the batter. Allow excess batter to drain off before placing it into the frying pan or deep fryer.

12. Fry the fish for about five to seven minutes or till it is golden brown on all sides.

13. Use a spatula to take the fish fillets out of the oil and place on absorbent paper for a minute before serving.

14. Serve the fried fish fillets with the salted chips and a bit of malt vinegar.

NOTES

_____
_____
_____
_____
_____
_____
_____
_____
_____
_____
_____
_____
_____
_____

Wales – Cawl

Cawl is a farmhouse stew that is popular in Wales. This Welsh dish contains seasonal vegetables and meat. Traditionally, farmers used bacon or goat meat to make Cawl, but nowadays lamb chops are the preferred choice. The traditional way to serve Cawl is in a wooden bowl. Some Welsh families serve Cawl like French pot–au–feu; where the broth is served as one course and the meat and vegetables are served as another. Cawl reportedly tastes better the day after it is prepared. It is eaten with bread and cheese.

SERVES 6

INGREDIENTS

medium potatoes (peeled and cut into chunks)	6
lamb shoulder / lamb neck	1 kg
carrots (peeled and diced)	3
small swede (peeled and chopped)	1
leeks (washed and sliced)	2
small bunch fresh parsley	1
Vegetable stock	
Salt	
Pepper	
Water	

DIRECTIONS

1. Place the meat into a large saucepan and pour in enough water to cover the meat.

2. Bring to a boil, then reduce to a simmer.

3. Simmer for about two (2:00) to three (3:00) hours.

4. Let the meat stand overnight.

5. The following day, remove any scum from the surface of the broth.

6. Use a spoon to dish out the meat from the broth.

7. Slice the meat off the bone and cut the meat into bite-sized chunks.

8. Discard the bones and return the meat chunks to the broth.

9. Bring the broth to a boil and add the carrots, potatoes, and swede.

10. Cook until the vegetables are tender, adding vegetable stock if necessary.

11. Season with salt and pepper.

12. Add the leeks to the pan.

13. Stir and cook for about eight (0:08) minutes.

14. Turn off the heat and sprinkle in the chopped parsley.

15. Divide the Cawl into bowls and serve with slices of bread and cheese.

NOTES

Argentina – Carbonada Criolla Stew

This famous Argentinian stew is a very hearty meal, made with beef, vegetables, and fruit.

SERVES 6

INGREDIENTS

stewing beef (cut into 1-inch chunks)	2 lbs.
large tomatoes (cut into big chunks)	4
large green pepper (cut into big chunks)	1
olive oil	3 tbsp.
large onion (diced)	1
bay leaves	2
cloves garlic (minced)	3
Salt	
dried oregano	1 tsp.
canned chicken stock	2 cups
potatoes (diced)	3
sweet potatoes (diced)	3
frozen corn kernels	2 cups
zucchinis (diced into ½ inch chunks)	2
peaches (diced into ½ inch chunks)	2
pears (diced into ½ inch chunks)	2

DIRECTIONS

1. Using a large, heavy pot or Dutch oven pot, cook the chunks of beef in hot oil.

2. Remove the meat from the pot and set aside. The beef may need to be cooked in batches to ensure that meat cooked evenly.

3. In this same pot, add the tomato, onion and green pepper chunks together with the minced garlic. The vegetables will cook in the natural fat released by the beef.

4. Allow the vegetables to cook until they are almost tender. Flavor the vegetables with a couple of bay leaves and dried oregano. Pour in the chicken stock, stir and bring to a boil.

5. Add the cooked beef to the vegetables in the pot as well as the chunks of potato and sweet potato. Cover the pot with a lid and let the stew simmer for about fifteen minutes.

6. Add the frozen corn and zucchini chunks. Let the stew simmer for ten more minutes.

7. When the vegetables are almost tender, add the peaches and pears. Cook the stew for five more minutes, stirring occasionally. Add salt to taste.

8. Carbonada Criolla Stew is served hot.

NOTES

_____
_____
_____
_____
_____
_____
_____
_____
_____
_____
_____
_____
_____
_____

Bolivia – Picante de Pollo

Bolivia's national dish is a spicy chicken stew. It originated in the western part of Bolivia and is characterized by its smoky aroma and spicy taste. A special type of pepper is used in Bolivia when preparing this dish; Aji Amarillo or yellow pepper sauce. Cayenne peppers are a good substitute for this ingredient.

SERVES 6

INGREDIENTS

chicken (cut into bite-sized pieces)	3 lbs.
Aji Amarillo sauce / 3 cayenne peppers whole or dried	4 tbsps.
yellow onions	2
small carrots (sliced into strips)	2
breadcrumbs	1 tbsps.
cumin powder	¾ tsp.
ground oregano	2 tsps.
black pepper	1 tsp.
salt	1 tsp.
vegetable oil	3 tsps.
Dash of cinnamon powder	
Water	

DIRECTIONS

1. Create a liquid mixture by combining the Aji Amarillo sauce, cumin powder, black pepper, and salt with a ¼ cup of water. Mix well and set aside in a small bowl.

2. Heat the vegetable oil in a large pot.

3. Peel the skin off the yellow onions and dice it. Add diced onions to the oil. Sauté the onions until they are limp and golden.

4. Pour the liquid Aji Amarillo mixture into the pot.

5. Add a dash of cinnamon powder, oregano and a cup of water, and bring to a boil.

6. Simmer until the liquid evaporates. Pour in another cup of water, place the lid on the pot and allow to simmer again until the liquid evaporates.

7. Spoon the chicken pieces into the pot. Mix thoroughly, so the chicken pieces are evenly coated with the cooked seasonings.

8. Cover the pot and cook for ten minutes. Pour in a cup of water and stir. Cover the pot and cook for approximately an hour.

9. Add the chopped carrots to the stew, cover the pot and cook for fifteen minutes. Add the breadcrumbs.

10. Plate and serve with steamed rice or potatoes.

NOTES

Brazil – Feijoada

In the sixteenth century, African slaves were introduced to Brazil for labor in the mining and agricultural industries. African, Portuguese and European cuisines came together over time as the slaves and native peoples altered the European dishes. Feijoada is one such dish. It was originally a dish that was cooked for prisoners and various parts of the pig such as snout, ears, tail and feet were used.

SERVES 12

INGREDIENTS

smoked ham hocks	1 lb.
black beans	1 lb.
Mexican chorizo / Portuguese linguica sausages	1 lb.
Canadian bacon / Brazilian Carne Seca	½ lb.
smoked ribs	½ lb.
pig's tail, ear, and snout (optional)	1
strips bacon	4
lean pork (cubed in ½ inch pieces)	½ lb.
beef (cubed in 1/2inch pieces)	½ lb.
wine vinegar	2 tbsps.
olive oil	3 tbsps.
large onion (diced)	1
garlic cloves	5
Salt	
Black pepper	
Water	
Hot sauce	

DIRECTIONS

1. Soak the black beans overnight in a bowl of water.

2. On low heat, cook the black beans for about four to five hours until they are soft.

3. Crush ½ cup of the beans. Set aside.

4. Fill a large pot of water and bring to a boil.

5. Add in the ham hocks, Carne Seca, chorizo and ribs. After some time, change the water and boil again. Repeat the process as this will tenderize the cured meats, and excess fat will be boiled off. Drain and set aside.

6. Heat the oil in a large skillet and sauté the onions and garlic. Add in bacon strips and fry for three minutes.

7. Add the pork and beef cubes - Cook for about three minutes.

8. In a separate pan, add a ½ cup of mashed black beans together with olive oil, vinegar, and hot sauce — Cook over medium heat for three minutes.

9. Stir in the bean paste in the skillet containing the pork and beef.

10. Add this to the boiled meats along with the whole, cooked black beans, and some fresh water. Let simmer on medium high heat for 1 ½ hour, once the meats cooked.

11. Serve over white rice. Add hot sauce if desired.

NOTES

_____
_____
_____
_____
_____
_____
_____
_____
_____
_____

Canada – Poutine

Poutine is essentially potato French fries topped with cheddar cheese curds and smothered in thick brown gravy. The dish originated in Warwick, Quebec by a restaurateur named Fernand Lachance. It is popular all over Canada and as such it is considered the country's national dish.

SERVES 4–6

INGREDIENTS

russet potatoes	4 lbs.
white cheddar cheese curds	3 cups
cans Canadian beer/water	2
unsalted butter	4 tbsps.
flour	¼ cup
shallot (finely chopped)	1
clove garlic (grated)	1
low sodium beef stock	4 cups
ketchup	2 tbsps.
balsamic vinegar	1 tbsp.
Worcestershire sauce	2 tsps.
Salt	
Pepper	
Canola oil/lard for frying	

DIRECTIONS

1. Wash and peel the Russet Potatoes. Slice the peeled potatoes into ¼ inch thick fries.

2. Put the fries into a bowl and pour in two cold cans of Canadian beer. Cold water can be used instead of beer. Refrigerate this for 1–2 hours.

3. Start making the gravy for the Poutine by first heating the butter in a saucepan on medium-high heat.

4. Make a roux by adding in the flour and whisking it until smooth.

5. Add the chopped shallot and grated garlic — Cook for two minutes or until tender.

6. Pour in the beef stock, ketchup, balsamic vinegar and Worcestershire sauce. Add a pinch of salt and pepper. Bring to a boil and stir until the gravy thickens, do this for approximately six minutes. Reduce the heat to keeps the gravy warm.

7. Fill a Dutch oven pot with canola oil or lard to fry the potatoes.

8. Drain the potatoes and use a paper towel to dry the fries. Cook the fries in batches, tossing them occasionally until crisp.

9. Use a slotted spoon to remove the fries and allow them to sit on paper towels to absorb excess oil. Sprinkle salt and pepper to taste.

10. Fill each serving dish with a portion of hot French fries.

11. Divide the three cups of cheese curds equally amongst the dishes and spoon the curds over each portion of fries.

12. Ladle hot gravy over each serving of fries and cheese curds. Eat the Poutine warm.

NOTES

_____
_____
_____
_____
_____
_____
_____
_____
_____
_____
_____
_____

Chile – Pastel de Choclo

Pastel de Choclo is a Chilean version of shepherd's pie that is made with corn and meat. Choclo is a specific type of corn with big starchy kernels. This hearty casserole dish is traditionally baked in a shallow clay pot and served with Chilean red or white wine.

SERVES 12

INGREDIENTS

large ears of corn	6
ground beef	1 lb.
hardboiled eggs (sliced)	4
pieces of chicken (seasoned with salt, pepper, and cumin and browned in oil)	12
raisins	1 cup
black olives	1 cup
large onions (chopped)	4
leaves basil (finely chopped)	8
milk	1 cup
oil	3 tbsps.
salt	1 tsp.
butter	3 tbsps.
cumin powder	1 tsp.
confectioner's sugar powder	2 tbsps.
Pepper	

DIRECTIONS

1. Grate the ears of corn and place in a large pot. Turn on the heat and mix in the chopped basil leaves, salt, and butter. Stir the mixture and pour in the milk, a little at a time until it thickens. Cook for five minutes on low heat. Set aside.

2. Heat a little oil and sauté the onions then add the ground beef. Sprinkle salt and pepper and add the cumin powder. When the beef browned, turn off the heat.

3. Grease a casserole dish and spoon the beef filling on the base it. Spread the meat evenly with a spoon or spatula. Arrange the hardboiled egg slices over the beef filling and then do the same with the olives and raisins. Remove the bones from the chicken, then arrange the pieces of cooked chicken on top of this.

4. Pour the cooked corn mixture over the filling. Use a spatula to spread the corn evenly over the filling. Dust the confectioner's sugar over the top. Bake at 400 degrees F° for about thirty-five minutes or until the crust is golden. Serve warm with additional sugar to sprinkle on the crust if desired.

NOTES

124

Colombia – Ajiaco

Colombian chicken and potato soup is called Ajiaco and because the dish is so popular in the capital city of Bogotá, it is considered one of the national dishes of the country. Three key Ingredients of Ajiaco are chicken, three varieties of potato and a flavorful herb called guascas or soldier gallant weed. Ajiaco is cooked on weekends or on special occasions.

SERVES 6–8

INGREDIENTS

chicken breasts	3
water	12 cups
frozen Andean potato (papa criolla)	2 cups
medium white potatoes	3
medium red potatoes	3
Guascas	1/3 cup
ears fresh corn (halved)	3
salt	¼ tsp.
chicken bouillon cubes	2
scallions (chopped)	3
cloves garlic (minced)	2
cilantro (chopped)	3 tbsps.
heavy cream	1 cup
capers	1 cup
Pepper	

DIRECTIONS

1. Remove the skin from the chicken breast and discard. Wash and peel the white and red potatoes. Slice the potatoes and set aside until ready to be used.

2. Begin cooking the Ajiaco by placing the chicken, corn, scallions, garlic, salt, pepper, and cilantro in a large soup pot. Crumble the chicken bouillon cubes over the meat. Pour twelve cups of water into the pot. Bring to a boil then reduce to medium heat. Stir occasionally and allow the chicken to cook for about forty minutes. Use a slotted spoon to take out the three cooked chicken breasts from the soup. Set the chicken aside in a separate container and allow the corn to cook for an additional thirty minutes.

3. Add the red potato and white potato slices to the soup. Add the guacas herb and stir well. Place the lid on the pot and cook for thirty minutes. Uncover the pot and dump in the frozen Andean potatoes. Let it simmer for fifteen or twenty minutes — season with salt and pepper.

4. Use a fork to shred the cooked chicken breasts. The chicken can also be cut into small cubes. Return the chicken to the pot or top the Ajiaco with the shredded chicken.

5. Serve the hot Ajiaco with a dollop of heavy cream and a sprinkle of capers.

NOTES

_____
_____
_____
_____
_____
_____
_____
_____
_____
_____
_____
_____
_____
_____
_____
_____
_____

Ecuador – Ceviche

Ceviche is a very popular dish in Ecuador. It is prepared with seafood such as shrimp, lobster or fish. Red onion, lime and cilantro are the main flavors in this dish. It is traditionally served cold alongside fried plantain chips, corn nuts or popcorn.

SERVES 6

INGREDIENTS

red onion (thinly sliced)	1 ½ cups
fresh lime juice	½ cup
fresh / thawed whole shrimp	1 ½ lb.
cilantro leaves (chopped)	¼ cup
ground black pepper	¼ tsp.
fresh orange juice	¾ cup
can (14.5 oz.) diced tomatoes	1
tomato ketchup	1/3 cup
yellow mustard	1 tbsp.
Extra virgin olive oil	2 tbsps.
salt	¼ tsp.
Cooking spray	

DIRECTIONS

1. Peel and de-vein the shrimp.
2. Set the shrimp aside.
3. Mix the onion slices, lime juice and salt in a small bowl.
4. Set this aside but stir occasionally.
5. Heat a large skillet over medium-high heat and spray it with enough cooking spray to sauté the shrimp.
6. Spoon the shrimp into the skillet and toss with the ground black pepper.
7. Sauté the shrimp for about four (0:04) minutes or until it curls and turns pink.
8. Remove the cooked shrimp from the skillet and set it in a shallow dish to cool.
9. Refrigerate the cooked shrimp for twenty (0:20) minutes until cold.
10. Open the can of tomatoes, then drain and discard the preserving liquid.
11. Place the diced tomatoes from the can in a large bowl.
12. Mix in the orange juice, tomato ketchup, cilantro leaves, olive oil, the marinated onion, and the yellow mustard together with the diced tomatoes.
13. Add the cold shrimp to this mixture.
14. Toss everything together until evenly mixed.
15. Serve this delicious and flavorful ceviche with fried plantain chips or popcorn.

NOTES

Greenland – Suaasat

The cuisine of Greenland is difficult to replicate because it utilizes much of the local produce and Ingredients that can be a challenge to find elsewhere. The national dish of Greenland is a type of meat and barley soup called Suaasat. Seal, whale, reindeer and musk ox are plentiful on the island and any of these are traditionally cooked in Suaasat. This dish is a favorite at Christmas time and can hardly be found in local restaurants; it is considered a hearty home – cooked meal that is nourishing for the cold climate. Suaasat is eaten by itself, without condiments or sides as it is a very filling meal.

SERVES 6

INGREDIENTS

Reindeer meat / seal meat / ox meat (cubed)	1 kg
water and extra for soaking the barley	2 L
pearl barley	200 ml
onions (peeled and chopped)	3
wild mushrooms	300 g
carrots (sliced)	2
dried cherries	200 g
chopped rosemary	1 tsp.
chopped thyme	1 tsp.
chopped sage	1 tsp.
Zest of a lemon	
Sea salt	
Pepper	

DIRECTIONS

1. Soak the barley in water overnight, then drain and set aside.

2. Pour the two liters of water in a large, heavy soup pot or Dutch oven and turn on the heat.

3. Add the reindeer meat to the pot, then add the dried cherries, mushrooms, carrots and onions.

4. When the Suaasat start boiling, season with salt, pepper, sage, rosemary, and thyme.

5. Reduce the heat and let it simmer on medium heat for about one (1:00) hour until the Reindeer meat becomes tender.

6. Stir in the pre-soaked barley to the Suaasat and add the lemon zest.

7. Adjust the seasoning to taste, then cook for an additional thirty (0:30) minutes until the soup thickens.

NOTES

Guyana – Pepperpot

Pepperpot was created by the Amerindians who were the native peoples of Guyana. This is a flavorful meat dish that is slow cooked for a long time. One of the key Ingredients is cassareep which is product of cassava. Guyanese traditionally cook this dish at Christmas. Pepperpot can be kept unrefrigerated for several days but has to be reheated at least twice each day.

SERVES 6–8

INGREDIENTS

pork shoulder chops (cut into bite-sized pieces)	1 lb.
stewing beef (cut into bite-sized pieces)	1 lb.
pigs' trotters (chopped into chunks)	3
cassareep	2/3 cup
Groundnut oil	3 tbsps.
cloves	12
large cinnamon stick (halved)	1
Brown sugar	4 tbsps.
West Indian pepper sauce	2 tsps.
Scotch Bonnet chili peppers (seeded and finely sliced)	2
whole Scotch Bonnet pepper (for garnish)	1
Salt	
Black pepper	
Water	

DIRECTIONS

1. Heat the groundnut oil in a large saucepan over medium heat.

2. Brown the meat in the oil.

3. Return the browned meat to the saucepan and season with the salt, sugar, black pepper, sliced peppers, cloves, cinnamon stick, and cassareep.

4. Stir together and pour in enough water to cover the meat.

5. Bring to a boil, then place the lid on the pot, reduce the heat and let simmer for one (1:00) hour, occasionally removing the scum that forms on the surface of the liquid.

6. After an hour of cooking, stir the Pepperpot and then replace the lid.

7. Let the meat cook for two (2:00) hours until tender and a dark, glossy gravy forms.

8. Remove the lid and stir the meat and gravy.

9. Adjust the seasoning to suit your tastes.

10. Turn off the heat and garnish with a whole Scotch Bonnet pepper.

11. Serve this dish with a large chunk of homemade bread.

NOTES

_____
_____
_____
_____
_____
_____
_____
_____
_____
_____
_____
_____
_____
_____
_____
_____

Honduras – Plato Tipico

Plato Tipico is a platter containing several separately prepared foods which are served together as one dish. It comprises mainly of stewed beans, fried plantains, chismol and grilled meat or sausage. Rice and corn tortillas are eaten with it. This dish is usually cooked on special occasions in Honduras and is considered the country's national dish.

SERVES 4

INGREDIENTS

beef sirloin (cut into long strips)	1 lb.
pork sirloin (cut into long strips)	1 lb.
chorizo sausages	4
cloves garlic (minced)	4
Olive oil	4 tbsps.
Vinegar	3 tbsps.
cans kidney beans	2
red onions (sliced separately)	2
bell peppers (sliced)	3
dried oregano	1 tsp.
pinch cayenne pepper	1
minced thyme	¼ tsp.
paprika	¼ tsp.
ketchup	1 cup
water	1 cup
large tomatoes (diced)	2
large green pepper (sliced)	1
sprigs coriander	3
cumin	¼ tsp.
lemon juice	2 tbsp.
plantains	2
Vegetable oil	4 tbsps.
Salt	
Black pepper	

DIRECTIONS

1. Mix the meat strips with olive oil, salt, pepper, garlic, and vinegar.

2. Marinate for one (1:00) hour.

3. Grill the meat and chorizo sausages together until cooked, then remove from the grill and set aside.

4. Heat two tablespoons of olive oil in a pot and sauté one diced red onion, half of the minced garlic and the sliced bell peppers until tender.

5. Add the canned beans.

6. Stir together, reduce the heat and let it simmer.

7. Add the ketchup, water, paprika, cayenne, thyme, salt, black pepper, and oregano.

8. Let simmer for fifteen (0:15) minutes, then turn off the heat and set aside.

9. Make the chismol by mixing the diced tomatoes and green pepper slices with lemon juice, coriander, diced red onion, cumin, salt, and black pepper.

10. Peel the plantains and slice in halves, then cut each half lengthwise into ½ inch slices.

11. Fry the plantain slices in vegetable oil until each side lightly browned.

12. Arrange the grilled meat, chorizo sausages, fried plantains, chismol and beans on four serving plates.

13. Serve with steamed rice, corn tortillas, avocado slices, farmer's cheese and a dollop of sour cream.

NOTES

_____
_____
_____
_____
_____

Mexico – Chiles en Nogada

Chiles en Nogada is one of Mexico's traditional chili pepper dishes. The peppers are stuffed with a mixture of dried fruit and meat. It is topped with a walnut sauce, pomegranate seeds and parsley. The colors in this dish mimic those in the Mexican flag and this dish is popularly prepared for Mexican Independence Day.

SERVES 4

INGREDIENTS

For the Stuffed Peppers

poblano chili peppers (roasted and peeled)	4
vegetable oil	1 tbsp.
skinless, boneless chicken breasts (diced)	2
diced onion	2 tsp.
diced apple	1 tsp.
dried apricots	1 tsp.
dried cranberries	1 tsp.
diced pear	1 tsp.
raisins	1 tsp.
clove garlic (minced)	1
tomato paste	2 tsp.
dry white wine	1 cup
Salt	
Black pepper	

For the Sauce

shallot (minced)	1
vegetable oil	½ tbsp.
clove garlic (minced)	1
dry white wine	1 cup
heavy cream	2 cups
almonds / walnuts (ground)	1/3 cup
fresh parsley leaves	1 tsp.
pomegranate seeds	1 tsp.
Salt	
Black pepper	

DIRECTIONS

For the Stuffed Peppers

1. Heat the vegetable oil in a sauté pan and add the diced chicken.

2. Cook the chicken for five (0:05) minutes and then add the onions.

3. When the onions become translucent, add the apples, apricots, pear, cranberries, raisins, and garlic.

4. Sauté together for about two (0:02) minutes, then add the tomato paste.

5. Stir together and cook for two (0:02) minutes.

6. Add the wine and cook for about five (0:05) minutes more or until the chicken is tender.

7. Sprinkle sugar, salt, and black pepper over the meat and fruits, then stir well.

8. Divide the cooked meat and fruit into four portions and stuff each roasted pepper with one-quarter of the mixture.

9. Set aside

For the Sauce

1. Heat the vegetable oil in a pan and sauté the shallots.

2. After three (0:03) minutes, add the garlic and cook the shallots and garlic for about five (0:05) more minutes.

3. Add the wine and cook for fifteen (0:15) minutes until almost all of the liquid evaporates.

4. Pour in the heavy cream.

5. Simmer for another fifteen (0:15) minutes.

6. Add the ground nuts, salt, and pepper.

7. Stir well and then turn off the heat.

8. Pour two tablespoons of sauce over each stuffed pepper.

9. Garnish the peppers with parsley and pomegranate seeds

10. Serve

Paraguay – Sopa Paraguaya

Sopa Paraguaya is Paraguay's most iconic dish. It is not a soup as the name suggests but a flavorful cheesy cornbread with hints of butter and onion. It is the perfect side dish to complement a hearty Paraguayan beef soup. This flavorful cornbread is the result of Guarani and Spanish influences in Paraguayan cuisine.

SERVES 6–8

INGREDIENTS

cottage cheese	1 cup
sweet onion (peeled and finely chopped)	1
butter	8 tbsp.
cornmeal	2 cups
grated corn kernels / 1 (16 oz.) can cream style corn	2 cups
salt	1 tsp.
grated Muenster cheese	1 cup
eggs (whites and yolks separated)	6
milk	1 cup
Lard (for greasing baking tray)	

DIRECTIONS

1. Heat four tablespoons of butter in a skillet.

2. Add the onions and sauté in the melted butter until tender and translucent, then set aside.

3. Place the cottage cheese and the remaining four tablespoons of butter in a bowl and mix well together.

4. Thoroughly combine the Muenster cheese with the butter and cottage cheese mixture.

5. Add the grated corn kernels or the can of cream style corn, along with the sautéed onions, cornmeal, and salt.

6. Pour in the cup of milk and thoroughly mix in the egg yolks.

7. Beat the egg whites separately until soft peaks form, then gently fold into the cheese batter.

8. Grease and flour a 25cm x 30 cm baking dish, then pour the batter into it.

9. Preheat the oven to 400 degrees F°.

10. Place the dish into the oven and bake for forty-five (0:45) to fifty-five (0:55) minutes or until a toothpick comes out clean.

11. Allow the cornbread to cool, then slice into squares or wedges.

12. Serve slices of Sopa Paraguaya alongside bowls of hearty beef soup.

NOTES

Peru – Ceviche

Ceviche is a delectable dish of raw fish cured in citrus juices and flavored with peppers and other seasonings. Essentially it is a type of fish salad. The acid in the citrus juice denatures the protein in the fish, giving it a cooked texture. It originated as a way for fishermen to eat some of their freshly caught fish while they were spending long days at sea. Ceviche is the national dish of Peru and there are many variations to the dish within the country. The dish is typically served with sweet potato, lettuce and corn.

SERVES 4

INGREDIENTS

ono / mahi mahi / blue nosed bass (diced)	1 ½ lb.
small red onion (peeled and slivered)	½
lime juice	¾ cup
salt	½ tsp.
ají Amarillo sauce	1 tbsp.
habanero chili pepper (seeded, thinly sliced)	1
cilantro leaves (chopped)	½ cup

DIRECTIONS

1. Place the cubes of fish and onions in a bowl together, top with cold water, then rinse and drain.

2. Pat the fish dry and return to the bowl with the onions.

3. Season the fish and onions with the salt and mix well.

4. Add the ají Amarillo sauce, sliced habanero pepper, and the lime juice.

5. Stir the Ceviche, then cover and place in the refrigerator for about twenty (0:20) minutes.

6. Add the chopped cilantro leaves and mix the cold Ceviche before serving.

7. Divide the Ceviche in four and place each into serving bowls.

8. Serve with butter lettuce, sweet potatoes, and boiled sweet corn.

NOTES

Puerto Rico – Mofongo

Mofongo is a garlic flavored plantain mash that also includes bacon and pork rinds. The dish has its roots in African cuisine as Puerto Rico was once a New World colony inhabited by African slaves. They introduced Fufu, a mash made of any starchy vegetable or root crop and over time, Mofongo was developed with plantains which were a major food source in Puerto Rico. Mofongo can be shaped into balls for serving and eaten alongside salad, rice and beans.

SERVES 4

INGREDIENTS

green plantains (peeled)	4
slice bacon (cooked and chopped)	1
canola oil	2 cups
olive oil	2 tbsp.
chopped, crisp, fried pork rinds / chicharrón	1 cup
cloves garlic	6
low sodium chicken stock	1 cup
Salt to taste	
Cilantro leaves (chopped)	

DIRECTIONS

1. Slice the plantains into one–inch rounds, then set aside.

2. Heat the canola oil to 350 degrees F° in a large saucepan or deep fryer.

3. Fry the plantain slices in the oil for about seven (0:07) minutes, turning once until they become light golden but not brown.

4. Remove the slices with a slotted spoon and place on paper towels.

5. Set aside the fried plantains.

6. Use a traditional mortar and pestle or a bowl and spoon to crush the cloves of garlic.

7. Add a pinch or two of salt to the crushed garlic and mix well.

8. Add the olive oil to the crushed garlic and mix well to marry the flavors.

9. Transfer the garlic aioli to a small bowl and set aside.

10. Mash the fried plantains in batches if necessary, using the same mortar and pestle or a bowl and potato masher.

11. Add the pork rinds, bacon, and the garlic aioli to the plantain mash and pound together, adding the chicken stock as necessary.

12. After the Mofongo is mixed, roll into small two-inch balls.

13. Garnish with chopped cilantro leaves.

14. Serve the Mofongo by itself or as a side dish to a rice meal.

NOTES

_____
_____
_____
_____
_____
_____
_____
_____
_____
_____

Suriname – Pom

Pom is the most popular meal in Suriname. It is a casserole made of meat and local root vegetables such as taro roots. Pom is traditionally prepared on Sundays and for festive occasions such as birthdays.

SERVES 8

INGREDIENTS

boneless and skinless chicken thighs (cut into bite sized pieces)	5
taro roots / eddoes (grated)	2 lbs.
cooking oil	3 tbsp.
nutmeg	2 tsp.
black pepper	½ tsp.
sour oranges	2
stalk celery (thinly sliced)	1
onion (peeled and chopped)	1
ripe plantain (peeled and grated)	1
tomato paste	1 tbsp.
chicken broth	3 cups
sugar	1 tsp.
lime	1
butter	2 tbsp.
Salt	

DIRECTIONS

1. Juice one of the oranges and pour this into the bowl of chicken.

2. Add a ¾ teaspoon of the nutmeg, the black pepper, and salt to the chicken.

3. Mix well, then set aside for thirty (0:30) minutes to allow the meat to marinate.

4. In a separate bowl, mix the grated taro root and plantain.

5. Add the remaining nutmeg, sugar and ½ teaspoon of salt.

6. Juice the next sour orange and lime and add the juices to the bowl.

7. Mix well and set aside.

8. Heat the oil in a pot and fry the chicken until brown on all sides.

9. Add the celery and onions to the chicken, then cook until soft and translucent.

10. Stir in the tomato paste and add the chicken broth to the pot.

11. Bring to a boil, then reduce the heat and allow to simmer for about twenty (0:20) minutes.

12. Transfer 5 tablespoons of the broth to the plantain/taro root mixture and combine well with a spoon.

13. Grease a casserole dish and place half of the taro root/plantain mixture in it.

14. Press the mixture lightly, then spread the chicken over this.

15. Place the rest of the taro root/plantain mixture over the chicken.

16. Preheat the oven to 350 degrees F°.

17. Bake the Pom for one (1:00) hour.

18. Brush the Pom with butter after baking.

19. Allow the Pom to cool slightly for five (0:05) minutes.

20. Slice and serve.

NOTES

_____
_____
_____
_____
_____
_____
_____
_____

United States of America – Apple Pie

One of America's most iconic foods is Apple Pie. Apple Pie was brought to American colonies during the 17th and 18th centuries by the Dutch, British and the Swedes. However, it only became a symbol of American pride in the 19th and 20th centuries. Since then, this baked treat is made especially for patriotic holidays such as Independence Day. Typical American Apple Pie has a crust designed with interwoven strips of pastry, similar to a lattice.

YIELDS 1 pie

INGREDIENTS

For the Pastry Crust

all-purpose flour	2 ½ cups
sugar	1 tbsp.
salt	¾ tsp.
chilled vegetable shortening (cubed)	1/3 cup
chilled, unsalted butter (cut into ½ inch pieces)	10 tbsp.
ice water	6 tbsp.

For the Filling

Granny Smith apples (peeled, cored, cut into ¼ inch thick slices)	3 ½ lbs.
sugar	½ cup
golden brown sugar	¼ cup
all-purpose flour	3 tbsp.
lemon juice	1 tbsp.
grated lemon peel	2 tsp.
ground cinnamon	1 ½ tsp.
ground ginger	1/8 tsp.
ground nutmeg	1/8 tsp.
milk	1 tbsp.
Granulated sugar (topping)	

DIRECTIONS

For the Pastry Crust

1. Blend the flour, sugar, and salt in a food processor.

2. Add the chilled butter and shortening.

3. Blend until the mixture resembles breadcrumbs.

4. Add the ice water and process mixture until a clumpy.

5. Shape the dough into a ball, then divide in half and roll each into a flat circle.

6. Wrap both circles of dough in plastic wrap, then chill for two (2:00) hours in the refrigerator.

7. Spread one sheet of dough onto a floured surface and roll out into a 12–inch round, then set aside.

8. Roll out the second sheet of dough into a 13–inch round.

9. Cut the second sheet of dough into twelve equal strips.

For the Filling

1. Place all of the filling Ingredients except the apples in a large bowl.

2. Mix thoroughly, then add the apples. Ensure all the apples coated with the other Ingredients.

3. Arrange the 12-inch round of pastry into a 9-inch glass pie dish.

4. Gently press the dough into the base of the dish and along the sides.

5. Spoon the filling into the pie dish.

6. Place six strips of pastry over the top of the pie, leaving gaps in between.

7. Form a lattice by placing the remaining six strips of pastry over the pie in the opposite direction.

8. Gently fold over the edges and press with a fork to seal.

9. Brush the lattice with milk and sprinkle with granulated sugar if desired.

10. Preheat the oven to 400 degrees Fº. Place the Apple Pie on the lowest rack in the oven, and Bake for ten (0:10) minutes.

11. Reduce the heat to 375 degrees F°.

12. Bake for one (1:00) hour and ten (0:10) minutes until the top is golden and the juices have thickened.

13. Cool for one (1:00) hour, then slice and serve.

U.S. Virgin Islands – Fish & Fungi

Fish and Fungi (Foon-Ji) is a traditional dish in the U.S. Virgin Islands. Despite its name, no mushrooms are used. Fungi is a smooth cornmeal mash which flavored with okra. This meal originated during the era of slavery when slaves were allowed six quarts of cornmeal and six salted herrings per week. African slaves on the U.S. Virgin Islands first created Fish and Fungi.

SERVES 6–8

INGREDIENTS

For Virgin Islands Style Fish

fish (scaled, gutted and sliced)	4 ½ lbs.
medium onions (peeled and chopped)	2
tomato (diced)	1
vinegar	1 tbsp.
lemon / lime juice	3 tbsp.
water	2 cups
butter	2 tsp.

For Okra Fungi

frozen okra	10 oz.
finely ground yellow cornmeal	1 ½ cups
boiling water	2 ½ cups
butter	2 tbsp.
salt	¼ tsp.
Pepper	

DIRECTIONS

For Virgin Islands Style Fish

1. Heat the butter in a pan until melted.

2. Add the fish slices and cook until they become a little brown on both sides.

3. Add the onions and tomatoes to the pan.

4. Add the vinegar, lemon juice and the water to the pan.

5. Allow the fish to cook gently for about thirty (0:30) minutes until the flesh is white and soft.

For Okra Fungi:

1. Place the frozen okras in a pot of boiling water and cook until tender.

2. Remove the okra from the hot water and set aside.

3. Allow the water in the pot to start boiling again.

4. In a separate bowl, mix a ¼ cup of cornmeal with a ¾ cup of water until smooth.

5. Add this mixture to the pot of boiling water.

6. Allow this to cook for one (0:01) minute.

7. Gradually add the rest of the cornmeal, continually stirring to prevent any lumps from forming.

8. Return the cooked okra to the cornmeal and stir well.

9. Add the butter, salt, and pepper to the pot.

10. Allow the Fungi to simmer for five (0:05) more minutes, then turn off the heat.

11. Serve the Fungi with the previously cooked fish.

Uruguay – Chivito

Uruguay is known for its Chivito, a beef steak sandwich that also includes ham and eggs. It originated in Punta del Este, in the year 1944.

It is said that a foreign customer visited a chef's restaurant and asked for goat meat, but the chef did not serve that type of meat. Determined not to lose the customer, the chef prepared a beef steak sandwich and called it Chivito, which means 'little goat.' Nowadays, there are many variations of this sandwich and is available in restaurants and cafés throughout Uruguay.

YIELDS 4 sandwiches.

INGREDIENTS

hamburger buns/ciabatta buns	4
thin cuts of top sirloin beef	4
oil	1 tbsp.
eggs	4
slices ham	4
thick slices Mozzarella cheese	4
lettuce leaves (rinsed and dried)	4
tomatoes	2
Salsa golf (Mixture of ketchup and mayonnaise)	
Mayonnaise	
Salt	
Black pepper	

DIRECTIONS

1. Slice the tomatoes and toss with a pinch of salt.

2. Set aside.

3. Heat the oil in a large skillet and add the beef — Cook for one (0:01) minute on each side.

4. Remove the beef and set aside.

5. Fry the eggs one at a time in the skillet.

6. Season the eggs with a pinch of salt and black pepper, and set aside when cooked.

7. Make the Chivito by first slicing open the buns and smearing mayonnaise on the insides of the buns.

8. Arrange the beef inside of the buns, then add the ham and cheese.

9. Place the open sandwiches under the broiler in an oven.

10. Allow the cheese to soften and melt slightly.

11. Remove the sandwiches from the oven and place the lettuce and tomato slices over the cheese.

12. Top each sandwich with a fried egg.

13. Dress with salsa golf and close the sandwiches.

14. Serve immediately.

NOTES

_____
_____
_____
_____
_____
_____
_____
_____
_____
_____
_____
_____
_____

137

Venezuela – Pabellón Criollo

Venezuela's traditional rice, meat and bean dish is called Pabellón Criollo. Pabellón means 'flag' and the rice, beans and meat is arranged side by side on the plate, to show the colors red, white and black of a tri–color flag. This dish is usually served along with plantains or a fried egg.

SERVES 6.

INGREDIENTS

flank steak	1 ½ lb.
tomatoes (diced)	2
beef bouillon cubes	2
chicken bouillon cube	1
cloves garlic (peeled and minced)	3
(15 oz.) can black beans	1
medium onions (peeled and chopped)	2–3
vegetable oil	2 tbsp.
ground cumin	1 ½ tsp.
garlic powder	½ tsp.
vinegar	1 tbsp.
butter	2 tbsp.
servings of cooked white rice	6
Salt	

DIRECTIONS

1. Submerge the beef steak into a saucepan of water and add the beef bouillon cubes.

2. Bring to a boil over medium heat, then allow to simmer over low heat for one (1:00) hour and thirty (0:30) minutes until tender.

3. Remove from the heat and set aside to cool.

4. Heat the oil in a clean skillet.

5. Sauté half of the onions and the minced garlic in the oil until soft.

6. Open the can of beans and add it to the pan, along with the liquid.

7. Add a ½ cup of water, cumin, garlic powder, vinegar, and the chicken bouillon.

8. Stir and add a pinch of salt.

9. Allow the beans to simmer for ten (0:10) minutes over low heat.

10. When the liquid has reduced, turn off the heat and set aside.

11. Slice the cooled steak against the grain into thin, long slices.

12. Shred any large pieces of steak into smaller pieces and set aside.

13. Melt the butter in a separate pan, then sauté the rest of the onions.

14. Add the shredded beef to the pan.

15. Stir and add the tomatoes.

16. Pour in a cup of the steak pan juices and allow it to simmer for about five (0:05) minutes.

17. When most of the liquid reduced, turn off the heat.

18. Arrange plates with portions of cooked white rice, beans, and the cooked steak.

19. Serve with fried plantain slices.

NOTES

_____

_____

_____

_____

_____

_____

_____

_____

_____

_____

Antigua and Barbuda – Fungee

Fungee is a cornmeal dish that cooked on the islands of Antigua and Barbuda. Eaten alongside vegetable mash and a sauce made from tomatoes, garlic, and salted codfish. It can also serve with Antiguan pepper pot, which is a spicy meat soup.

SERVES 5

INGREDIENTS

cornmeal	2 cups
water	4 cups
salt	1 tsp.
okras (finely chopped)	6
Butter or olive oil	

DIRECTIONS

1. Add water to the dry cornmeal until it becomes a wet paste. There should not be any pockets of dry cornmeal in this paste.

2. Boil 4 cups of water in a large non–stick pot. Add the chopped okras and salt.

3. When the okras are cooked use a wooden spoon to stir in the wet cornmeal paste, reduce the heat and allow to cook for about five minutes with the lid on the pot.

4. Uncover and start stirring the cornmeal mixture continuously.

5. The mixture may become reasonably difficult to stir because of its thick consistency, but it is essential to keep stirring as this will prevent the cornmeal from forming lumps. Additional water can be added occasionally as the mixture thickens.

6. After about thirty minutes, continue adding water as needed, by this point, the cornmeal should be cooked.

7. Continue to stir the mixture for another five minutes, pressing the spoon against the sides of the pot to crush any cornmeal lumps.

8. The cornmeal should be cooked at this point. Turn off the heat.

9. Spoon a pat of butter or a teaspoon of olive oil into a small bowl. Take some of the cooked fungee and place it into the buttered bowl. Swirl the fungee in the bowl till it forms a little ball. Set the ball aside on a platter. Repeat with the balance of the cooked fungee. The balls can be plated and served with pepper pot, vegetables, or salted codfish.

NOTES

_____
_____
_____
_____
_____
_____
_____
_____
_____
_____
_____
_____
_____
_____
_____

Aruba – Keshi Yena (Stuffed Cheese)

Keshi Yena is a popular main course cheese dish cooked in Aruba. Keshi Yena may have originated from the slaves of the Dutch West Indies who stuffed discarded Edam and Gouda cheese rinds with table scraps to make a meal. Modern recipes use sliced cheese on the base and top of the chicken filling.

SERVES 5–8

INGREDIENTS

whole 2 pound Edam cheese	1
eggs	2
cooked, shredded chicken	1 lb.
canned tomatoes (peeled and chopped)	2
tomato paste	2 tsp.
sliced green olives	2 tbsp.
whole capers	1 ½ tsp.
parsley (chopped)	1 ½ tsp.
habanero chili pepper (minced)	1 tsp.
raisins	¼ cup
vegetable oil	2 tbsp.
onion (sliced)	1 cup
garlic (minced)	1 tsp.
bell pepper (diced)	1/3 cup
Worcestershire sauce	1 tsp.
mustard	1 tbsp.
mustard	1 tbsp.
Salt and pepper	

DIRECTIONS

1. Place the whole Edam cheese on a board and use a sharp knife to slice it into ¼ inch slices. Line the base of a square 11-inch baking tray with 2/3 of the cheese slices.

2. Start cooking the chicken filling by heating the oil in a skillet and adding the onions, garlic, bell pepper, and habanero chili. Sauté these vegetables in the oil for about six minutes or until soft. Add the olives, tomato paste, chopped canned tomatoes, parsley, olives, and capers. Stir in the ketchup, mustard and Worcestershire sauce. Mix in the shredded chicken. Place the lid on the skillet and cook for about twenty minutes for the chicken to absorb all of the flavors. Stir to prevent it from burning. Sprinkle salt and pepper to taste.

3. Once the chicken filling cooked, allow it to cool.

4. Whisk two eggs in a separate bowl and pour this on the chicken filling. Stir well.

5. Spoon the filling onto the cheese slices in the baking tray. Spread it evenly.

6. Arrange the remaining slices of Edam to cover the chicken filling.

7. Bake in a preheated oven at 350° for forty minutes or until the melted cheese top is golden brown.

8. Serve hot with tortillas or toasted French bread.

NOTES

_____

_____

_____

_____

_____

_____

_____

_____

_____

_____

_____

_____

_____

_____

_____

_____

Barbados – Flying Fish & Cou Cou

The island of Barbados is known for its exotic seafood, and one such delicacy is flying fish, cooked in a creole sauce. Served with another local dish called Cou Cou made from fine cornmeal and okra.

SERVES 6

INGREDIENTS

For Fried Flying Fish

flying fish fillets	12
eggs (beaten)	3
flour	1 cup
breadcrumbs	1 cup
soybean oil	2 cups
salt	2 tbsps.
limes	2

For Creole Sauce

cloves garlic (crushed)	2
onion (sliced)	1
olive oil	3 tbsps.
bell peppers (sliced)	2
thyme (finely chopped)	1 tbsp.
stewed tomatoes	8 Oz.
sugar	
pepper sauce (vinegar, mustard, salt, pickled hot pepper)	1 tbsps.
parsley (chopped)	4 tbsps.
stock	½ cup
Salt	

For Cou Cou

fine yellow cornmeal	8 Oz.
okras (sliced ¼ inch thick)	12
water	4 cups
Olive oil	
Salt	

DIRECTIONS

For Flying Fish

1. Marinate the flying fish fillets in a mixture of water, lime juice, and salt for ten minutes.

2. Remove the fillets and pat dry with a paper towel.

3. Coat each filet in dry flour, then the beaten egg mixture and lastly in breadcrumbs.

4. Heat the soybean oil and fry each fish filet until golden brown. Set aside.

For Creole Sauce

1. To make the creole sauce, begin by adding oil to a skillet or frying pan. Sauté the onions, bell peppers and garlic in the hot oil for about a minute.

2. Add the thyme, sugar, stock, and pepper sauce. Cover the pan and let the sauce simmer for about fifteen to twenty minutes.

3. Add the salt and chopped parsley. Turn off the heat.

For Cou Cou

1. Pour three cups of water into a pot. Add salt and the sliced okra. Bring to a boil and then turn off the heat.

2. Use a slotted spoon or strainer to remove the okra and set aside. Retain the salted water.

3. In another pot on low heat, combine the fine cornmeal and one cup of water. Use a wooden spoon or whisk to stir this mixture. Break up any lumps of cornmeal.

4. As the cornmeal mixture begins to thicken, gradually add the salted water. Continue whisking. After three minutes, mix in the cooked okra.

5. Turn off the heat. Spoon some Cou Cou into a bowl greased with olive oil. As the Cou Cou begins to get firm, overturn the bowl onto a serving dish to plate it.

6. Serve the Cou Cou with fried flying fish fillets.

7. Pour the creole sauce over the fish and cut two lime slices for a garnish.

8.

Belize – Boil Up

The Kriol people of Belize descended from the African slaves and Scottish woodcutters who settled there in the 17th century, and as such, the local dishes like this Belizean Boil Up is influenced mainly by both Scottish and African cuisine.

SERVES 4

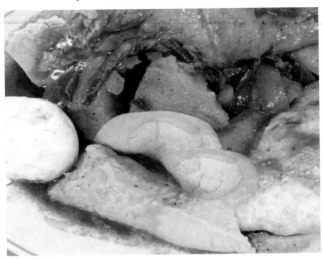

INGREDIENTS

fish (sliced)	2 lbs.
small piece of salted pork (diced)	1
eggs	2
yam	1
cassava	1
large sweet potatoes	2
ripe plantains	2
green bananas	4
onion	1
tomatoes / can of diced tomatoes	3
baking powder	2 tsps.
Water	
Pepper	
Salt	

DIRECTIONS

1. Prepare the boil cakes by combining the flour, baking powder and water to form a soft dough. Separate the dough into three-inch balls and flatten each.

2. Prepare a tomato sauce by first sautéing onions and then adding diced tomatoes. Add salt and pepper to taste.

3. Peel the yam, cassava, and sweet potatoes, and chop them into chunks measuring about three inches.

4. Remove the skin from the green bananas and slice.

5. Peel the ripe plantains and cut into cubes.

6. Fill a Dutch oven pot with water and bring to a boil.

7. Add the cubes of salted pork to the pot.

8. Pour in the chopped ground provisions together with the green bananas and plantain cubes.

9. Cook the pork, bananas, plantains and ground provisions until tender.

10. A few minutes before cooking, place the boil cake dough in the water.

11. When cooked, use a slotted spoon to remove everything besides the salted pork.

12. Add the raw fish slices to the pot containing the water and salted pork. Cook together until the fish becomes tender.

13. Place the eggs in the pot and hard-boil them. After 8-10 minutes, remove the eggs from the pot and drench in cold water. Remove the shells, and slice the eggs in halves.

14. Plate the boiled provisions, bananas, plantains, boil cakes, fish, and salted pork foods on a shallow dish. Finish by pouring the tomato sauce over the food.

NOTES

_____
_____
_____
_____
_____
_____
_____
_____
_____
_____
_____

Bermuda – Fish Chowder

A unique blend of spices and seafood, Bermudian Fish Chowder is a hearty meal that is enjoyed by locals and island visitors alike.

SERVES 6

INGREDIENTS

red snapper fillets (cut into 1-inch pieces)	1 lb.
bay leaf	1
clam juice	4 cups
tomato paste	3 tbsps.
cloves garlic (minced)	3
bell pepper (sliced)	1
onion (finely chopped)	1
carrots (cubed)	2
stalks celery (chopped)	3
potatoes (peeled and diced)	2
vegetable oil	2 tbsps.
peeled and diced tomatoes	1 can
Worcestershire sauce	2 tbsps.
jalapeno pepper	1
ground black pepper	1 tbsp.
shot of black rum	1
Dash of Sherry Pepper Sauce (a blend of pickled bird peppers and cooking sherry)	

DIRECTIONS

1. In a large soup pot, pour in the vegetable oil. Heat on medium-high and add the minced garlic, carrot cubes, chopped onion, celery, and bell pepper slices.

2. Sauté the vegetables for about eight minutes or until the vegetables are partially cooked.

3. Add the tomato paste and allow it to cook for a minute. Stir well before pouring in four cups of the clam juice.

4. Add the diced potatoes, jalapeno pepper, ground black pepper and Worcestershire sauce. Open the can of tomatoes and empty all the contents into the chowder. Stir and add a bay leaf to the chowder.

5. Place a lid on the soup pot, reduce the heat, and allow to simmer. Occasionally, remove the lid and stir.

6. When the potatoes are tender, add the pieces of red snapper. Let the chowder continue to simmer for about ten to fifteen minutes or until the fish is cooked.

7. When done, the snapper should flake easily with a fork.

8. Ladle the hot fish chowder in a serving bowl and add a dash of Sherry Pepper Sauce and a shot of black rum.

NOTES

Costa Rica – Gallo Pinto

Gallo Pinto is the most popular meal in Costa Rica. It is a one pot dish of seasoned rice and beans that are cooked together. The name of this dish translates to "Spotted Rooster" and it may have been named so because of the speckled mix of colors of the black beans against the white rice. This meal is commonly served with fried plantains, scrambled eggs, avocado slices and tortillas. In Costa Rica, it is eaten as a hearty breakfast.

SERVES 6

INGREDIENTS

cooked long grain white rice	3 cups
cooked black beans / canned black beans	2 cups
cumin powder	1 tsp.
canola oil or vegetable oil	2 tbsps.
medium onion (finely diced)	1
red or green bell pepper (diced)	1
cloves garlic (minced)	2
celery (diced)	½ cup
coriander leaves (dried and ground)	1 tsp.
Worcestershire / Lizano sauce	3 tbsps.
ginger (minced)	½ tsp.
Green onions for garnish (sliced)	
Fresh cilantro for garnish (chopped)	
Salt	
Pepper	

DIRECTIONS

1. Pour the canola oil in a large skillet. Turn up the heat to medium-high.

2. Add the diced onions and sauté until soft and translucent.

3. Add the minced cloves of garlic and sauté for an additional five minutes.

4. The onions should become golden at this point.

5. Add the diced bell pepper, celery, ground coriander, powdered cumin, and minced ginger to the skillet. Stir in three tablespoons of Worcestershire sauce.

6. Stir the vegetables and spices together.

7. Spoon the black beans into the skillet and then add the cooked white rice. Toss the beans, rice, and spices until evenly mixed. Let the rice and beans cook for a short while. Season generously with salt and pepper. Garnish the Gallo Pinto with fresh cilantro and green onions.

8. Serve this exotic breakfast dish with sides such as fried plantains, avocado slices, and eggs.

NOTES

_____
_____
_____
_____
_____
_____
_____
_____
_____
_____
_____
_____
_____
_____
_____
_____
_____
_____

Cuba – Arroz con Pollo

Arroz con Pollo is a Cuban dish of rice and chicken that is cooked together with fresh herbs and flavorful spices. In Cuba, it is prepared in every home as a comfort food or dinner party meal.

SERVES 8

INGREDIENTS

chicken legs or thighs	8
rice	2 cups
large onion (diced)	1
salt	1 ½ tsps.
black pepper	½ tsp.
cloves garlic (crushed)	4
Oregano	2 tsps.
(8 oz.) can tomato sauce	1
chicken broth	2 cups
Cumin powder	2 tsps.
bay leaf	1
frozen green peas	½ cup
large red pepper (diced)	1
olive oil	½ cup
annatto condiment	½ tsp.

DIRECTIONS

1. Season the chicken with adequate salt, black pepper, and cumin powder.

2. Heat the olive oil over medium-high heat and lightly fry the seasoned pieces of chicken until brown on all sides.

3. Set the cooked chicken aside but retain the oil, keep the heat on and sauté the onion and red pepper.

4. When the onion is tender, add the crushed garlic and stir.

5. Sauté together for two minutes.

6. Place the fried chicken back into the pan.

7. Pour in the chicken broth and tomato sauce.

8. Stir in the annatto, bay leaf, and cumin powder.

9. Season with salt and pepper.

10. Rinse the rice in water and then add to the pan.

11. Stir together so that the rice becomes submerged in the liquid.

12. Bring to a boil, then reduce the heat and let it cook.

13. Stir occasionally, when the rice has absorbed most of the liquid, cover the pan and let it simmer for about thirty (0:30) to forty-five (0:45) minutes or until the rice is tender.

14. Five minutes before it is fully cooked, stir in the frozen peas.

15. Serve hot.

NOTES

_____
_____
_____
_____
_____
_____
_____
_____
_____
_____
_____
_____
_____
_____
_____

Dominica – Mountain Chicken

Mountain Chicken is an endangered frog species native to the island of Dominica. The natives of the island have prepared and eaten Mountain Chicken for many years until it is now considered the national dish of the country. The cooked frog is traditionally eaten with provisions, rice and peas.

SERVES 5

INGREDIENTS

fresh frog legs	12 – 16
cloves whole garlic	2
minced garlic	1 tsp.
lime (sliced in half)	1
flour	¼ cup
vinegar	1 tsp.
small onion (sliced)	1
butter	1 tbsp.
water	1 cup
dasheen roots (each cut into 4 pieces)	2
yams (each sliced into 4 pieces)	2
green pepper (sliced)	1
fresh thyme (minced)	¼ tsp.
Salt	
Pepper	

DIRECTIONS

1. Rinse the frog legs in the water.

2. Use a sharp knife to cut and peel away the skin from the flesh.

3. Discard the skin and wash the frog legs with lime juice.

4. Rinse the legs with cold water.

5. Place the frog legs into a bowl and season with the thyme, vinegar, minced garlic, salt, and pepper.

6. Allow the seasoned legs to sit for two (2:00) hours.

7. Put the flour in a shallow dish and coat each leg in flour.

8. Heat the oil to high in a skillet.

9. Fry the flour coated legs until golden brown and set aside.

10. Prepare a gravy for the legs by first sautéing the onion in a mixture of melted butter and one tbsp of oil.

11. Add a cup of water, bring to a boil, and then add flour to thicken the gravy.

12. Let it simmer for five (0:05) minutes on medium heat.

13. Add the fried frog legs to the gravy, cook for a minute and turn off the heat.

14. Boil the provisions (yams and dasheen root) in salted water together with the sliced green pepper.

15. Test the provisions with a fork and when it is tender, turn off the heat and drain.

16. Serve the Mountain Chicken and provisions with rice and peas.

NOTES

_____
_____
_____
_____
_____
_____
_____
_____
_____
_____
_____
_____

Dominican Republic – Chicharrones de Pollo

Chicharonnes de Pollo or fried chicken chunks is a tasty meal that is quite popular in the Dominican Republic. This fried chicken dish contains rich Spanish flavors as the Dominican Republic was first inhabited by the Spanish. In this country, Chicharrones de Pollo is enjoyed with tostones (fried plantain slices) or rice and beans.

SERVES 5

INGREDIENTS

skinless, boneless chicken breast	1 lb.
dark rum	½ cup
corn oil	4 cups
Worcestershire sauce	¼ cup
lime or lemon juice	½ cup
minced garlic	½ cup
Garlic powder	3 tbsps.
adobo seasoning	1 tsp.
onion powder	1 tsp.
ground black pepper	1 tsp.
all-purpose flour	3 cups
ground coriander	1 tsp.
packets (0.18 oz.) of dried achiote and coriander seasoning	2

DIRECTIONS

1. Use a sharp knife to cut the raw chicken breasts into bite-sized cubes.

2. Create a flavorful marinade for the chicken by combining Worcestershire sauce, lime or lemon juice, rum, minced garlic, onion and garlic powder, black pepper, coriander, adobo and contents of the seasoning packets.

3. Immerse the raw chicken cubes in the marinade and mix with a spoon allowing all pieces to coat.

4. Refrigerate the marinated chicken in a covered bowl for four (4:00) hours.

5. Lay the flour in a shallow dish and coat each piece of marinated chicken in flour before frying.

6. Pour the corn oil into a large pan and heat to medium high, about 300 degrees F°.

7. Fry the chicken cubes in small batches, occasionally flipping until golden brown on all sides.

8. Use a slotted spoon to remove the chicken cubes from the pot and set them on paper towels to absorb the oil.

9. Serve delicious Chicharonnes de Pollo with rice and beans or hot slices of fried plantain.

NOTES

_____
_____
_____
_____
_____
_____
_____
_____
_____
_____
_____
_____
_____
_____
_____
_____
_____
_____
_____
_____

El Salvador – Pupusa

A Pupusa is a thick fried tortilla that is stuffed with a hearty filling of cheese, meat or refried beans. This popular El Salvadorian dish was first prepared by the Pipil tribes who were the country's first native peoples. Pupusas are traditionally eaten with a cabbage relish called Curtido.

YIELDS 8 pupusas

INGREDIENTS

For the Curtido

head cabbage (shredded)	½
large carrot (grated)	1
apple cider vinegar	½ cup
medium yellow onion (thinly sliced)	½
water	¼ cup
brown sugar	½ tsp.
red pepper flakes	1 tsp.
dried oregano	1 tsp.
salt	½ tsp.

For the Pupusas

Masa Harina/corn flour	2 cups
grated mozzarella / Monterey jack cheese	1 cup
warm water	1 ½ cups
Vegetable oil	
Salt	

DIRECTIONS

1. For the Curtido
2. Prepare the Curtido by first tossing the cabbage, onions, and carrot together in a bowl.
3. Mix the apple cider vinegar, water, brown sugar, salt, oregano, and red pepper flakes altogether.
4. Pour this over the cabbage mixture and mix well.
5. Refrigerate in a covered dish for at least a day until serving.
6. For the Pupusas
7. Knead together the flour, salt, and water to form a smooth, moist dough adding additional water or flour gradually if needed.
8. Work into a ball, place in a bowl, cover and let it rest for ten (0:10) minutes.
9. Oil the hands and divide the dough into eight pieces. Roll in two-inch diameter balls.
10. Make an indentation in each ball, by pressing in with the thumb to make a small cup.
11. Spoon one tablespoon of grated cheese in the indentation and seal the dough shut.
12. Flatten the ball into a thick tortilla about a ¼ inch thick.
13. Heat a little vegetable oil and fry the pupusas for three (0:03) minutes on each side.
14. Serve the hot pupusas with a generous serving of Curtido.

NOTES

_____
_____
_____
_____
_____
_____
_____
_____
_____
_____
_____

Guatemala – Fiambre

Considered to be Guatemala's national dish, this cold platter of vegetables, cheese, deli meats and eggs is traditionally served on All Saints Day. Fiambre is served cold.

SERVES 12 – 16

INGREDIENTS

skinless and boneless poached chicken breasts (cubed)	1 lb.
boiled shrimp (unpeeled with heads on)	1 lb.
cooked chorizo sausage (cut into ¼ inch slices)	8 oz.
cooked linguica sausage (cut into ¼ inch slices)	8 oz.
salami (cut into ½ inch strips)	3 oz.
ham (cut into ½ inch strips)	3 oz.
hardboiled eggs (cut into quarters)	4
farmer's cheese/feta	8 oz.
radishes (cut into quarters)	5
Pacaya (palm tree blossoms)	3
Spanish olives (pitted)	3 oz.
mini gherkins (drained)	3 oz.
frozen peas	1 cup
small head red leaf lettuce	1
small head green leaf lettuce	1
medium roasted beets (peeled and cut into quarters)	4
head cauliflower (cut into florets and boiled)	1
ribs celery (boiled and cut into ½ inch slices)	4
medium carrots (boiled and cut into ½ inch slices)	4
green beans (trimmed and boiled)	4 oz.
Yukon Gold potatoes (boiled and cut into halves)	1 lb.
olive oil	1 cup
knob ginger (thinly sliced)	1
clove garlic (thinly sliced)	1
scallions (chopped)	6
(17 oz.) jar pimientos (drained)	1
Dijon mustard	1 tbsp.
capers (drained)	1 tbsp.
white wine vinegar	½ cup
chopped parsley	¾ cup

DIRECTIONS

1. Start making a vinaigrette by first pureeing the parsley, vinegar, mustard, capers, ginger, garlic and pimientos in a blender.

2. Add oil until emulsified and season with adequate salt and pepper, then set aside.

3. In a large bowl, mix the chicken cubes, chorizo, linguica sausage, shrimp, green beans, ham, peas, carrots, celery, potatoes and cauliflower florets with a ¾ cup of the pre-made vinaigrette.

4. In a separate bowl, mix a ¼ cup of the vinaigrette and the beets.

5. Cover both bowls with plastic wrap and refrigerate for thirty (0:30) minutes.

6. Arrange the lettuce leaves on a large serving platter.

7. Remove the bowls from the refrigerator and arrange the cold meats and vegetables on top of the bed of lettuce.

8. Garnish the Fiambre with the beets, cheese, olives, papayas, eggs, radishes and gherkins.

9. Sprinkle chopped parsley over the Fiambre and serve.

NOTES

_____

_____

_____

_____

_____

Grenada – Oil Down

Oil Down is a cooked breadfruit dish and is considered Grenada's national dish. It is made with fresh vegetables and herbs cooked together with a mixture of both fresh and salted meats. This island meal is eaten by itself, without condiments or sides.

SERVES 4–6

INGREDIENTS

chicken	2 lbs.
salted pork or fish	½ lb.
breadfruit (peeled and cut into large wedges)	1
bunch dasheen / taro leaves (chopped)	½
green bananas (peeled)	8
cabbage (cut into eight chunks)	1
flour	2 cups
turmeric powder	1 tbsp.
carrots (chopped into 1-inch rounds)	2
cloves garlic (finely chopped)	6
onion (diced)	½
sweet peppers (seeded and sliced)	5
yams (peeled and cut into chunks)	2
coconut milk	3 cups
water	3 cups
sprigs celery (roughly chopped)	2
sprig fresh thyme (chopped)	1
sprig basil (chopped)	1
hot pepper (seeded and sliced)	1

DIRECTIONS

1. Soak the salted pork or fish in water and set aside.

2. Cut the chicken into parts, rinse and place in a large Dutch oven pot.

3. Put the garlic cloves into the pot with the chicken, along with the thyme, celery, hot pepper slices, basil, onion, and sweet peppers.

4. Rinse the breadfruit wedges and place them over the herbs and chicken in the pot.

5. Add the green bananas to the pot.

6. Next, add the carrots and yams to the pot.

7. Remove the salted pork or fish from the water and use a knife to scrape off any unwanted parts before slicing and rinsing in clean water.

8. Add the salted pork or fish to the pot.

9. In a separate bowl, combine the coconut milk, water, and the turmeric.

10. Reserve ¾ cup of this liquid and pour the rest over the Ingredients in the pot.

11. Place the pot on the stove, turn on the heat, and allow it to start simmering.

12. Add the pieces of cabbage.

13. Make flour dumplings by kneading the flour with the reserved coconut and turmeric liquid.

14. Add the dumplings to the pot and cover everything with the chopped dasheen leaves.

15. Place the lid on the pot and let it cook for about one (1:00) hour until the starches absorb the liquid.

16. Serve hot.

NOTES

_____

_____

_____

_____

_____

_____

_____

Haiti – Diri ak Djon Djon

Diri ak Djon Djon is a popular Haitian rice dish, also called Black Mushroom Rice. Its key ingredient is a type of black mushroom native to Northern Haiti. This mushroom forms a black stock when boiled and gives food a unique color, aroma and flavor. The mushrooms are considered a delicacy and are not used in everyday cooking.

SERVES 6

INGREDIENTS

dried Djon Djon (dried black mushrooms)	2 cups
rice	3 cups
water	5 cups
cloves garlic (chopped)	2
jumbo shrimps (peeled and de-veined)	12
shallots (finely chopped)	2
green pepper (roughly chopped)	1
cloves	3
Oil	4 tbsps.
salted lard (cubed)	¼ cup
large onion (peeled and finely diced)	1
sprig thyme	1
chicken/beef stock cubes	2
pigeon peas	1 ½ cups
butter	1 tbsp.
salt	1 tsp.
black pepper	1 tsp.
pinch cayenne pepper	1
whole hot pepper	1

DIRECTIONS

1. Boil five cups of water in a small saucepan.

2. Add the dried Djon Djon mushrooms to the boiling water and turn off the heat.

3. Soak the mushrooms in hot water for thirty (0:30) minutes.

4. Transfer the liquid and mushrooms to a blender and blend roughly, then strain through a fine strainer.

5. Collect and reserve the black liquid stock.

6. Discard the solids.

7. In a large saucepan, heat the oil and lard together.

8. When the lard melts, add the shallots, onions, peas, garlic, green pepper, and shrimps.

9. Sauté together for about five (0:05) minutes.

10. Add the black mushroom stock to the saucepan, and season with the cloves, hot pepper, thyme, salt, cayenne and black pepper. Bring to a boil.

11. Rinse the rice in water and add it to the pan.

12. Stir frequently for two (0:02) minutes.

13. Cook with the cover of until the rice absorbs the liquid.

14. Stir in the butter.

15. Reduce the heat, cover the pan, and cook for an additional fifteen (0:15).

16. Serve the Diri Ak Djon Djon with meat or fish.

NOTES

_____

_____

_____

_____

_____

_____

_____

_____

_____

_____

Honduras – Plato Tipico

Plato Tipico is a platter containing several separately prepared foods which are served together as one dish. It comprises mainly of stewed beans, fried plantains, chismol and grilled meat or sausage. Rice and corn tortillas are eaten with it. This dish is usually cooked on special occasions in Honduras and is considered the country's national dish.

SERVES 4–6

INGREDIENTS

beef sirloin (cut into long strips)	1 lb.
pork sirloin (cut into long strips)	1 lb.
chorizo sausages	4
cloves garlic (minced)	4
Olive oil	4 tbsps.
Vinegar	3 tbsps.
cans kidney beans	2
red onions (sliced separately)	2
bell peppers (sliced)	3
dried oregano	1 tsp.
pinch cayenne pepper	1
minced thyme	¼ tsp.
paprika	¼ tsp.
ketchup	1 cup
water	1 cup
large tomatoes (diced)	2
large green pepper (sliced)	1
sprigs coriander	3
cumin	¼ tsp.
lemon juice	2 tbsp.
plantains	2
Vegetable oil	4 tbsps.
Salt	
Black pepper	

DIRECTIONS

1. Mix the meat strips with olive oil, salt, pepper, garlic, and vinegar.

2. Marinate for one (1:00) hour.

3. Grill the meat and chorizo sausages together until cooked, then remove from the grill and set aside.

4. Heat two tablespoons of olive oil in a pot and sauté one diced red onion, half of the minced garlic and the sliced bell peppers until tender.

5. Add the canned beans.

6. Stir together, reduce the heat and let it simmer.

7. Add the ketchup, water, paprika, cayenne, thyme, salt, black pepper, and oregano.

8. Let simmer for fifteen (0:15) minutes, then turn off the heat and set aside.

9. Make the chismol by mixing the diced tomatoes, green pepper slices, lemon juice, coriander, diced red onion, cumin, salt, and black pepper.

10. Peel the plantains and slice in halves, then cut each half lengthwise into ½ inch slices.

11. Fry the plantain slices in vegetable oil until lightly browned on both sides.

12. Arrange the grilled meat, chorizo sausages, fried plantains, chismol and beans on four serving plates.

13. Serve with steamed rice, corn tortillas, avocado slices, farmer's cheese and a dollop of sour cream.

NOTES

_____

_____

_____

_____

_____

_____

_____

Jamaica – Ackee and Salt fish

Ackee is the national fruit of Jamaica and it is used to prepare the national dish of Ackee and Salt fish. The ackee is prepared with vegetables and savory salt fish. It is usually eaten for breakfast with Caribbean dumplings, homemade bread, fried plantains and boiled green bananas.

SERVES 3–4

INGREDIENTS

ackee / 2 cups fresh, boiled ackee	1 can
boneless salted codfish	½ lb.
paprika	1 tsp.
freshly ground black pepper	1 tsp.
small onion (peeled and thinly diced)	1
small bell pepper (diced)	1
tomatoes (diced)	2
sprig fresh thyme	1
slices bacon (sliced)	4–6
vegetable oil	¼ cup
scallions (finely sliced)	2
minced garlic	1 tsp.
Scotch Bonnet pepper / ½ tsp. cayenne pepper	1
Hot water	

DIRECTIONS

1. Soak the salted codfish in a bowl of hot water for one (1:00) hour.

2. Drain and soak again in hot water for an additional hour to remove some of the salt.

3. Drain and transfer the codfish to a shallow dish.

4. Use a fork to shred the codfish into smaller bits.

5. Set the shredded codfish aside.

6. Place a skillet over medium heat and add the bacon when hot.

7. Fry the bacon until brown and crisp, then remove from the skillet and set aside.

8. Remove the bacon drippings and return the cooked bacon to the skillet together with the vegetable oil.

9. Add the garlic, onions, scallions, and thyme.

10. Sauté together, occasionally stirring to prevent burning.

11. Add the tomatoes and bell peppers to the skillet and cook for about three (0:03) minutes.

12. Add the Scotch Bonnet slices or cayenne pepper.

13. Sprinkle in the paprika and black pepper, then stir together and let cook for about five (0:05) minutes.

14. Add a little water if needed.

15. Place the shredded salt fish into the skillet and mix with the vegetables.

16. Cook for about two (0:02) minutes, then stir in the ackee.

17. Finish cooking for an additional three (0:03) minutes before turning off the heat.

18. Serve hot.

NOTES

_____
_____
_____
_____
_____
_____
_____
_____
_____
_____
_____

Nicaragua – Gallo Pinto

Gallo Pinto is the official dish of Nicaragua. It is a delicious meal of boiled rice and fried beans which are cooked together. Red beans or black beans are traditionally used. Gallo Pinto translates to "spotted rooster" in Spanish and the name was given to this dish because the mix of white rice and colored beans resembles the speckled feathers of a rooster. This dish is usually eaten with corn tortillas or alongside carne asada.

SERVES 6

INGREDIENTS

Gallo pinto beans (red/black beans)	I cup
bay leaf	1
clove	1
small whole onion (peeled)	1
small onion (peeled and finely chopped)	1
cloves garlic (peeled)	2
long grained white rice	1 ½ cups
olive oil	4 tbsp.
Black pepper	
Salt	
Water	

DIRECTIONS

1. Soak the beans in a bowl of cold water for four (4:00) hours.

2. Drain the water and discard.

3. Transfer the beans to a pot and cover with two quarts of fresh water.

4. Stick the bay leaf with the clove onto the whole, peeled onion and place into the pot of beans and water.

5. Add the garlic cloves to the pot.

6. Gradually bring the beans to a boil and skim off any foam that may rise to the surface of the water.

7. Reduce the heat and let the beans simmer for about one (1:00) hour and thirty (0:30) minutes until tender.

8. Add salt to taste a few minutes before turning off the heat.

9. Drain the water from the pot and discard the onion, clove, bay leaf and garlic.

10. Rinse the beans under cold water, then set aside.

11. In a heavy saucepan, pour in two and a half cups of water and add a teaspoon of salt.

12. Bring to a boil and add the rice.

13. Cook the rice for about eighteen (0:18) minutes until tender.

14. Set the rice aside uncovered for five (0:05) minutes, then fluff with a fork.

15. Heat the oil in a frying pan, then brown the chopped onion for about five (0:05) minutes.

16. Add the rice and beans to the pan and mix.

17. Cook for five (0:05) minutes until the rice begins to brown.

18. Add additional salt and black pepper if desired, mix well, then turn off the heat.

19. Serve Gallo Pinto immediately with corn tortillas.

NOTES

_____
_____
_____
_____
_____

Panama – Sancocho de Gallina

Sancocho de Gallina is Panama's beloved national dish. It originated in the Azuero region of the country. The dish is a delicious chicken soup that is usually eaten for lunch. Traditionally, homegrown chickens are used to make Sancocho and the soup is cooked over an outdoor open fire where it absorbs a natural smoky flavor. Steamed rice is served with Sancocho, along with patacones or fried plantains.

SERVES 8

INGREDIENTS

chicken (cut into pieces)	1
cloves garlic (crushed)	3
salt	3 tsp.
ears corn (broken into 1-inch pieces)	2
Yucca root/green occasionally flipping (peeled and cut into bite-sized pieces)	3 lbs.
large onion (diced)	1
cilantro / culantro leaves (chopped)	4 tbsp.
black pepper	1 tsp.
fresh oregano	2 tbsp.
cooking oil	1 tbsp.

DIRECTIONS

1. Season the chicken parts with black pepper, oregano, and the garlic.

2. Heat the cooking oil in a large pot and add the chicken and allow brown on all sides.

3. Reduce the heat and cover the pot to allow the herbs and meat to sweat (Reserve a little cilantro/Culantro to garnish the finished Sancocho and add the rest to the pot.)

4. Add the onions and stir well, then add enough water to cover the chicken.

5. Bring to a boil, then reduce the heat and simmer for about twenty (0:20) minutes.

6. Add the yucca root / green plantains/yams to the pot and mix with the chicken and herbs.

7. Cook the Sancocho for one (1:00) hour until the meat and vegetables are tender, adding more water if necessary.

8. Add the pieces of corn to the soup.

9. Cook for fifteen (0:15) minutes until the corn is tender.

10. Season the soup with salt.

11. Turn off the heat and garnish with the reserved cilantro/Culantro leaves.

12. Serve with steamed rice and Tostones/ Patacones (Thick green plantain chips).

St. Kitts and Nevis – Salt fish, Spicy Plantains, Breadfruit & Coconut Dumplings

The national dish of St. Kitts and Nevis is an assortment of separately prepared foods; namely stewed saltfish, spicy plantains, cooked breadfruit chunks, and coconut dumplings. These are all served together as one meal.

SERVES 4–5

INGREDIENTS

Stewed Saltfish

saltfish	1 lb.

green pepper (seeded and diced)	1
cloves garlic (chopped)	5
tomatoes (diced)	1 lb.
scallions (finely chopped)	6
chopped parsley	2 tbsp.
margarine	2 tbsp.
vegetable oil	4 tbsp.
Salt	
Pepper	

Spicy Plantains

medium-sized ripe plantains (peeled and cut into ½ inch slices)	3
fresh minced ginger	2 tbsp.
small onion (peeled and grated)	1
salt	¼ tsp.
hot sauce	¼ tsp.
Vegetable oil for frying	

Seasoned Breadfruit Chunks

boiled breadfruit chunks (1-inch pieces)	3 cups
diced red bell pepper	½ cup
medium onion (peeled and chopped)	1
cloves garlic (crushed)	4
chopped parsley	2 tbsp.
freshly ground black pepper	1 tsp.
chicken stock	½ cup
fresh thyme leaves	1 tbsp.
vegetable oil	2 tbsp.
unsalted butter	1 tbsp.
salt	¼ tsp.

Coconut Dumplings

grated coconut	½ cup
flour	1 ½ cups
margarine	1 tbsp.
water	½ cup
oil	1 tbsp.
salt	¼ tsp.

DIRECTIONS

Stewed Saltfish

1. Soak the salt fish overnight, then drain and boil in fresh water until tender.
2. Clean the saltfish by removing any scales, bones, and viscera.
3. Use a fork to flake the saltfish, then set aside.
4. Heat the oil in a saucepan, then add the pepper, scallions, onion, and garlic.
5. Stir well, then cover and cook for five (0:05) minutes.
6. Add the tomatoes and simmer for three (0:03) minutes.
7. Add the saltfish together with the butter and season with salt and pepper.
8. Cover the pot and cook for five (0:05) minutes.

Spicy Plantains

1. Season the plantain slices with the onion, salt, hot sauce, and ginger by combing together in a bowl.
2. Heat the oil in a skillet and fry the seasoned plantains in batches until golden brown.
3. Drain on paper towels before serving.

Seasoned Breadfruit Chunks

1. Melt the butter in a saucepan, then add the oil.
2. When the fat is hot, add the onions and cook for about six (0:06) minutes until golden brown.
3. Add the chopped peppers, garlic and thyme to the onions.
4. Sauté the Ingredients for about one (0:01) minute, then add the breadfruit chunks.
5. Add the chicken stock and stir gently.
6. Season with salt and pepper, then turn off the heat.

Coconut Dumplings

1. Combine the flour, grated coconut, salt, butter and oil in a bowl.
2. Add water and knead into a stiff dough for about two (0:02) minutes.
3. Shape into dumplings.
4. Place the dumplings into a pot of boiling water, cover and let it boil for about fifteen (0:15) minutes or until cooked, then drain.
5. Serve the dumplings with portions of stewed saltfish, seasoned breadfruit chunks, and spicy plantains.

St. Lucia – Green Fig & Salt fish

Green figs are the local name for green bananas. This dish had its roots in 19th-century slavery when bananas were plentiful and dried; salted codfish was cheaply imported from Canada to serve as rations for slaves. Over time, the slaves added their spices to the dish, and it became so popular on the island, that it was eventually recognized as the national dish of St. Lucia. The dish is typically prepared on weekends and especially for the Creole Day Festival held in October.

SERVES 4

INGREDIENTS

saltfish	1 lb.
green bananas	8-12
vegetable / coconut oil	¼ cup
medium bell pepper (seeded and chopped)	1
large onion (peeled and diced)	1
pimento peppers (seeded and thinly sliced)	4
finely chopped chives	¼ cup
cloves garlic (grated)	3
fresh thyme	2 tsp.
Salt	
Black pepper	
Parsley (garnish)	

DIRECTIONS

1. Rinse the green bananas and slice off both ends.

2. Make one slice lengthwise in each banana and place in a heatproof bowl.

3. Cover the bananas with hot water and let rest for about ten (0:10) minutes, then drain and allow to cool.

4. Carefully peel the bananas and place in a pot of boiling water with a ½ teaspoon of salt and a ¼ teaspoon of oil.

5. Bring to a boil and cook for fifteen (0:15) minutes until tender, then drain and cool.

6. Diagonally slice each banana into three pieces, then set aside.

7. Rinse the saltfish, then simmer in boiling water for fifteen (0:15) minutes to remove excess salt.

8. Drain the water and repeat the previous step.

9. Clean the saltfish by removing any scales, bones, and viscera, then flake the fish with a fork and set aside.

10. Heat the remaining oil in a saucepan over medium heat.

11. Sauté the peppers, onions and half of the grated garlic for five (0:05) minutes until soft and fragrant.

12. Add the flaked saltfish, half of the thyme and half of the chives.

13. Stir well and cover the pan, allowing the herbs to cook for ten (0:10) minutes.

14. Uncover and add the remaining thyme, chives, and garlic to the pot.

15. Season with salt and pepper, stir well and turn off the heat.

16. Plate a portion of the green bananas and top with generous servings of saltfish.

17. Garnish with chopped parsley and serve.

NOTES

_____

_____

_____

_____

_____

_____

St. Vincent & the Grenadines –
Roasted Breadfruit and Fried Jackfish

The national dish of St. Vincent and the Grenadines is Roasted Breadfruit and Fried Jackfish. Breadfruit has grown on these islands since 1793 when it was brought to feed the slave populations. Since then, breadfruit has been prepared in a variety of delicious methods. Roasting the breadfruit is the most common way and it is traditionally done over an outdoor charcoal or wood fire. Jackfish is a common fish caught locally. This dish is usually prepared for the annual Breadfruit Festival.

SERVES 4

INGREDIENTS

large whole breadfruit	1
jackfish (cleaned and sliced or left whole)	1 lb.
cup flour	1
salt	1 tbsp.
minced seasoning blend (onion, chive, garlic, thyme)	¼ cup
medium onion (peeled and minced)	1
clove garlic (minced)	1
sprig thyme	1
medium ripe tomato (sliced)	1
margarine	½ oz.
water	1 cup
ketchup	1 tsp.
Lemon / Lime juice	
Salt	
Pepper	
Vegetable oil	

DIRECTIONS

1. Pierce the breadfruit in several places with a skewer.
2. Roast the breadfruit in an outdoor fire or bake in an oven at 350 degrees F° for one (1:00) hour and thirty (0:30) minutes.
3. Insert a skewer from top to bottom of the breadfruit and remove from the oven or fire if it comes out clean.
4. Peel the breadfruit and slice into wedges, then set aside.
5. Marinate the fish slices in a small bowl of lime or lemon juice for fifteen (0:15) minutes.
6. Rinse the fish and pat dry with paper towels.
7. Make a rub with the seasoning blend and salt, then coat the fish slices.
8. Dredge the fish slices in flour and shake off the excess.
9. Heat vegetable oil in a pan over medium heat, then fry the fish for four (0:04) minutes on each side.
10. Place the fried fish on paper towels and set aside.
11. In a clean saucepan, heat a tablespoon of oil and sauté the garlic, thyme and sliced tomato until tender.
12. Add the margarine and stir until it melts.
13. Add the ketchup and water.
14. Season with salt and pepper.
15. Reduce the heat and allow the sauce to simmer for a few minutes until it thickens.
16. Plate the roasted breadfruit and fried jackfish.
17. Drizzle the sauce over it and serve immediately.

The Bahamas – Crack Conch with Peas & Rice

Queen conch is a giant sea creature found in the ocean surrounding the islands of the Bahamas. It is a versatile and flavorful delicacy. Bahamian prepare conch in a variety of delicious ways. The flesh of the conch is tough and chewy, but 'cracking' or pounding it with a meat mallet causes it to become tender. Fried conch strips are eaten with Bahamian style peas and rice.

SERVES 4–6

INGREDIENTS

For Conch and Tempura Batter

queen conch flesh (tenderized using a meat mallet)	1 lb.
Oil for frying	
water	2–4 cups
flour	1 lb.
black pepper	1 tsp.
garlic powder	1 tsp.
egg (whisked)	1
fresh thyme (minced)	1 tsp.

For Bahamian Style Peas and Rice

pigeon peas	1 cup
water	3 cups
rice	1 ½ cups
medium onion (diced)	1
tomato paste	½ cup
fresh thyme (minced)	2 tsp.
slices bacon (diced)	2
ripe tomato (sliced)	½
Salt	
Pepper	

DIRECTIONS

For Conch and Tempura Batter

1. Combine flour, egg, salt, black pepper, garlic powder, thyme and water to form a batter. Add a small amount of water at a time to make a thick batter that resembles a paste.

2. Chop the tenderized conch into 2-inch strips. Coat the pieces in tempura batter and deep fry in oil until golden brown. Set aside.

For Bahamian Style Peas and Rice

1. Begin by adding the bacon to a pan. Fry until golden brown. Add the sliced tomato, onion, tomato paste, pepper, and thyme. Sauté together with the bacon. Add the peas. Sprinkle salt and pepper to taste. Add 3 cups of water. Stir and bring to a boil. Add the rice, cover and cook on medium heat for about thirty minutes or until the rice is tender and the water is absorbed.

2. Serve the fried conch with Bahamian style rice and peas.

NOTES

_____
_____
_____
_____
_____
_____
_____
_____
_____
_____
_____
_____
_____

Trinidad & Tobago – Callaloo

Callaloo is the national dish of Trinidad and Tobago. It is a thick stew with the consistency of a soup. Callaloo is made from dasheen leaves and cooked with an assortment of herbs and spices. Traditionally, crabs are included in Callaloo, but meats such as chicken and salted pork can also be incorporated in the stew. Callaloo can be eaten alone but it is also commonly eaten with macaroni pie, a Caribbean pasta dish.

SERVES 8.

INGREDIENTS

bundle young dasheen/taro leaves (approximately 18 leaves)	1
okra pods (sliced)	12
blue crabs (cleaned and halved)	4
large onion (peeled and chopped)	1
sprigs fresh thyme	4
cloves garlic (peeled and crushed)	6
peeled, cubed pumpkin	½ cup
water	1 cup
habanero pepper	1
coconut milk	3 cups
chives (chopped)	4
Salt	

DIRECTIONS

1. Remove the skin from the dasheen leaf stalks and discard.

2. Rinse the leaves and stalks, then chop into bite-sized pieces.

3. Place the leaves in a large pot.

4. Add the onions, garlic, thyme, pumpkin, coconut mil, and okras to the pot.

5. Pour a cup of water into the pot and add the whole habanero pepper.

6. Cover the pot and simmer over low heat for thirty (0:30) minutes.

7. Remove the lid, then add the crabs.

8. Stir the Ingredients but do not puncture the habanero pepper.

9. Replace the lid on the pot and allow the Callaloo to cook for another thirty (0:30) minutes.

10. Remove the habanero pepper and discard it.

11. Season the Callaloo with the salt and chives.

12. Use an immersion blender to puree the stew, excluding the crabs.

13. Stir well, then turn off the heat.

    Serve the Callaloo with macaroni pie.

NOTES

_____
_____
_____
_____
_____
_____
_____
_____
_____
_____
_____
_____
_____
_____
_____
_____
_____
_____

Angola – Moamba de Galinha

Moamba de Galinha is a flavorful chicken stew which is considered to be Angola's national dish. One of its distinguishing Ingredients is red palm oil which gives the stew a unique aroma and taste. This ingredient may be difficult to find in modern supermarkets but can be substituted with paprika infused peanut oil.

SERVES 4

INGREDIENTS

chicken (cut in quarters)	1
red palm oil/mixture of ½ cup peanut oil and 1 teaspoon paprika	½ cup
okra (sliced)	½ lb.
onions (diced)	3
whole chili pepper	1
tomatoes (largely diced)	3
butternut squash / pumpkin (cut into 1 ½ inch cubes)	1 lb.
chili powder	1 ½ tsps.
cloves garlic (minced)	4
fresh lemon juice	3 tbsps.
chicken broth	1 cup
salt	½ tsp.

DIRECTIONS

1. Create a marinating paste for the chicken by combining the lemon juice, salt, two minced garlic cloves, and the chili powder.

2. Rub the paste on the pieces of chicken and marinate for about an hour or two (it can also be marinated overnight).

3. In a large Dutch oven pot, heat the red palm oil.

4. Brown the chicken pieces skin side down, flip every three to five (0:03-0:05) minutes. It is best to cook only a few pieces at a time to ensure each piece evenly browned.

5. Add the chopped onions, the remaining minced cloves of garlic, tomatoes and the whole chili pepper.

6. Pour in a little water and bring to a boil. Cover the pot, reduce the heat, and allow the vegetables and meat to simmer for about an hour or until the chicken becomes tender.

7. Add the diced squash or pumpkin cubes, and the sliced okra. Stir the stew.

8. Pour in the chicken stock and cook for about fifteen minutes till the vegetables become tender.

9. Serve hot over steamed rice or boiled cassava.

NOTES

_____

_____

_____

_____

_____

_____

_____

_____

_____

_____

_____

Benin – Kuli Kuli

Kuli Kuli is a savory groundnut snack popularly eaten in Benin. It was first made by the Hausa people of Nigeria. It is made by frying peanut paste into hard crunchy sticks, pellets or balls. Its high peanut content makes this snack a healthy option as it is rich in protein. Kuli Kuli is traditionally eaten with other snacks such as cassava flakes soaked in water. Although this snack is also eaten in Ghana and Nigeria, it is considered to be the national dish of Benin and apart from being made in almost every household, the snack is also sold in nylon bags.

SERVES 4

INGREDIENTS

peeled, salted and roasted groundnuts/peanuts	2 cups
ground chili pepper	1 tsp.
ginger powder	1 ½ tsp.
Groundnut/peanut oil for frying	

DIRECTIONS

7. Place the groundnuts and ginger powder into a food processor until it turns into a paste. This paste is called "Labu."

8. Spoon the nut paste into a dry piece of muslin cloth. Wring the muslin to remove as much of the natural oil as possible. Less oil in the peanut paste will make the Kuli Kuli crunchier. Discard the oil.

9. Empty the peanut paste into a bowl.

10. Sprinkle the ground chili pepper onto the peanut paste and mix thoroughly with the hands.

11. Shape the thick paste into balls, pellets, or long sticks. Set aside.

12. Pour adequate peanut or groundnut oil into a non-stick pan to fry the Kuli Kuli.

13. Add the garlic cloves in the oil to flavor it.

14. Spoon the peanut balls or sticks into the pot and fry until golden brown.

15. Use a slotted spoon to remove the fried Kuli Kuli from the pot.

16. Allow the Kuli Kuli to cool and harden.

17. Serve this snack with Garri (cassava flakes soaked in cold water).

NOTES

_____
_____
_____
_____
_____
_____
_____
_____
_____
_____
_____
_____
_____
_____
_____
_____
_____
_____
_____
_____

Botswana – Seswaa

A beef dish served at important events in Botswana such as weddings, funerals and Independence Day celebrations, Seswaa is a traditionally cooked in a three legged pot over an open fire. The dish was usually prepared by men who were responsible for pounding and shredding the cooked beef. Only three Ingredients was traditionally used to prepare Seswaa in Botswana; salt, beef and water.

SERVES 5–6

INGREDIENTS

beef (bone in and cut into pieces)	2.2 lbs
salt	2 tsp.
onion	1
bay leaves	4
teaspoon black pepper	¼ tsp.
Water	

DIRECTIONS

1. Combine the salt and pepper before adding it to the container of meat. Mix well so that the meat is properly seasoned.

2. Place the meat in a slow cooker, add the onion and the bay leaves. Pour in enough water to cover the beef — Cook on high for approximately four hours.

3. Test the meat after four hours. If the meat is still attached to the bone, continue cooking. When cooked, the meat should fall off the bones.

4. Remove the beef from the slow cooker and allow the meat to cool down to room temperature. Remove the bones.

5. Use a mortar and pestle to pound the meat until shredded. (A more natural way to do this is to use a couple of forks to pull apart the meat.) Seswaa is complete when all of the beef is shredded.

6. Alternatively, Seswaa can be prepared by cutting the beef into chunks and cooking it in a cast iron casserole dish, first browning the meat, then allowing it to simmer in water and seasonings, then bake it for about four hours.

7. In Botswana, Seswaa is commonly served with pap or sadza; both are cornmeal dishes. Green vegetables are also served with this dish.

NOTES

_____
_____
_____
_____
_____
_____
_____
_____
_____
_____
_____
_____
_____
_____
_____
_____
_____
_____
_____
_____
_____

Burkina Faso – Riz Gras

Riz Gras or fat rice as it is sometimes called is the national dish of Burkina Faso. The dish originated from a similar one prepared in Senegal. In the urban regions of Burkina Faso, Riz Gras is served at parties.

SERVES 4

INGREDIENTS

beef or chicken (cubed)	1 lb.
long grained white rice	2 ½ cups
tomatoes (chopped)	4
cloves garlic (peeled)	3
onion (chopped)	½
habanero peppers	2
vegetable oil	½ cup
tomato paste	4 tbsps.
bouillon /stock cube	1
water	4 ½ cups
Salt	
Pepper	

DIRECTIONS

1. Put the habanero peppers, garlic cloves, tomatoes, and onion into the food processor. Pulse into a paste.

2. Cook the paste for approximately eight minutes in vegetable oil on medium heat, and set aside.

3. Cook the meat in a separate cooking pan.

4. Rinse the food processor container which held the paste with some water. Utilize this water by pouring it into the cooking pan and add the cubes of beef or chicken. Bring to a boil, then reduce the heat, cover the pan, and let it simmer for fifteen minutes (0:15).

5. Reheat the pan which holds the seasoning paste and oil. Add the meat to this pan. Stir the chicken or beef so that it becomes coated with the seasonings. Add water and the tomato paste. Crumble one bouillon cube into the pan. Stir with a wooden spoon.

6. Place the rice into a bowl of water. Wash the rice. Drain the liquid. Repeat several times or until the water runs clear. Add the wet rice to the pan. Bring to a boil. Reduce the heat, then place the lid on and let it simmer for about fifteen minutes again. Monitor, stirring occasionally. After ten minutes, the meat and rice should be tender, and the water should be absorbed.

7. Dish the Riz Gras on a plate. Cut thin onion rings for a garnish and serve hot.

NOTES

_____
_____
_____
_____
_____
_____
_____
_____
_____
_____
_____
_____
_____
_____
_____
_____
_____

Burundi – Elephant Soup

In rural Burundi, the natives hunt and kill wild elephants for food. Burundi's national dish, Elephant soup, can feed many people in a village. Elephant soup is traditionally cooked with elephant meat that has been coated with salt and honey and dried in the hot African sunshine. This dried meat is called biltong. The dried elephant meat can be replaced with dried beef as elephant meat may be difficult to obtain outside of Burundi.

SERVES 4–6

INGREDIENTS

biltong (dried elephant meat or dried beef)	½ lb.
beef stock	6–8 cups
mixed vegetables – diced onions, carrots, celery, and other herbs	1 cup
onions (finely chopped)	2
peanuts (shelled and roasted) or ½ cup peanut butter	1 cup
boiled lentils / dried beans of any kind	1 cup
small leek (finely chopped)	1
Wumubu mushrooms (black African mushrooms)	1 cup
butter	2 tbsp.
Water	
cream	½ cup
Salt to taste	
Black pepper to taste	

DIRECTIONS

1. Soak the biltong or dried meat in hot water for a few minutes. Remove from the boiling water and place on a cutting board.

2. Use a sharp knife to chop the meat into bite-sized pieces.

3. Place the chopped meat into a large Dutch oven pot. Pour in sufficient water to cover the meat.

4. Turn on the heat beneath the pot and allow the meat to cook for twenty to thirty minutes.

5. Add the cup of mixed vegetables to the soup and then pour in the beef broth. Place a lid on the pot and let the soup simmer for two hours.

6. Uncover the pot and add the chopped leek, onions, Wumubu mushrooms, and the lentils or dried beans. Stir in the peanuts.

7. Continue cooking the soup until the lentils or beans have disintegrated entirely.

8. Stir in the butter and cream. Sprinkle in salt and pepper to taste.

9. Serve the elephant soup hot.

NOTES

_____
_____
_____
_____
_____
_____
_____
_____
_____
_____
_____
_____
_____
_____

Cameroon – Ndolé

Ndolé is a popular Cameroonian soup dish made from meat, peanuts, seafood and bitter leaves from a wild plant that is native to the country. This thick soup dish is both nutritious and tasty. In Cameroon, it is served with boiled plantain slices, provisions or rice.

SERVES 5–6

INGREDIENTS

raw groundnuts/peanuts	1 cup
bitter leaves (kale or spinach can be used)	1 lb.
large onions (1 diced, 1 whole)	2
cloves garlic	4
stockfish (dried fish)	½ lb.
shrimp (peeled and de-veined)	½ lb.
crayfish meat (minced)	¾ cup
beef	½ lb.
vegetable oil	3 cups
bouillon cubes (crumbled)	2 tbsps.
Salt	
Water	

DIRECTIONS

1. Dice the beef and season it with salt, one tablespoon of the crumbled bouillon cubes and diced onion.

2. Add the meat to a large pot filled with water. Boil the beef until tender.

3. In a separate pan, boil the stockfish in salted water, and then add it to the pan containing the cooked beef.

4. Let the fish and beef simmer. Reserve the liquid fish stock for use in other dishes.

5. Fill a separate saucepan with water and add the raw peanuts.

6. Boil the peanuts for ten minutes, then drain and allow it to cool.

7. Blend the peanuts into a thick paste, adding a little water if necessary.

8. Add the peanut paste to the beef and fish mixture.

9. Peel an onion, chop into quarters and blend with a clove of garlic until it forms a fine paste.

10. Spoon this paste into the pot containing the beef, fish and peanut paste. Stir well.

11. Add the minced crayfish and allow this to simmer together for ten minutes. Stir occasionally and season with salt and the rest of the crumbled bouillon cubes.

12. Chop the bitter leaves, kale or spinach into strips. Wash, drain and add the leaves to the pot.

13. Allow the soup to simmer for several minutes.

14. While the soup is cooking, heat a little vegetable oil in a skillet, and sauté a small amount of chopped onion with the shrimp.

15. Add the cooked shrimp and onions to the top of the simmering ndolé. Turn off the heat.

16. Serve hot with boiled plantains.

NOTES

_____

_____

_____

_____

_____

_____

_____

_____

_____

_____

Cape Verde – Cachupa

Cachupa is a rich, slow cooked stew consisting of mainly corn, pork, beans, ground provisions, and tuna. It is both delicious and nutritious as it is rich in proteins and vitamins. This national dish has its origins in Portuguese cuisine as the Cape Verde islands were colonies of Portugal until 1975.

SERVES 6

INGREDIENTS

dry corn kernels/hominy	2 cups
dry red beans	¾ cup
piece (250 g) chorizo (cut into chunks)	1
salted pork (cut into chunks)	500 g
can flaked tuna	1
tomatoes (peeled and diced)	2
carrots (cubed)	2
white cabbage (sliced)	¼
onions (finely chopped)	2
bay leaves	2
small potatoes (peeled and cut into quarters)	4
sweet potato (peeled and cut into quarters)	1
cloves garlic (minced)	3
water	4 cups
chicken stock	4 cups
olive oil	8 tbsps.
chili powder	1 tbsps.

DIRECTIONS

1. Mix the corn and red beans together and wash twice in clean water. Drain the water and set aside.

2. Place four tablespoons of olive oil in a pressure cooker. Add half of the chopped onions together with a bay leaf.

3. Sauté these two Ingredients for about a minute until the onions are soft. Add the washed corn and red beans. Stir everything together, then pour in the chicken stock and water.

4. Allow the corn and beans to cook for about forty minutes. Add more water if necessary.

5. In a separate pot, heat the remaining four tablespoons of olive oil. Sauté the onions, garlic and one bay leaf until the onions are translucent and soft.

6. Sprinkle the chili powder and add the chorizo and salted pork chunks. Reduce the heat and stir the meat and seasonings together. Let it cook for about twenty minutes.

7. Transfer the corn and red bean mixture to the seasoned chorizo and pork.

8. Add the sliced cabbage and the potato chunks, together with the diced tomatoes. Open the can of flaked tuna and empty it into the pot. Mix and allow the vegetables to cook properly. Add additional salt if needed and turn off the heat.

9. Let the Cachupa rest for a few minutes, then serve warm with chilled Vinho Verde (Portuguese green wine).

NOTES

_____
_____
_____
_____
_____
_____
_____
_____
_____
_____
_____
_____

Chad – La Bouillie

The national dish of Chad is a hot peanut and wheat porridge traditionally eaten for breakfast. It is simple to make and served in bowls with canned or fresh fruit. Red tea made from hibiscus blossoms, cinnamon, ginger and cloves is consumed alongside La Bouillie.

YIELDS 4 bowls

INGREDIENTS

ground rice	1 cup
water	5 cups
smooth and creamy peanut butter	3 tbsps.
corn flour/wheat flour	1tbsp.
whole milk	1/3 cup
brown sugar	2 tbsps.
lemon juice	1 ½ tbsps.
ripe bananas	4

DIRECTIONS

1. Combine peanut butter, corn flour and one cup of water in a bowl. Use a fork to mix the Ingredients thoroughly. The mixture should not have pockets of flour or lumps. Once it is evenly mixed, set aside.

2. Fill a saucepan with four cups of water. Turn on the heat and bring to a boil.

3. Add the ground rice gradually to the hot water, stirring continuously with a wooden spoon. After adding the ground rice to the pot, and the water starts bubbling, add the mixture of peanut butter and corn flour to it. Use a whisk to mix the porridge and let it cook until it thickens, stirring frequently. Turn off the heat.

4. Pour in the milk and brown sugar.

5. Add the lemon juice to the porridge and stir until the sugar crystals dissolve. Let it sit for a few minutes.

6. Ladle the porridge equally into four serving bowls. Peel the four ripe bananas. Slice into chunks and place on top of the La Bouillie. Make hot red tea by steeping dried hibiscus flowers, cinnamon, cloves and ginger in hot water. Strain into teacups and add sugar. Enjoy with the La Bouillie.

NOTES

168

Comoros – Langouste a la Vanille

Langouste a la Vanille is a famous dish that is prepared in the Comoros Islands. It is made with fresh South African lobster that is caught regularly in the Comorian waters and newly harvested vanilla beans which is a major agricultural crop there. The dish has its origins in French cuisine.

SERVES 5–6

INGREDIENTS

live lobsters (1 ¼ – 1 ½ lb each)	2
vanilla bean (sliced lengthwise)	½
tender spinach (stems removed)	¾ lb.
olive oil	1tbsp.
white wine	¼ cup
medium shallots (peeled and finely diced)	3
unsalted butter	7 tbsps. & 2 tsps.
tablespoons white wine vinegar	1 ½ tbsps.
Black pepper to taste	
Kosher salt to taste	
Vidalia onions (sliced)	
Clover sprouts	

DIRECTIONS

1. Prepare the lobsters for cooking by piercing between the eyes with a sharp knife.

2. Use a hammer or cleaver to crack the claws.

3. Preheat a large roasting pan in the oven at 450 degrees and place the lobsters in it.

4. Drizzle with olive oil and roast for fifteen minutes until they become red.

5. Remove the pan from the oven and set aside to cool.

6. Melt two teaspoons of unsalted butter in a saucepan.

7. Sauté the shallots in the butter for about three minutes until soft. Pour in the wine and vinegar.

8. Cook on medium high heat for about five minutes. Turn off the stove after the liquid has reduced to about a tablespoon.

9. Stir in six tablespoons of butter, one at a time.

10. Prod the seeds out of the halved vanilla bean and add to the sauce.

11. Strain the sauce into a clean saucepan, and discard the diced shallots.

12. Season the sauce with a sprinkle of salt and black pepper. Set aside.

13. Remove the meat from the lobster claws. Detach the heads and tails. Slice the tails lengthwise in half. Remove the meat and chop it into ¼ inch chunks.

14. Place the meat chunks into a container and cover with aluminum foil to keep warm.

15. Melt a tablespoon of butter in a pan and sauté the spinach and onions. Cook until the spinach is tender. Season with salt and pepper.

16. Arrange the greens onto the serving dish, then place the warm lobster on top of it.

17. Reheat the sauce and pour it over the lobster.

18. Garnish with tender clover sprouts and serve.

NOTES

_____

_____

_____

_____

_____

_____

_____

_____

_____

169

Djibouti – Skoudehkaris

Skoudehkaris is a one–pot lamb and rice dish that is very popular in the small African nation of Djibouti. The country used to be a French colony at one point in time and due to this, its cuisine has French influence.

SERVES 4

INGREDIENTS

lamb meat	1 lb.
long grained white rice	½ cup
onion (peeled and chopped)	1
ghee / vegetable oil	1 tbsp.
whole cloves	1 tsp.
cayenne pepper powder	¼ tsp.
ground cinnamon	½ tsp.
cumin powder	½ tsp.
1 tsp. ground cardamom	
can of diced tomato	15 oz.
Salt	
Water	
Pepper	
Cilantro leaves (chopped)	

DIRECTIONS

1. Heat a Dutch oven pot on medium-high, then add the ghee or oil.

2. Sauté the chopped onions in the ghee together with cumin, cinnamon, cloves, cardamom, and cayenne pepper.

3. Cook until the onions are soft and translucent.

4. Cut the lamb meat into cubes using a sharp knife.

5. Put the lamb meat into the pot and toss with the sautéed onions and spices.

6. Brown the lamb and then add the canned tomatoes.

7. Season with pepper.

8. Pour in enough water to cover the meat.

9. Place the pot in an oven preheated to 350 degrees F°.

10. After forty-five (0:45) minutes, test the tenderness of the lamb.

11. Adjust cooking time and add more water if necessary.

12. When the meat is tender, remove the pot from the oven and place it on the stove over medium-high heat.

13. Rinse the rice in water and add it to the pot. Stir, season with salt and cover the pot.

14. Allow to cook for about fifteen (0:15) minutes or until the rice is tender and sticky, and all the water absorbed.

15. Spoon the cooked meal onto serving plates and garnish with chopped cilantro leaves.

16. Serve Skoudehkaris hot.

NOTES

_____
_____
_____
_____
_____
_____
_____
_____
_____
_____
_____
_____
_____
_____

Equatorial Guinea – Succotash

Succotash consists of lima beans and other vegetables sautéed together with butter and fresh herbs. The cuisine of Equatorial Guinea is one that is influenced by both the Spanish and the native tribespeople. This dish is made without meat in Guinea but crumbled bacon can be added for extra flavor.

SERVES 6

INGREDIENTS

fresh lima beans	2 cups
small yellow onion	½
medium sweet onion (chopped)	1
clove garlic	1
sprigs fresh thyme	4
slices bacon	3
halved cherry tomatoes	2 cup
fresh corn kernels	3 cup
red wine vinegar	1 tbsp.
Fresh dill weed (chopped)	1 ½ tbsps.
Chives (chopped)	1 ½ tbsps.
Unsalted butter	2 tbsps.
Water for boiling	
Salt	
Pepper	

DIRECTIONS

1. Fill a saucepan with water, heat over medium-high heat, and bring to a boil.

2. Add the lima beans, a clove of garlic, half of the yellow onion, and the sprigs of fresh thyme.

3. Simmer on low heat, occasionally stirring for twenty (0:20) minutes until the beans are tender.

4. Drain the beans but reserve ¾ cup of the cooking liquid.

5. Remove and discard the thyme, yellow onion and garlic.

6. Heat a little oil in a skillet and fry the slices of bacon.

7. Cook the bacon for about seven (0:07) minutes or until crisp.

8. Remove the bacon from the skillet and set aside on paper towels.

9. Reserve two tablespoons of the bacon fat and discard the rest.

10. Sauté the chopped sweet onions in the bacon fat for about five (0:05) minutes.

11. Add the corn kernels and cook for six (0:06) minutes over medium high heat until the corn cook and tender.

12. Stir in the cherry tomatoes.

13. Add the cooked lima beans and reserved cooking liquid.

14. Cook for five (0:05) minutes, stirring occasionally.

15. Add the butter, chives, dill, and red wine vinegar.

16. Season with salt and pepper.

17. Chop the cooked bacon and sprinkle over the succotash.

18. Serve warm.

NOTES

_____
_____
_____
_____
_____
_____
_____
_____
_____
_____
_____

Eritrea – Zigini with Injera

Zigini is a very spicy meat stew that is considered to be the national dish of Eritrea. One of its key Ingredients is Berbere, a famous blend of spices used in African cuisine. Zigini is traditionally eaten with a type of flatbread called Injera.

SERVES 4–6

INGREDIENTS

For Berbere Spice Blend

small onion (diced)	1
cloves garlic (minced)	2
water	1 cup
salt	1 tbsp.
paprika	1 tbsp.
chili powder	1 tbsp.
allspice	1 tbsp.
minced ginger	1 tsp.
white pepper	½ tsp.
cloves	2
cardamom seeds	8
ground fenugreek	½ tsp.
ground coriander	½ tsp.
ground nutmeg	¼ tsp.
pinch ground cinnamon	1
Oil	

For Zigini

beef (cut into cubes)	2 lbs.
cloves garlic	4
can (14 oz.) diced tomatoes	1
scallions (minced)	3
berbere spice blend	4 tbsps.
Oil	5 tbsps.
bunch cilantro	1
Salt	

For Injera

teff flour	½ lb.
warm water	2 cups
sachet yeast	½
salt	½ tsp.
pinch baking soda	1

DIRECTIONS

For Berbere Spice Blend

1. In a shallow pan, roast the cardamom, coriander, ginger, fenugreek, cloves, nutmeg and cinnamon on low heat for two (0:02) minutes.
2. Cool the roasted spices.
3. Add garlic, half of the salt, onion and two tablespoons of water to the cooled spices, then mix and set aside.
4. Toast the chili pepper, white pepper, paprika, allspice and remaining salt in a pan for one (0:01) minute.
5. Pour in the rest of the water, stir and let simmer for fifteen (0:15) minutes, then cool.
6. Pour the cooled berbere in a jar, top with a layer of oil and store in the refrigerator.

For Zigini

1. Brown the beef cubes in a hot pan containing the oil.
2. Add onions and garlic.
3. After two (0:02) minutes, add the berbere.
4. Cook for an additional two (0:02) minutes and then add the can of tomatoes and its liquid.
5. Season with salt and pepper, then toss in the scallions.
6. Simmer on low heat for two (2:00) hours.
7. Add the cilantro and cook for an additional thirty (0:30) minutes.

For Injera

1. Blend all the Ingredients except the salt for one (0:01) minute.
2. Sprinkle in the salt and blend for fifteen seconds.
3. Transfer the mixture to a bowl, cover and refrigerate for forty-eight (48:00) hours.
4. Heat a griddle or skillet to high heat.
5. Smear the Griddle with a little oil.
6. Use a ladle to spoon the injera batter onto the griddle; it should resemble a pancake.
7. Cook for a minute or two, then flip.
8. Continue making the injera pancakes till there is no more batter.
9. Serve the Zigini stew with injera.

Ethiopia – Fit Fit

Fit Fit is a spicy Ethiopian flatbread dish which is so popular there; it is considered the country's national dish. Fit Fit is made from crumbled injera, which is a type of African flatbread and seasoned with berbere spice blend; a key ingredient in African cuisine. Traditionally this dish is eaten for breakfast.

SERVES 4

INGREDIENTS

large injera flatbread	1
green jalapenos (seeded and chopped into strips)	2
canola oil	¼ cup
tomatoes (chopped)	2
can (3 oz.) tomato paste	½
large onions (peeled and chopped)	2
water	¼ cup
berbere spice blend / red pepper paste	1–2 tsp.
cloves garlic (minced)	4
minced ginger	2 tsp.
Salt	

DIRECTIONS

1. Heat the canola oil in a pot on medium-high heat.

2. Add the onions and sauté until soft and translucent.

3. Add the berbere spice blend or red pepper paste.

4. After a few minutes, stir in the tomato paste and allow to cook for about four (0:04) minutes.

5. Add the chopped tomatoes, minced garlic, and ginger to the pot.

6. Sprinkle a dash of salt.

7. Cook on medium-low heat until the tomatoes are tender.

8. Pour in the water, reduce the heat, and allow to simmer.

9. While the liquid simmers, set the injera flatbread on a flat surface.

10. Use a knife to slice the injera into small pieces, either squares or thin, short strips.

11. Crumbled the injera using your hands.

12. Put the sliced or crumbled injera into the pot.

13. Mix so that the injera starts to soak up the spicy liquid.

14. Maintain the pot on low heat, stirring gently as the liquid absorbed by the injera flatbread.

15. Once all the liquid is absorbed, turn off the heat.

16. Garnish with the chopped jalapenos.

17. Serve the Fit Fit with a mug of hot coffee for a delicious breakfast.

NOTES

_____
_____
_____
_____
_____
_____
_____
_____
_____
_____
_____
_____
_____

Gabon – Poulet Nyembwe

This spicy chicken dish is the national dish of Gabon. The word Nyembwe means palm oil in the Myene language which is spoken in Gabon. Essentially, Poulet Nyembwe is chicken cooked and flavored with palm oil. Smoked chicken is usually used to prepare it. People of Gabon usually serve hot rice, plantain or mashed yams with this dish.

SERVES 6

INGREDIENTS

smoked chicken (cut into pieces)	1
can palm nut puree	1
red palm oil	1 tbsp.
onions (peeled and diced)	2
cloves garlic (finely chopped)	3
water	1 L
bouillon cubes	2
mustard	2-3 tbsp.
tomatoes (diced)	3
okras (sliced)	12
Vegetable oil for frying	
Salt	
Black pepper	
whole chilies	3

DIRECTIONS

1. In a large bowl, add the mustard, one crumbled bouillon cube and a dash of black pepper to the pieces of chicken.

2. Mix well so that the chicken pieces are thoroughly seasoned.

3. Heat a skillet and add vegetable oil to fry the chicken.

4. Add the pieces of chicken to the oil and fry for ten (0:10) minutes or until all sides are brown.

5. Remove from the oil and set aside.

6. In another cooking pot, heat the red palm oil over low heat.

7. Add the diced onions and chopped garlic, then sauté together until tender.

8. Add the chopped tomatoes and sliced okra.

9. Stir in the palm nut puree, and pour in the water and mix.

10. Crumble the second bouillon cube into the stew.

11. Increase the heat to high and place the lid on the pot.

12. Allow the sauce to thicken and remove the lid.

13. When the red palm oil appears on the surface of the stew, place the fried chicken into the sauce.

14. Add the whole chilies.

15. Season with salt.

16. Reduce the heat and let simmer for twenty (0:20) minutes.

17. Serve with hot steamed rice.

NOTES

_____
_____
_____
_____
_____
_____
_____
_____
_____
_____
_____
_____

Ghana – Jollof Rice

Jollof Rice is a popular dish in West African cuisine but each region prepares it differently. Ghanian Jollof Rice can be made with or without meat. It is nutritious, flavorful and easy to prepare.

SERVES 6

INGREDIENTS

basmati rice	3 ½ cups
palm or olive oil	1 tbsp.
Tomato puree	2 ½ tbsps.
onions (1 diced, 2 quartered)	3
cloves garlic	2
Scotch Bonnet chili peppers	4
canned plum tomatoes	2
stock cube	1
bay leaf	1
finger of ginger	1
water	2 cups
bouillon cube	1
Dried mixed herbs (nutmeg, thyme, dill weed, parsley)	
Salt	

DIRECTIONS

1. Heat the oil in a non–stick pan and add the diced onion.

2. Sauté until tender and golden brown.

3. Stir in the tomato puree and let cook for four (0:04) minutes.

4. Blend the ginger, garlic, chilies, the onion quarters and canned tomatoes.

5. Add the blended mixture to the pot and cook till the tomatoes are tender, and the oil appears on the surface.

6. Add the stock cube together with the bouillon cube.

7. Sprinkle two or more pinches of the dried herbs.

8. Stir everything together, so that is well seasoned and let it simmer for three (0:03) minutes.

9. Rinse the raw rice in cold water to remove some of the starch.

10. Add the rinsed rice to the pot, stir thoroughly allowing the rice to coat in the flavorful mixture.

11. Add two cups of water to the pot.

12. Stir and add salt to taste.

13. Let the rice cook until most of the water has absorbed.

14. Cover the pot, reduce the heat, and allow it to simmer until the rice is tender, then turn off the heat.

15. Serve Jollof Rice with fried plantain slices and a crisp green salad.

NOTES

_____
_____
_____
_____
_____
_____
_____
_____
_____
_____
_____
_____

Guinea – Poulet Yassa

Poulet Yassa is a simple chicken dish that is popular in the West African region. It is distinguished by an onion and lemon infused marinade which tenderizes the tough meat of the African fowls found in these regions. This dish is considered to be the national dish of Guinea although it is also prepared in neighboring countries like Senegal.

SERVES 4–6

INGREDIENTS

chicken (cut into pieces)	1
large lemons (juiced)	6
large onions (peeled and sliced)	6
cloves garlic (minced)	5
water	4 cups
bay leaf	1
Peanut oil	3 tbsps.
chili pepper (seeded and finely chopped)	1
chicken bouillon cubes (crumbled)	3
Vegetable oil	
Salt	
Pepper	
Cooked white rice	

DIRECTIONS

1. Make the marinade by mixing the peanut oil, chili pepper, lemon juice, sliced onion, salt, pepper, bay leaf, garlic and bouillon cubes in a large glass bowl.

2. Place the pieces of chicken into the bowl and mix until coated all over with the marinade.

3. Cover the meat with plastic wrap and let it chill overnight in the refrigerator.

4. Heat a skillet and pour in enough vegetable oil to fry the chicken.

5. Fry the chicken pieces until cooked and golden brown (you can bake the chicken as well).

6. Set the chicken aside and sauté the onions from the marinade in a separate saucepan.

7. When the onions are brown and caramelized, add the marinade to the pan.

8. Add the water to this and stir everything together.

9. Reduce the heat and allow to simmer for thirty (0:30) minutes.

10. Place the fried chicken into the sauce and let it simmer for just a few minutes more.

11. Turn off the heat.

12. Plate the white rice and top with the tangy Poulet Yassa.

NOTES

Guinea Bissau – Jollof Rice

Jollof Rice is a very common dish in West Africa and it is considered the national dish of many of the continent's countries. One such country is Guinea Bissau. This flavorful rice dish can be made with or without meat but is traditionally prepared without meat.

SERVES 4

INGREDIENTS

long grain rice	2 ½ cups
dried thyme	1 tbsp.
bay leaves	2
curry powder	1 tsp.
onion powder	1 ½ tbsp.
garlic powder	1 ½ tsp.
hot ground chili powder	1 ½ tsp.
salt	1 ½ tsp.
minced ginger	½ tsp
palm oil	½ cup
small red bell peppers (diced)	3
medium onion (peeled and finely chopped)	½
medium tomatoes (roughly chopped)	2
habanero pepper	1
Water	

DIRECTIONS

1. Blend the tomatoes, habanero pepper, and onions to form a puree.

2. Reserve half of the puree.

3. Add the bell peppers to the puree in the blender and blend again until smooth.

4. Add to the reserved puree and mix.

5. Add the palm oil to a pot, heat to medium high on the stove and spoon the puree into the pot.

6. Add the salt, ground chili powder, curry powder, onion powder, garlic powder, bay leaves, ginger, and thyme.

7. Stir with a wooden spoon.

8. Allow this to simmer for a few minutes.

9. Rinse the rice in water, then drain.

10. Put the rinsed rice in the pot and mix.

11. Reduce the heat, add enough water for cooking, and place the lid on the pot.

12. Cook for about thirty (0:30) minutes and stir it.

13. If there is still liquid in the pot, remove the lid, increase the heat, and allow the excess water to cook off quickly.

14. Cook for five (0:05) more minutes and allow the rice at the base of the pot to char; this will give the rice a smoky flavor.

15. Serve Jollof Rice with fried plantains and cooked meat or eggs.

NOTES

_____
_____
_____
_____
_____
_____
_____
_____
_____
_____
_____
_____
_____
_____
_____

Ivory Coast – Kedjenou

Kedjenou is a slow cooked poultry dish that was invented by the Baoulé ethnic group in Ivory Coast. The dish is cooked in a sealed terra cotta pot or canari over a wood fire. Instead of chicken, Guinea hen is used in some parts of Ivory Coast to prepare it. Kedjenou means to shake and the pot is not stirred, but shaken during cooking to prevent the sauce from sticking to the pan. Today, this succulent stew is the country's national dish.

SERVES 4–6

INGREDIENTS

chicken thighs	6
can (24 oz.) diced tomatoes	1
eggplant (chopped)	1
chicken stock	2 cups
sliced okra	1 cup
minced ginger	1 tbsp.
small onions (peeled and diced)	2
cloves garlic (minced)	2
bay leaf	1
dashes soy sauce	3
pinches dried thyme	3
Vegetable/peanut oil	
Salt	
Black pepper	

DIRECTIONS

1. In a large pot, sauté together with the onions, garlic, and ginger in some vegetable oil.

2. When the onions are tender, place the chicken thighs in the pot, skin side down first.

3. Brown the chicken on all sides, then add the chopped eggplant, tomatoes, the bay leaf, and thyme.

4. Add the soy sauce.

5. Pour in the chicken stock, reduce the heat and place the lid on the pot.

6. Lift the pot and give a proper shake, then return to the stove.

7. Allow the Ingredients to simmer together for about forty-five (0:45) minutes

8. Add the sliced okra ten (0:10) minutes before the stew is finished cooking

9. Add adequate salt and black pepper to season the stew

10. Shake the pot once more so that the Ingredients incorporate in the stew

11. Turn off the heat when the meat is tender and falling off the bone

12. Serve Kedjenou with Attieke, a cassava side dish or hot steamed white rice.

NOTES

_____
_____
_____
_____
_____
_____
_____
_____
_____
_____
_____
_____
_____
_____
_____
_____

Kenya – Sukuma Wiki

Sukuma Wiki is one of Kenya's national dishes. It is essentially braised greens and tomatoes. Traditionally, kale, spinach or collard greens are used which makes this dish very nutritious. The name of the dish is actually a phrase which means to "stretch the week," in Swahili. Sukuma Wiki is eaten with other Kenyan dishes such as ugali and roasted meat or fish.

SERVES 4

INGREDIENTS

kale	1 lb.
medium tomatoes (diced)	2
large white onion (peeled and diced)	1
peanut / vegetable oil	1 tbsp.
cumin	1 tsp.
ground coriander	½ tsp.
saffron powder	½ tsp.
kosher salt	1½ tsp.
Lemon juice	3 tbsps.
water	1 cup
Freshly ground black pepper	

DIRECTIONS

1. Rinse the kale in cold water, then chop into one-inch pieces, including the ribs.

2. Heat the oil in a deep pot or wok, then add the diced onions.

3. Sauté the onions for about eight (0:08) minutes on medium-high heat until soft.

4. Add the coriander, cumin and saffron powder

5. Add the diced tomatoes and mix well with the spices and onions.

6. Add the chopped kale one handful at a time, stirring continuously so that each set is well seasoned.

7. After adding the kale to the pot, add the salt and some freshly ground black pepper.

8. Add one cup of water to the pot.

9. Place the lid over the pot and reduce the heat to medium-high.

10. Let the kale cook for about fifteen (0:15) minutes or until tender.

11. Remove the lid and turn off the heat.

12. Add the lemon juice to the kale and toss together.

13. Serve the Sukuma Wiki with extra diced tomatoes on top, ugali and any roasted meat or meat stew.

NOTES

_____
_____
_____
_____
_____
_____
_____
_____
_____
_____
_____
_____
_____
_____
_____
_____

Liberia–Dumboy

Dumboy is considered Liberia's national dish. Cassava is one of the country's main agricultural crop and it is used to make dumboy, although plantains and yams are also utilized. Essentially, this dish is boiled cassava that has been pounded into a viscous dough and shaped into balls. Dumboy is usually eaten with pepper soup.

SERVES 4

INGREDIENTS

For Dumboy

cassava roots	2–3
Water	

For Pepper Soup

goat meat, beef or chicken (cut up)	1 lb.
uncooked shrimp	1 lb.
water	3- 4 cups
medium onion (peeled & quartered)	1
habanero peppers	2
whole okras	3
beef flavored bouillon cubes	2
bay leaves	2
Salt	

DIRECTIONS

For Dumboy
1. Peel the cassava roots with a sharp knife

2. Cut the cassava into chunks and rinse in water

3. In a large saucepan, boil the pieces of raw cassava in water for twenty (0:20) minutes

4. Drain and allow the cassava to cool

5. Slice the boiled cassava into smaller pieces

6. Place the chunks of boiled cassava into a mortar and use a pestle to mash it into a sticky dough, occasionally moistening with water if necessary

7. When the desired consistency is reached, mold the dough into balls and set aside.

For Pepper Soup

1. Place the meat, onions, bay leaves and peppers into a large Dutch oven pot

2. Add the water to the pot, then season with a generous pinch of salt and crumbled bouillon cubes

3. Bring the soup to a boil

4. Cover the pot and allow it to simmer for about thirty (0:30) minutes until the meat is tender

5. Add the shrimp to the soup

6. Add the okras

7. Stir the soup, then let it cook for ten (0:10) minutes on medium high heat

8. Let the soup simmer on low heat until it is ready to be served

9. Serve the dumboy with hot pepper soup.

NOTES

_____

_____

_____

_____

_____

_____

_____

_____

_____

_____

_____

_____

_____

Madagascar – Romazava

Romazava is a stew made with meat and leafy greens. It is considered to be the national dish of Madagascar and is served with steamed rice at almost every meal, together with sakay, a spicy condiment made of chilies, garlic and ginger. Authentic Romazava is made with zebu meat and local greens grown there such as paracress, mustard greens and anamamy but spinach and arugula are good substitutes.

SERVES 4

INGREDIENTS

beef chuck/zebu meat (cut into pieces)	1 lb.
pork loin (cut into bite-sized pieces)	1
skinless chicken breast (cut into pieces)	1
(14 oz.) can diced tomatoes	1
vegetable oil	2 tbsp.
beef/chicken stock	2 cups
yellow onions (diced)	½ cup
cloves garlic (minced)	5
inch piece of ginger (peeled and minced)	2 ½
serrano chili peppers (finely chopped)	3
bunch mustard greens (chopped)	1
bunch Spinach/Anamamy greens	1
bunch arugula/paracress greens	1
Salt	
Pepper	

DIRECTIONS

1. Heat the oil in a large Dutch oven pot

2. Add the beef/zebu meat to the pot and cook until brown on all sides

3. Stir in the can of diced tomatoes to the beef

4. Add the chili peppers, onion, garlic and ginger to the beef and tomatoes

5. Pour in the stock, cover the pot and let the Ingredients simmer over low heat for thirty (0:30) minutes

6. Add the chicken and pork to the stew, then bring to a boil

7. Reduce the heat and let it simmer for fifteen (0:15) minutes

8. Add the greens to the pot, then place the lid on the pot and allow them to wilt into the stew

9. Cook the stew for ten (0:10) minutes more

10. Season the stew with salt and pepper

11. Stir the Ingredients together and then turn off the heat.

12. Serve the Romazava over hot steamed rice, together with a bit of Sakay condiment.

NOTES

_____
_____
_____
_____
_____
_____
_____
_____
_____
_____
_____
_____
_____
_____
_____
_____
_____
_____
_____

Malawi – Nsima

The staple food of Malawi is a thick cornmeal porridge known as Nsima which is shaped into mounds or patties. One of the country's major agricultural crops is corn so Nsima is widely prepared as cornmeal is the main ingredient. The dish is usually eaten with sautéed greens, roasted fish or groundnuts.

SERVES 4

INGREDIENTS

For the Nsima

cornmeal, corn flour or ground maize	4 cups
Water	

For the Sautéed Greens (Side dish)

	4
greens (sweet potato leaves, bean leaves, Chinese cabbage, kale, mustard greens)	3 cups chopped
small onion (chopped)	1
small tomatoes (chopped)	2
oil	1 tbsp.
water	1 cups
Salt	

DIRECTIONS

For the Nsima

1. Pour ten cups of water into a large pot.

2. Turn on the heat and bring to a boil

3. Reduce the heat and begin adding the cornmeal to the water, one spoon at a time.

4. After half of the cornmeal has been added, stir the water and cornmeal continuously with a wooden spoon until the mixture bubbles, and the lumps disappear.

5. After a few minutes of cooking, add the remaining cornmeal to the pot, one spoon at a time and continue to stir the mixture

6. Stir the mixture until it becomes thick and smooth.

7. When the desired consistency is reached, turn off the heat, cover the pot and allow the Nsima to rest for a few minutes.

For the Sautéed Greens

1. Heat the oil in a pan

2. Sauté the onions in the oil until tender

3. Add the greens and tomatoes to the onions

4. Sauté together quickly, then add the salt

5. Pour in the water and let it simmer for about five (0:05) minutes until the greens are tender

6. Serve Nsima and greens together.

NOTES

_____
_____
_____
_____
_____
_____
_____
_____
_____
_____
_____
_____
_____
_____
_____
_____
_____
_____
_____

Mali – Tiguadege Na

Mali's national dish is called Tiguadege Na. It is a meat dish made with beef but chicken or goat can be used. The signature characteristic of this dish is that the meat is cooked in a rich peanut sauce. Groundnuts are integral to African cuisine as it is locally grown in many of the African regions including Mali.

SERVES 8

INGREDIENTS

beef / goat meat / chicken (cut into pieces)	2 lb.
onions (peeled and chopped)	2
vegetable oil	2 tbsp.
cloves garlic (peeled and crushed)	2
can tomatoes / 4 large tomatoes (peeled, seeded and diced)	1
tomato paste	2 tsp.
vegetable / beef stock	4 cups
peanut butter	4 tbsp.
Herbs de Provence (a spice mix containing bay leaves, thyme, rosemary, cloves, sage, marjoram, and basil)	1 tsp.
carrots (chopped into chunks)	2
potatoes (chopped into chunks)	2
eggplant (sliced)	1
Parsley leaves (chopped)	
Salt	
Pepper	

DIRECTIONS

1. Heat the oil in a stewing pot and add the meat.

2. Brown the meat on all sides, then add the onions and garlic.

3. Sprinkle salt and pepper to season the meat and stir the Ingredients together.

4. When the onions have softened, add the can of tomatoes or the fresh tomatoes.

5. Bring the liquid to a boil, then reduce the heat and let it simmer for about six (0:06) minutes, stirring occasionally.

6. Stir in the Herbs de Provence and the tomato paste.

7. Add the vegetable/beef stock to the pot and then add the peanut butter.

8. Mix well and add the carrots, eggplant, and potatoes to the Tiguadege Na.

9. Place the lid on the pot and let the stew simmer over low heat for about one (1:00) hour until the meat and vegetables are tender.

10. Serve the stew over warm rice and garnish with chopped parsley.

NOTES

_____
_____
_____
_____
_____
_____
_____
_____
_____
_____
_____
_____
_____
_____
_____
_____
_____
_____
_____

Mauritius – Octopus Curry

Octopus curry is a traditional Mauritian dish. It is prepared from freshly caught octopus and a multitude of dried spices and fresh herbs. Octopus curry is served with steamed rice and tomato chutney.

SERVES 4–5

INGREDIENTS

kg fresh octopus	1
onion (peeled and chopped)	1
tomatoes	6
cloves garlic	4
ginger paste	1 tbsp.
curry leaves	4
bay leaves	3
fresh thyme (minced)	1 tsp.
turmeric powder	3 tsp.
cumin powder	2 tsp.
coriander powder	2 tsp.
hot paprika	1 tsp.
curry powder	3 tsp.
chili pepper (chopped)	1
Corn flour	
Coriander leaves	
Vegetable oil	
Pepper	
Water	
Salt	

DIRECTIONS

1. Wash and cut away any unwanted parts of the octopus.

2. Rub the octopus with corn flour and freeze overnight.

3. Rinse the frozen octopus to remove the corn flour

4. Fill a large saucepan of water and bring to a boil.

5. Add the octopus to the boiling water and cook until tender and pink.

6. Use a sharp knife to slice the cooked octopus into small bite-sized pieces, then set aside.

7. Add a little vegetable oil to a clean saucepan and heat over medium heat.

8. Add the bay leaves, onions, fresh thyme, curry leaves, cumin, turmeric powder, coriander powder and the hot paprika to the pan.

9. Stir the herbs and spices together in the oil, then cover the pan for three (0:03) minutes to let the flavors marry.

10. While this simmers, blend the tomatoes, garlic, ginger and six tablespoons of water.

11. Add this mixture to the pan of tender onions and spices.

12. Add the chopped chili pepper to the pan, stir the sauce and let it cook for about five (0:05) minutes over medium heat.

13. Mix the curry powder with three tablespoons of water and add this mixture to the pan.

14. Cook for five (0:05) minutes, then add the chopped octopus to the sauce.

15. Replace the lid on the pan and cook for seven (0:07) minutes, stirring occasionally.

16. Transfer the Octopus curry to a serving dish and top with fresh coriander leaves

17. Serve with steamed rice.

NOTES

_____

_____

_____

_____

Mozambique – Frango a Portuguesa

The cuisine of Mozambique is highly influenced by the Portuguese who colonized the country for hundreds of years before it gained independence. It is no surprise that its national dish is considered to be Frango a Portuguesa which is a Portuguese chicken dish. The chicken is usually marinated, then roasted or grilled before it is placed in a red sauce consisting of tomatoes, chili peppers and spices. This dish is served with rice.

SERVES 2–3

INGREDIENTS

half chickens	2
large onion (peeled and chopped)	1
clove garlic (minced)	1
butter	3 ½ tbsp.
flour	1 tbsp.
vine tomatoes (skinned and diced)	5
(68g) can tomato paste	1
cooking sherry	2 tbsp.
sea salt	4 tsp.
black pepper	1 tsp.
smoked paprika	1 tsp.
red chili pepper (deseeded & cut into strips)	1

DIRECTIONS

1. Season, the chicken with two teaspoons of sea salt, the black pepper, and the paprika

2. Place the two chicken halves on the grill for thirty (0:30) minutes, occasionally flipping each piece to roast properly on all sides

3. While the chicken is grilling, prepare the sauce by first heating the butter in a pot

4. Sauté the onions and garlic in the butter until tender

5. Stir in the flour, then add the vine tomatoes, the can of tomato paste, the cooking sherry, the chopped chili pepper, and the remaining salt

6. Stir well and bring to a boil

7. Reduce the heat, cover the pot and let it simmer for twenty-five (0:25) minutes

8. Remove the lid and place the roasted half chickens into the sauce, ensuring the meat is completely coated with the sauce

9. Let the chicken simmer in the sauce for twenty (0:20) minutes, then turn off the heat

10. Serve Frango a Portuguesa over steamed white rice.

NOTES

_____
_____
_____
_____
_____
_____
_____
_____
_____
_____
_____
_____
_____
_____
_____
_____
_____
_____
_____

Namibia – Sweet Millet Porridge

Millet is one of the main food crops in Namibia. The main dish prepared in Namibia with millet is porridge. Sweet Millet Porridge or Süßer Hirsebrei is considered to be the national dish of the country. Seasonal fresh fruit and sweet fruit preserves are usually added to the porridge. This porridge is usually served cold. It can be eaten for breakfast or as a snack.

SERVES 4

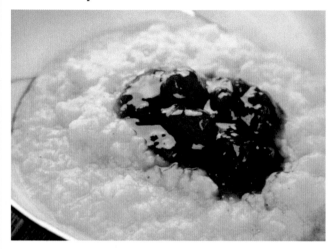

INGREDIENTS

millet	2 ¼ cups
single cream	1 cup
water	2 cups
brown sugar	3 tbsp.
vanilla pod	1
nectarine (sliced)	1 ½
Kiwi (peeled and sliced)	1 ½
banana (peeled and sliced thinly)	1
Dates (deseeded and chopped)	

DIRECTIONS

1. Place the millet into a colander and wash thoroughly under cold, running water

2. Put the rinsed millet into a saucepan and fill with two cups of water

3. Set the saucepan over high heat and bring to a boil

4. Reduce the heat and let simmer for approximately fifteen (0:15) minutes

5. Turn off the heat and set aside

6. Split the vanilla pod into halves and remove the seeds

7. Place the vanilla seeds into a bowl and add the sugar and cream

8. Stir these Ingredients with a spoon until the sugar dissolves

9. Pour this sweet, creamy mixture into the saucepan of boiled millet.

10. Stir the porridge, then place the lid on the pan and set the pan over low heat.

11. Let the porridge simmer for an additional four (0:04) minutes, then turn off the heat.

12. Divide the porridge into four equal portions in serving bowls and let cool.

13. Top each bowl of millet porridge with chopped dates and slices of nectarine, kiwi, and banana

14. Serve cold.

NOTES

_____
_____
_____
_____
_____
_____
_____
_____
_____
_____
_____
_____
_____
_____
_____
_____
_____
_____
_____

Niger – Djerma Stew

Djerma Stew is the official dish of Niger. It can be made with meat or without. Traditionally, if a meat version is being cooked, chicken is usually the meat of choice. In Niger, rice is the main staple and many stews like Djerma are eaten with it.

SERVES 7

INGREDIENTS

chickens (cut into parts)	3 (3 ½ lb.)
medium onion (sliced)	1
clove garlic (minced)	1
paprika	1 tbsp.
Roma tomatoes/2 cups tomato puree	5-6
dried thyme	1 ½ tsp.
curry powder	¼ tsp.
bay leaf	1
crumbled bouillon cubes	1 tbsp.
sliced carrots	1-2 cups
Chopped parsley leaves	3 tbsp.
chives (sliced)	2
peanut butter	2 ½ tbsp.
oil	¼-½ cup
Salt	
Pepper	

DIRECTIONS

1. Wash the chicken pieces and season with salt and pepper, then set aside.

2. Heat the oil in a large Dutch oven pot and add the chicken.

3. Fry the chicken until brown on all sides.

4. Create a tomato and seasoning mixture by blending the fresh tomatoes, onions, and garlic, then add this to the chicken and stir well.

5. If using tomato puree, add the onions to the chicken and brown, then add the puree and garlic.

6. Add the smoked paprika, curry powder, bay leaf, and crumbled bouillon cubes.

7. Bring to a boil, then reduce to a simmer.

8. Cook the chicken for about thirty (0:30) minutes or until it is tender.

9. Add two cups of water to the stew, then add the parsley, carrots, and chives.

10. Cook for five (0:05) minutes until the carrots are tender.

11. Remove a cup of liquid from the stew and whisk with the peanut butter in a separate bowl.

12. Pour this peanut butter and sauce mixture back into the pot.

13. Allow the stew to simmer until thick.

14. Adjust the salt and pepper, then remove and discard the bay leaf.

15. Serve Djerma Stew over steamed rice.

NOTES

_____
_____
_____
_____
_____
_____
_____
_____
_____
_____
_____
_____
_____

Nigeria – Egusi Soup

Egusi Soup is a melon seed stew that is popular in Nigeria. There are many versions of the dish and the end result may range from a typical soup, to a fried, chunky stew of vegetables, egusi curdles and meat. Egusi Soup is eaten with pounded yam, plantains, rice or fufu.

SERVES 4–5

INGREDIENTS

ground Egusi melon seeds	1 cup
smoked turkey	½ lb.
smoked beef	½ lb.
medium onion (finely chopped)	1
canola oil	½ cup
medium tomatoes (diced)	2–3
cloves garlic (minced)	3
smashed crayfish	1/3 cup
spinach leaves	2/3 cup
paprika	3 tsp.
Salt	
Pepper	

DIRECTIONS

1. Season the beef and turkey with salt, half of the onions, pepper, and paprika in a bowl.

2. Bring a saucepan of water to a boil, then transfer the seasoned meat to the water and boil until tender.

3. Reserve three to four cups of meat stock and discard the rest.

4. Set the cooked meat aside.

5. In a separate saucepan, heat the oil, then add the rest of the onions and sauté for five (0:05) minutes until translucent.

6. Add the cooked beef and turkey to the pan.

7. Add the smashed crayfish and sauté together with the onions and meat.

8. Stir in the tomatoes and garlic together with two cups of the beef and turkey stock that was previously reserved.

9. Bring to a boil, then let simmer for five (0:05) minutes.

10. Add the ground Egusi seeds and continue to simmer for about ten (0:10) minutes over medium heat.

11. While simmering, add more meat stock if required to maintain the desired consistency.

12. Add the spinach to the pan and stir well — Cook for five (0:05) minutes over low heat.

13. Adjust the salt and pepper to taste, then turn off the heat.

14. Serve the Egusi Soup with pounded yam, boiled plantains or rice.

NOTES

_____
_____
_____
_____
_____
_____
_____
_____
_____
_____
_____
_____
_____
_____
_____

Republic of Congo – Poulet a la Moambe

Poulet a la Momabe is a type of savory chicken stew which embraces the potent African flavors of nutmeg and peanut. Traditionally, free range chicken is used in this dish which takes a longer time to cook. Poulet a la Moambe is considered to be the national dish of the Democratic Republic of Congo. It is typically eaten with cooked white rice.

SERVES 6

INGREDIENTS

chicken parts (cut into stewing pieces)	3–4 lbs.
(8 oz.) can tomato sauce	1
butter	1 tbsp.
creamy peanut butter	1 cup
onion (peeled and finely diced)	1
pinch ground nutmeg	1
pinch black pepper	1
Salt	
Cayenne pepper	
Water	

DIRECTIONS

1. Place the chicken in a large pot and cover the meat with water.

2. Add salt and pepper, then bring to a boil.

3. Reduce the heat and bring to a gentle simmer.

4. Boil the chicken for about one (1:00) hour and thirty (0:30) minutes or until the meat is tender.

5. Remove the chicken from the pot with a slotted spoon and set aside.

6. Reserve a cup and a half of the cooking liquid (chicken stock) and set aside.

7. Melt the butter in a separate pan and add the onions, cayenne pepper, and ground nutmeg.

8. Add black pepper and then sauté these Ingredients together.

9. Add the can of tomatoes and mix well, then cook for about three (0:03) minutes.

10. Transfer the chicken to the pan.

11. Pour in the reserved chicken stock and stir.

12. Cover the pan with a lid and let the stew cook for fifteen (0:15) minutes.

13. Remove the lid and add the peanut butter to the stew.

14. Stir well so that the peanut butter is incorporated thoroughly into the stew.

15. Preheat the oven to 350 degrees F°.

16. Transfer the pan from the stove to the preheated oven and bake for thirty (0:30) minutes or until the sauce has thickened.

17. Serve Poulet a la Moambe on a bed of steamed rice.

NOTES

_____
_____
_____
_____
_____
_____
_____
_____
_____
_____
_____
_____
_____
_____
_____

São Tomé and Principé – Palm Oil Stew

The cuisine of São Tomé and Principé is greatly influenced by traditional Sub–Saharan African cooking and Portuguese influences. Palm Oil Stew is considered the country's national dish as palm oil is plentiful on the islands and is a key ingredient in many dishes. This rich, red stew is usually prepared with smoked meats or fish.

SERVES 3–4

INGREDIENTS

red palm oil	1–2 cups
dried, smoked fish / smoked chicken parts	2 lb.
onions (peeled and diced)	3
cloves garlic	4
diced tomatoes	2 ½ cups
large red bell pepper (diced)	1
scotch bonnet chili pepper (seeded and finely chopped)	1
lemon juice	1 tbsp.
bunch basil (chopped)	1
bouillon cube (crumbled)	1
Salt	
Water/meat stock	

DIRECTIONS

1. Blend the diced tomatoes, scotch bonnet pepper, red bell pepper, garlic cloves and three-quarter of the onions.

2. Place this blended mixture into a pot and set over low heat to allow the moisture to evaporate.

3. Once the consistency of a thick puree has achieved, turn off the heat and set aside.

4. Heat the red palm oil in a separate saucepan and then add the rest of the onions.

5. Sauté the onions until softened, then add the tomato and onion puree to the pot.

6. Cook for a few minutes, then pour in some water or meat stock if the puree is too thick.

7. Stir and let it cook for about five (0:05) minutes.

1. Add the smoked chicken parts or prepared smoked fish.

2. Season the stew with salt and crumbled bouillon cube.

3. Sprinkle the lemon juice over the stew and stir well.

4. Cook the stew for an additional ten (0:10) minutes, adding more stock or water if it becomes too thick.

5. Add the chopped basil leaves and cook for one (0:01) minute more until fragrant, then turn off the heat.

6. Serve the Palm Oil Stew with boiled rice or plantains.

NOTES

_____
_____
_____
_____
_____
_____
_____
_____
_____
_____
_____
_____
_____
_____
_____
_____

Senegal – Thieboudienne

Thieboudienne is a hearty one-pot dish of rice, fish and vegetables simmered in tomato sauce. It is known as the national dish of Senegal. This dish is traditionally eaten with the hands.

SERVES 6–8

INGREDIENTS

(4 oz.) fish fillets (grouper, snapper, tilapia)	8
basmati rice	4 cups
finely chopped parsley	¼ cup
cloves garlic (minced)	6
scallions (minced)	2
medium onions (peeled and coarsely chopped)	2
small onion (peeled and finely diced)	¼
crushed red chili flakes	2 tsp.
palm oil	½ cup
Tamarind paste	2 tbsp.
fish sauce	2 tbsp.
medium green pepper (seeded and diced)	1
can (12 oz.) tomato paste	1
fish stock	6 cups
small carrots (halved crosswise)	6
large eggplant (cut into chunks)	1
cassava root (cut into 1 ½ inch chunks)	½
turnip (peeled and cut into 12 wedges)	1
dried hibiscus flowers (optional)	1/3 cup
Kosher salt	
Black pepper	
Lime wedges	

DIRECTIONS

1. Prepare stuffing for the fish by combining the parsley, chili flakes, scallions, salt, black pepper and the finely diced onion in a bowl.

2. Make a 2–inch cut lengthwise into each of the fish fillets.

3. Stuff the fillets with the herb mixture and set aside.

4. Heat the palm oil in an 8–quart Dutch oven and sauté the coarsely chopped onions, minced garlic and the chopped green pepper for ten (0:10) minutes until soft.

5. Add the tomato paste and cook for ten (0:10) minutes, then add the fish stock and bring to a boil.

6. Reduce the heat and add the stuffed fish fillets.

7. Cook the fish for about eighteen (0:18) minutes, then remove from the pot and set aside.

8. Add the carrots, turnips, eggplant and cassava pieces to the pot and cook for forty (0:40) minutes until tender.

9. Use a slotted spoon to remove the vegetables and set them aside in a bowl.

10. Add the hibiscus flowers, tamarind paste, and fish sauce to the pot.

11. Cook for five (0:05) minutes, occasionally stirring until the hibiscus flowers soften.

12. Add the rice to the pot, stir and allow to cook for forty-five (0:45) minutes until the rice is soft.

13. Remove the pot from the stove and fluff the rice with a fork.

14. Put together servings of rice, fish, and vegetables on plates.

15. Garnish with lemon wedges and serve hot.

NOTES

_____
_____
_____
_____
_____
_____
_____

Seychelles – Ladob

Ladob is a popular sweet dessert made of sweet potatoes, bananas, or plantains cooked in coconut milk. The dish is infused with flavors of vanilla and cinnamon. There are savory versions of Ladob which are made with selfish, breadfruit and cassava. Locals regularly eat both the sweet and savory versions in Seychelles. It is a one of the country's most traditional dishes. Served Ladob hot or cold.

SERVES 4

INGREDIENTS

large, firm plantains (peeled and halved lengthways)	3
freshly grated nutmeg	1 tsp.
brown sugar	3 tbsp.
vanilla pod (split in half lengthways)	1
salt	1 tsp.
cinnamon leaves/4 cinnamon sticks	6
coconut milk	2 ½ cups
Ground cinnamon (for garnish)	

DIRECTIONS

1. Slice each of the plantain halves into two pieces.

2. Line the base of a large saucepan with the pieces of plantains.

3. Add the cinnamon leaves or sticks to the pan.

4. Sprinkle the grated nutmeg, salt, and sugar over the plantains

5. Add the vanilla pod to the pan

6. Pour the coconut milk over the plantains and spices.

7. Bring to a boil and cook for ten (0:10) minutes.

8. Reduce the heat and allow to simmer uncovered for thirty (0:30) minutes.

9. Stick the plantains with a fork or knife to check if they are tender.

10. Turn off the heat when the plantains are soft.

11. Remove the vanilla pod as well as the cinnamon sticks or leaves and discard.

12. Divide the Ladob into four servings.

13. Garnish each serving with a dusting of extra ground cinnamon if desired.

14. Serve the Ladob immediately or chill in the refrigerator before serving.

NOTES

_____
_____
_____
_____
_____
_____
_____
_____
_____
_____
_____
_____
_____
_____
_____
_____
_____
_____
_____

Sierra Leone – Cassava Leaf Stew

Cassava Leaf Stew is an exotic African dish that is widely consumed in Sierra Leone. Other names for this dish are Pondu and Saka Saka. Shrimp, groundnut paste and dried or smoked meats are cooked together with cassava leaves to make this dish. It is typically eaten with rice.

SERVES 5.

INGREDIENTS

frozen cassava leaves (rinsed)	3 lbs.
beef (cut into bite-sized pieces)	1 lb.
smoked chicken / turkey / fish (cut into bite sized pieces)	½ lb.
ground crayfish / dried shrimp	½ cup
fresh shrimp (peeled and deveined)	½ lb.
groundnut paste/peanut butter	5 tbsp.
Scotch bonnet pepper (seeded and finely diced)	1
palm oil	1 cup
crumbled chicken bouillon cubes	1 tbsp.
medium onion (peeled and chopped)	1
Salt	

DIRECTIONS

1. Use a blender to mince the cassava leaves to a fine consistency, then set aside.

2. Place the beef and smoked meat into a saucepan.

3. Season the meats with salt, pepper, half of the onions and the crumbled bouillon cubes.

4. Add water to the pot and boil the meats until cooked.

5. Reserve two cups of stock, then drain and set aside the cooked meats.

6. Heat the palm oil in a separate saucepan over medium heat.

7. Sauté the onions and dried crayfish in the oil for two (0:02) minutes or until fragrant.

8. Add the beef and smoked meats.

9. Stir in the groundnut paste or peanut butter, then add one cup of the meat stock.

10. Cook for five (0:05) minutes then add the blended cassava leaves to the pan.

11. Add the second cup of stock and cook for five (0:05) minutes more.

12. Add the fresh shrimp to the stew and cook until they turn pink.

13. Adjust the salt and pepper.

14. Turn off the heat.

15. Serve over warm rice.

NOTES

_____
_____
_____
_____
_____
_____
_____
_____
_____
_____
_____
_____
_____
_____
_____
_____
_____
_____

South Africa – Doro Wat

Doro Wat is a traditional South African chicken stew made with a spice paste (berberé) and spicy clarified butter (nitter kibbeh). Berberé and nitter kibbeh is not easily found in other places, than South Africa, where Doro Wat is popularly cooked.

SERVES 4

INGREDIENTS

chicken Weighing approximately 3 lbs.	1
onions (finely chopped)	2
lemon (Juiced)	1
nitter kibbeh or butter	4 tbsps.
salt	2 tsps.
cloves garlic (finely chopped)	4
chopped ginger root	1 tsp.
teaspoon nutmeg	½ tsp.
teaspoon cardamom	½ tsp.
teaspoon fenugreek	½ tsp.
teaspoon berberé or a mixture of paprika and cayenne pepper	½ tsp.
chicken stock, water or dry red wine	1 cup
small tomato (chopped)	1
hardboiled eggs (each pierced with a fork)	4

DIRECTIONS

1. Clean the chicken and cut into pieces. Make small cuts in the meat so it can marinate successfully.

2. Marinate the chicken in a bowl for forty–five minutes in a mixture of the lemon juice and one teaspoon of salt.

3. Set a Dutch oven pot on medium heat and add the chopped onions. Do not add oil to the pot.

4. Cook the onions for a few minutes, constantly stirring to prevent burning.

5. Add the nitter kibbeh or butter to the pot, along with the garlic, fenugreek, cardamom, ginger, the remaining teaspoon of salt and the nutmeg. Also, add the tomato and the berberé if available or cayenne and paprika mixture as a substitute.

6. Sauté the Ingredients in the pot for a few minutes.

7. Once the onions are translucent, add the chicken stock, water or dry red wine.

8. Cook for a few minutes, stirring gently. Then reduce the heat and bring it to a boil.

9. Add the marinated chicken to the pot and cook for 40 minutes, turning the chicken occasionally to ensure it is cooked evenly.

10. Twenty minutes before the chicken cooked thoroughly, add the hard-boiled eggs, and ladle the sauce over them.

11. Traditionally, Doro Wat is served hot with injera, a spongy flatbread made of grain flour (commonly called teff flour). Doro Wat can also be paired with couscous, rice, or Indian flatbread.

NOTES

_____
_____
_____
_____
_____
_____
_____
_____
_____
_____
_____
_____
_____

Sudan – Ful Medames

Ful Medames is a fava bean breakfast dish that is popular in Sudan. It is prepared in large quantities for the holy month of Ramadan and eaten before sunrise to prepare for daytime fasting. Ful Medames is believed to have originated in Egypt but is considered to be Sudan's national dish. Typically, boiled eggs are served with it, along with flatbread. Dried beans are traditionally used but Ful Medames can also be prepared using canned fava beans.

SERVES 4

INGREDIENTS

(14 oz.) cans fava beans	3
olive oil	3 tbsp.
large yellow onion (peeled and diced)	1
cumin	2 tsp.
cloves garlic (minced)	6
smoked paprika	2 tsp.
vegetable stock	½ cup
medium tomatoes (diced)	2
parsley	¼ cup
boiled eggs (shelled and sliced)	4
Juice of 2 lemons	
Salt	
Pepper	

DIRECTIONS

1. Drain each can of fava beans and place in a bowl.

2. Rinse the beans with water, and separate in two halves.

3. Use a fork and crush half of the beans.

4. Set aside all of the beans.

5. Heat the olive oil in a skillet over medium-high heat.

6. Add the diced onion and minced garlic to the skillet.

7. Sauté for five (0:05) minutes until the onions are tender.

8. Add the mashed and whole beans to the skillet.

9. Season the beans with lemon juice, salt, cumin, pepper, and smoked paprika. Then cook for five (0:05) minutes over medium high heat, stirring the beans occasionally.

10. Gradually add the vegetable stock until the desired consistency of gravy is achieved.

11. Spoon the cooked beans onto a serving platter.

12. Arrange slices of boiled eggs over the beans.

13. Top with chopped raw tomatoes and parsley.

14. Serve Ful Medames with flatbread such as pita or chapatti.

NOTES

_____
_____
_____
_____
_____
_____
_____
_____
_____
_____
_____
_____
_____
_____

Swaziland – Karoo Roast Ostrich Steak

Ostrich meat is popularly eaten in Swaziland as this wild bird is common to certain parts of Africa and it is also farmed in certain parts of the country. Swazi cuisine is heavily influenced by French cooking techniques such as the use of cream sauces and meat marinades. Karoo Roast Ostrich Steak is considered to be the country's national dish and it is prepared alongside pumpkin mash and topped with a rich cream sauce.

SERVES 4–6

INGREDIENTS

ostrich steaks (thinly sliced)	2
onion (peeled and thinly sliced)	1
heavy cream	½ cup
white wine	1 cup
green peppercorns (lightly crushed)	6
juniper berries (lightly crushed)	5
pumpkin (peeled and cubed)	1
red wine	¾ cup
ground maize	½ cup
Butter for frying	
Water	
Salt	
Pepper	

DIRECTIONS

1. Combine the red wine, juniper berries, salt and pepper in a bowl.

2. Add the strips of ostrich meat to this and mix well.

3. Cover the bowl with plastic wrap and refrigerate overnight.

4. Combine the pumpkin and ground maize in a pot, then pour in enough water to cover the pumpkin

5. Boil for thirty (0:30) minutes, adding more water if necessary.

6. When the pumpkin softens, drain off any excess liquid.

7. Mash the cooked pumpkin and ground maize together, then set aside.

8. Melt some butter in a clean skillet.

9. Sauté the onions in the melted butter until brown.

10. Add the peppercorns.

11. Stir in the white wine and heavy cream, then bring to a gentle simmer.

12. Season this cream sauce with salt and pepper if desired, then set aside.

13. Discard the liquid marinade from the bowl of ostrich meat.

14. Heat some butter in a separate frying pan and flash-fry the marinated ostrich strips.

15. Serve the ostrich steaks with portions of pumpkin mash.

16. Drizzle the cream sauce over the top and serve immediately.

NOTES

_____
_____
_____
_____
_____
_____
_____
_____
_____
_____
_____
_____
_____
_____

Tanzania – Ugali na Maharage ya Nazi

Ugali is a staple in many African countries. It is a bland side dish which is made from cornmeal, banana, or semolina and cassava flour. The consistency of Ugali can vary from doughy to porridge–like. In Tanzania, Ugali is typically eaten with a kidney bean stew. This dish is usually prepared on December 9th, which is Tanzania's Independence Day.

SERVES 4

INGREDIENTS

water	1 L
corn flour	2 cups
canned kidney beans (drained)	2 ½ cups
vegetable oil	5 tbsp.
onions (peeled and diced)	2
tomatoes (diced)	2
large carrot (diced)	1
coconut milk	1 cup
Salt	
Black pepper	

DIRECTIONS

1. Warm the water for three (0:03) minutes in a large pot, but do not allow it to boil.

2. Add half of the corn flour to the water and stir with a wooden spoon until thick.

3. When the mixture resembles a bubbling porridge, cover the pot and cook for four (0:04) minutes over medium heat.

4. Remove the pot from the heat and stir in the remaining flour.

5. Stir the mixture well and remove any lumps.

6. Spread the doughy mixture over the base of the pot and return it to the stove.

7. Cover the pot and allow it to cook for four (0:04) minutes.

8. Flip the mixture to the other side, then repeat the previous step.

9. Shape the Ugali into a neat ball and set aside on a serving dish.

10. In a separate pan, heat the vegetable oil and sauté the onions in the oil.

11. Add the tomatoes to the onions.

12. When the tomatoes begin to soften, add the carrots and cook for two (0:02) minutes.

13. Add the canned beans, then season with salt and pepper.

14. Stir in the coconut milk.

15. Reduce the heat and simmer for three (0:03) minutes, stirring occasionally.

16. Turn off the heat.

17. Serve the bean stew with the Ugali.

NOTES

_____

_____

_____

_____

_____

_____

_____

_____

_____

_____

_____

_____

_____

The Gambia – Benachin

Benachin is a popular Gambian dish that is prepared in one pot alone. It consists of rice, vegetables and meat that is cooked together.

SERVES 6–8

INGREDIENTS

chicken (cut into pieces)	½
boneless beef (diced)	½ lb.
cups rice	3
onions (peeled and diced)	4
large tomatoes (chopped)	2
bay leaves	2
cloves garlic (minced)	3
hot peppers (minced)	2
tomato puree	3 tsp.
vegetable oil	1 ½ cups
bell peppers (sliced)	2
large eggplant (chopped)	1
small cabbage (chopped)	½
water	6 cups
Salt	
Black pepper	
Vinegar	

DIRECTIONS

1. Put the chicken and beef pieces into a bowl.

2. Season the meats with salt, black pepper, garlic and a dash of vinegar, then leave undisturbed for thirty (0:30) minutes.

3. Heat a large pot, add the vegetable oil and fry the chicken until golden brown on all sides.

4. After the chicken cooked, remove and set aside, then brown the beef in the same pot.

5. Add the onions to the beef and cook until brown.

6. Add the tomatoes and the tomato puree together with the minced hot pepper.

7. Stir these Ingredients together and cook for fifteen (0:15) minutes.

8. Pour in the water and bring to a boil.

9. Add the chicken to the pot.

10. Add the chopped cabbage, chopped eggplant and the bay leaves to the pot.

11. Sprinkle salt to taste.

12. Use a large spoon to dish out the vegetables and chicken pieces, then set these aside.

13. Rinse the raw rice in cold water, then add to the pot.

14. Add the sliced bell peppers and bring to a boil.

15. Reduce the heat and let the Ingredients simmer.

16. When the liquid absorbed, and the rice is tender, turn off the heat and place in a serving dish.

17. Arrange the chicken and vegetables on top of the rice and beef.

18. Serve hot.

NOTES

_____
_____
_____
_____
_____
_____
_____
_____
_____
_____
_____
_____
_____

Togo – Yeyebessissi

Hot peppers such as chilies and habaneros are major Ingredients in Togolese cuisine. Sauces are particularly popular in Togolese cooking especially hot pepper sauces. The most iconic hot pepper sauce in Togo is called Yeyebessissi. It is a mix of hot peppers, herbs, oil and tomatoes. Yeyebessissi is typically eaten as a condiment. It is also added to Togolese meat and poultry stews.

YIELDS 1 jar.

INGREDIENTS

habanero / Scotch bonnet peppers	10
medium onion (peeled and coarsely chopped)	1
cloves garlic	4
basil leaves	2
Roma tomatoes (coarsely chopped)	1- 3
chopped parsley	2 tbsp.
crumbled bouillon cubes	2 tbsp.
vegetable oil	½1 cup
Salt	

DIRECTIONS

1. Remove the stems of the peppers and discard.

2. Put the whole peppers in the food processor or blender and add the tomatoes, onion, garlic, basil, bouillon cubes and parsley.

3. Pour in the oil and blend all of the Ingredients.

4. Pour the pepper sauce into a small saucepan.

5. Bring to a boil and allow to simmer for fifteen (0:15) minutes, frequently stirring to prevent burning.

6. Adjust the salt if necessary.

7. Allow the Yeyebessissi to cool.

8. Transfer the Yeyebessissi to a clean glass jar or lidded container.

9. Store in the refrigerator.

10. Serve cold with cooked dishes or add it to stews and soups to make them more spicy and flavorful.

NOTES

_____

_____

_____

_____

_____

_____

_____

_____

_____

_____

_____

_____

_____

_____

_____

_____

_____

_____

_____

_____

_____

_____

_____

Uganda – Matoke

Matoke is a variety of banana which is indigenous to Uganda. Locals typically consume these bananas when they are unripe. This starchy banana is cooked until yellow, then mashed. Matoke can either be prepared alone or with beef. Matoke is traditionally served with groundnut sauce. A particular tribe in Uganda called the Buganda, is famous for preparing the best Matoke dishes in the country.

SERVES 4–6

INGREDIENTS

matoke / green bananas (peeled)	8–10
ground beef	1 lb.
beef broth	1 cup
onion (peeled and chopped)	1
tomatoes (chopped)	2–3
green bell pepper (chopped)	1
cloves garlic (peeled and chopped)	3–4
chili pepper (chopped)	1
Juice of 1 lemon	
Oil	
Salt	
Water	
Black pepper	

DIRECTIONS

1. Use a sharp knife to cut the matoke/green bananas into cubes.

2. Rinse the bananas with lemon juice and water.

3. Boil the bananas in a pan of salted water for ten (0:10) minutes.

4. Drain and set aside.

5. Heat the oil in a large frying pan and add the onions, garlic, chili pepper, green pepper, and tomatoes.

6. Sauté the vegetables in the oil until tender.

7. Add salt and black pepper.

8. Add the ground beef and the beef broth to the pot.

9. Mix well to break up any clumps.

10. Allow the beef to cook, stirring occasionally.

11. When the beef is almost done, reduce the heat, and add the bananas.

12. Cover the pan and simmer over low heat.

13. When the bananas are tender and yellow, stir the Ingredients together.

14. Depending on the consistency desired, use the spoon to mash the banana chunks.

15. Once the meat is tender and no longer pink, turn off the heat.

16. Serve the Matoke immediately.

NOTES

_____

_____

_____

_____

_____

_____

_____

_____

_____

_____

_____

_____

_____

_____

_____

Zambia – Nshima

Nshima is a popular Zambian dish made from white cornmeal and water. It is typically eaten with a vegetable or meat side dish. It is a dish that is usually eaten with the hands.

SERVES 4

INGREDIENTS

white cornmeal	4 cups
water	10 cups
salt	2 tsp.

DIRECTIONS

1. Pour the water into a large saucepan and begin boiling it.

2. When the water is warm, gradually add half of the cornmeal, adding it a spoonful at a time while stirring.

3. Continue to stir the mixture until it begins to bubble.

4. Reduce the heat to medium high and allow the mixture to cook for a few minutes.

5. Gradually add the remaining cornmeal, adding it a spoonful at a time while stirring.

6. Stir until the Nshima is thick and free of any lumps, adding more water or cornmeal if necessary.

7. Sprinkle in the salt while stirring.

8. Once the desired consistency is achieved, turn off the heat.

9. Place the lid on the pot and allow the Nshima to rest for a few minutes.

10. Serve the Nshima hot, with a meat or vegetable side dish.

Zimbabwe – Sadza

A staple dish in Zimbabwean cuisine is Sadza, a cornmeal food, primarily eaten with curries or stews. Sadza has the consistency of porridge. It is one of the first foods eaten by children in Zimbabwe. Sadza can be eaten for any meal during the day.

SERVES 4

INGREDIENTS

water	4 ½ cups
salt	1 tsp.
white cornmeal (finely ground)	2 cups

DIRECTIONS

1. Pour the water into a large saucepan and add the salt.

2. Bring the salted water to a boil.

3. Gradually add the white cornmeal to the boiling water one spoonful at a time.

4. While adding the cornmeal, use a whisk to stir the mixture.

5. Cook for about fifteen (0:15) to thirty (0:30) minutes or until a thick, smooth consistency.

6. After cooking, let the Sadza rest for a few minutes in the covered pot.

7. Scoop the Sadza onto serving plates.

8. Serve hot with stewed/curried vegetables, mushrooms or meat.

The Central African Republic – Cassava Sticks / Bâton de Manioc

Cassava is extensively farmed in Central Africa, and it has become a staple food there. Cassava or manioc as it is referred to is present in many African dishes as it is an abundant food crop and is versatile enough in that it can be prepared in many different ways. One of the most popular dishes made in the Central African Republic is Bâton de Manioc or Cassava Sticks. This national dish is essentially cassava pulp which is wrapped in banana leaves and steamed for hours until cooked. The sticks are flavored with the banana leaves while steaming.

SERVES 8

INGREDIENTS

fresh cassava tubers	2 lbs.
Banana leaves / Aluminum foil	

DIRECTIONS

1. Wash the cassava tubers to remove the dirt

2. Peel the skin off each tuber with a sharp knife, and rinse.

3. Soak the cassava tubers in a basin of water for three days.

4. Grate the flesh of each tuber. The tough fibers in the core of the tubers should not be grated as they contain traces of cyanide which can be poisonous.

5. Discard the ungrated fibers and retain the cassava pulp.

6. Use a potato masher to grind the pulp into a fine paste further (In Central Africa, a large mortar and pestle are used to do this).

7. Rinse the banana leaves, use a paper towel to pat dry and cut into pieces. If using aluminum foil, tear into large chunks.

8. Spoon a ¼ cup of the cassava paste onto the banana leaf or foil. Shape the paste into a log.

9. Fold into 1" x 4" packets and tie with string. Traditionally, the packets are measured about 2" x 12".

10. Place the wrapped packets into a large pot.

11. Steam for approximately 6 hours.

12. Unwrap, slice and serve the Bâton de Manioc with meat stew

NOTES

_____
_____
_____
_____
_____
_____
_____
_____
_____
_____
_____
_____
_____
_____
_____
_____
_____
_____
_____
_____
_____
_____

American Samoa – Luau Palusami

Coconut trees and taro plants grow abundantly on the islands of American Samoa. Both coconuts and leaves of the taro plant are used to make the national dish; Luau / Palusami.

YIELDS 10

INGREDIENTS

Taro leaves (approximately)	40
coconuts	5
Onion (minced)	
warm water	1 cup
Salt	
Aluminum foil	
Baking Tin	
A thin cloth or Tauaga (used to strain liquid)	
A coconut scraper	

DIRECTIONS

Preparing the Coconut Cream

8. Halve the coconuts and use a coconut scraper to remove the white flesh.

9. Place the coconut flesh into the baking tin. Bake this until it becomes brown.

10. Pour a cup of warm water onto the brown coconut flesh.

11. Scoop up the mass of wet coconut flesh and place in a thin cloth or Tauaga.

12. Squeeze the cloth and extract the cream into a large bowl.

13. Add salt and onion to taste.

Preparing the Luau / Pulsami

1. Stack 4 taro leaves one on top of the other. Use a large taro leaf at the base and three smaller ones on top of it.

2. Hold the stack of leaves together and make it into a cone/bowl like container. Once done, pour a small amount of coconut cream into the taro leaf container, and close the leaves by folding them shut over the cream.

3. The enclosed leaf container will resemble a ball. Hold the top of the ball carefully so it will not unfold.

4. Place the ball onto a square piece of aluminum foil and wrap the foil around the ball. Twist the foil at the top to seal it and hold it tightly.

5. Repeat this to create ten taro and coconut cream packages, each wrapped in foil.

6. Place them in a baking tin and bake for one hour at 475°F°.

7. Unwrap the foil and enjoy the delicious, gooey fusion of taro leaves and coconut cream.

NOTES

_____
_____
_____
_____
_____
_____
_____
_____
_____
_____
_____
_____
_____

Australia – Meat Pie

Australia's national dish is a savory pastry pie with a base and top crust that sandwiches a generous helping of minced meat.

YIELDS 8 pies.

INGREDIENTS

Pie Crust (Base)

Flour	2/3 cups
water	2/3 cup
salt	½ tsp.
beef fat	2 oz.

Pie Filling

ground beef	¾ lb
pinch nutmeg	1
beef bouillon cubes	2
water	3¾ cups
flour	2 tbsp.
soy sauce	1 tsp.
Salt and pepper to taste	

Pie Crust (Top)

puff pastry	14 Oz
egg yolk	1
water	1tsp.

DIRECTIONS

Pie Crust (Base)

1. Sift the flour and salt in a bowl.

2. Heat the beef fat in a saucepan, occasionally stirring until the fat melts.

3. Make a well in the flour and salt mixture and pour the melted beef fat.

4. Combine the fat and the dry Ingredients on a floured board.

5. Roll out the pastry.

6. Grease 8 pie tins and line the base of each tin with the pastry. Trim the excess pastry from the edges.

Pie Filling

1. Cook the ground beef in a pan. Remove the excess fat by pouring it out.

2. Crumble the bouillon cubes and add to the pan.

3. Add salt, pepper, and nutmeg to flavor the beef and, pour in 2 cups of water and stir well.

4. When it starts boiling, reduce the heat, cover the pan, and allow it to simmer for twenty minutes.

5. Add the flour and 1 ¾ cups of water and stir.

6. Add the soy sauce to give the meat more color.

7. Simmer for ten minutes and set aside to cool.

8. Add the meat filling to each of the pie tins previously prepared with pastry

Pie Crust (Top)

1. Prepare the puff pastry by rolling it out on a floured board.

2. Cut circular shapes of pastry for the top of each meat pie.

3. Moisten the edges of the base crust with a little water and press the top crust into place.

4. Trim the edges and pierce the center of each pie.

5. Bake the pies for five minutes at 350°F°.

6. Brush the tops of the pies with an egg yolk wash and bake them further for ten minutes at moderate heat.

East Timor – Ikan Pepes

Ikan Pepes is a national fish dish in East Timor. Ikan means fish and Pepes refers to the method of steaming it in banana leaves, then grilling. Ikan Pepes is made with a whole fish cooked in exotic Eastern spices.

SERVES 4

INGREDIENTS

whole red snapper (gutted and rinsed)	2 lb.
Banana leaves	
salt	1 tsp.
lime Juiced	1

For Curry Paste

tamarind pulp (soaked for 5 minutes)	1 tbsp.
warm water	2 tbsp.
large chili peppers (chopped)	6–10
stalk lemongrass (thinly sliced)	1
candlenuts / macadamia nuts	5
small ripe tomato	1
palm sugar / brown sugar	1 tbsp.
saffron powder	½ tsp.
dried shrimp paste	½ tsp.
basil leaves (chopped)	½ cup

DIRECTIONS

1. Use a knife to score the fish on both sides.

2. Rub the fish with salt and lime juice.

3. Set aside.

4. Make a curry paste by combining the tamarind pulp, warm water, chili peppers, lemongrass, basil leaves, nuts, tomato, sugar, saffron powder and shrimp paste in the food processor.

5. Mince for two (0:02) minutes until a smooth paste is formed.

6. Rinse the banana leaves in cold water.

7. Spread a layer of the curry paste over one side of the banana leaf.

8. Rub adequate curry paste over the fish as well as inside the belly.

9. Place the fish on the smeared banana leaf.

10. Wrap the fish in the banana leaf, securing it with pre-soaked strings.

11. Steam the banana leaf packet in a bamboo steamer for twenty (0:20) minutes.

12. Remove from the steamer.

13. Lay the packet on a hot grill for a total of six (0:06) minutes.

14. Cut the strings and unwrap the packet.

15. Remove the cooked fish and set it on a serving dish.

16. Serve Ikan Pepes with warm white rice sprinkled with chopped basil leaves.

NOTES

_____
_____
_____
_____
_____
_____
_____
_____
_____
_____
_____
_____
_____
_____
_____
_____

Fiji – Fijian Kokoda

Fijian Kokoda is a raw fish ceviche that is served in a half coconut shell or giant clam shell in the tropical islands of Fiji. It is usually made with fresh white fish such as mahi–mahi or snapper, both of which are found in the seas surrounding the islands. The Kokoda in Fiji is prepared with plenty of citrus and coconut flavors.

SERVES 10

INGREDIENTS

white fish fillets (Mahi–Mahi, cod or snapper)	4
fresh lime/lemon juice	¾ cup
ripe tomatoes (diced)	2
large chili pepper	1
coconut cream	100 ml
onion (peeled and finely diced)	1
green capsicum pepper	1
green oak leaf lettuces	3
Salt	
Black pepper	

DIRECTIONS

1. Remove the bones from the fish filet and discard.

2. Use a sharp knife to cut the fish into small 1 cm cubes.

3. Mix the fish cubes with the lemon or lime juice in a ceramic or glass bowl as metal bowls will react with the lime and lemon juice.

4. Cover the bowl with plastic wrap and refrigerate for eight (8:00) hours or overnight.

5. Mix occasionally with a wooden spoon.

6. After marinating, the fish will appear white, as if cooked in the lime and lemon juice.

7. Cut the chili and capsicum peppers into halves, then remove the seeds and chop finely.

8. Add the chopped peppers to the marinated fish, along with the diced onions.

9. Pour in the coconut cream.

10. To ensure all the Ingredients properly flavor the fish, give it a thorough stir.

11. Season the Kokoda with adequate salt and black pepper.

12. Remove the stems from the lettuce leaves, rinse them in water, and then pat dry with a paper towel.

13. Line the serving platter with the lettuce leaves and then transfer the Kokoda onto it.

14. Alternatively, line half coconut shells with lettuce and spoon the Kokoda into each, then serve

NOTES

_____
_____
_____
_____
_____
_____
_____
_____
_____
_____
_____
_____
_____
_____
_____
_____

Hawaii – Lau Lau

Lau Lau is a dish that is at the heart of the Hawaiian people. It is considered soul food and utilizes natural Ingredients from the islands. The main Ingredients are taro leaves, meat or fish and Hawaiian Alea salt. The phrase Lau Lau translates to "leaf – leaf" which relates to the taro and ti leaves used in the dish. Hawaiian Alea salt is native to Hawaii and consists of sea salt and red organic volcanic clay which was used in both cooking practices and purifying rituals by the native Hawaiians. Traditionally, this dish is prepared in an underground oven or imu.

SERVES 6

INGREDIENTS

taro leaves	30
large ti/banana leaves	6
boneless chicken thighs	6
pork belly chops (cut into 6 pieces)	1 lb.
salted butterfish (cut into 6 pieces)	¼ lb.
Hawaiian Alea salt	1 ½ tsp.
soy sauce/Shoyu sauce	1 tsp.
Toothpicks, rubber bands or butcher's twine to seal	
Water	

DIRECTIONS

1. Wash the taro leaves and remove the fibrous veins and stems, then set aside.

2. Place the pork, chicken, and fish into a large bowl and season well with the soy sauce and Hawaiian Alea salt.

3. Layer five taro leaves together and places a piece of pork, butterfish, and a chicken thigh in the center of the leaves.

4. Wrap the taro leaves over the meat and fish to form a neat bundle, then set seam side down on a dish.

5. Prepare the rest of the taro and meat bundles.

6. Wrap each Lau Lau bundle in a ti or banana leaf.

7. Secure the Lau Lau bundle with toothpicks, rubber bands or tie tightly with butcher's twine and set aside.

8. Pour some water in a steamer and bring to a boil.

9. Place the Lau Laus in the steamer, reduce the heat, and let them simmer for approximately six (6:00) hours until cooked.

10. Unwrap the ti or banana leaves and discard them as these are not edible.

11. Serve the taro and meat bundle on a bed of steamed rice.

NOTES

_____
_____
_____
_____
_____
_____
_____
_____
_____
_____
_____
_____
_____
_____
_____
_____

Kiribati – Palusami

Palusami is a dish that is common in the Pacific Islands. It is considered the national dish of Kiribati. The two main Ingredients of Palusami are coconut milk and taro leaves as coconuts and taro are plentiful on the populated parts of the islands. The coconut cream and taro filled bundles are traditionally baked in an underground earthen oven.

SERVES 4–5

INGREDIENTS

young taro leaves	36
coconut cream / coconut milk	2 cups
curry powder	1 tsp.
wilted banana leaves	6
breadfruit leaves	6
medium onion (peeled and finely diced)	1
Hot water	
Salt	
Black pepper	

DIRECTIONS

1. In a medium-sized bowl, combine the onions and the coconut cream.

2. Add the curry powder to this and mix well, then set aside.

3. Remove the thick stems of the taro leaves.

4. Dip each leaf for half a minute in a container of hot water; this will make them more pliable.

5. Lay six taro leaves together, using a larger leaf as the base.

6. Fold the leaves into a cone or cup.

7. Pour half cup of the seasoned coconut cream mixture into the taro leaf cone.

8. Secure the open top by folding delicately, then place in a banana leaf.

9. Fold the banana leaf around the taro cone and secure the top.

10. Place the leaf bundle in the center of a breadfruit leaf, wrapping the leaf around the bundle and securing it at the top with toothpicks.

11. Wrap the bundle in foil paper to secure it further if needed.

12. Place the finished bundles in a baking tray, and bake in the oven for thirty (0:30) minutes in moderate heat.

13. Remove from the oven and place the bundles on a serving platter; unwrap them to reveal the creamy taro leaf and coconut cream filling.

14. Serve Palusami hot or cold.

NOTES

_____
_____
_____
_____
_____
_____
_____
_____
_____
_____
_____
_____
_____
_____
_____
_____
_____

The Marshall Islands –
Macadamia Nut Pie

The National dish of The Marshall Islands is Macadamia Nut Pie. Although macadamia nuts are not native to the country, it is fairly popular in locally baked goods. Coconut is native to the islands and since it pairs well with these nuts, Macadamia Nut Pie has become an iconic sweetmeat there. It is a crunchy dessert, made primarily from macadamia nuts and infused with coconut. It can be eaten either hot or cold.

YIELDS 1 pie

INGREDIENTS

store bought 9" pie crust	1
shredded, unsweetened coconut	¼ cup
macadamia nuts (roughly chopped)	1 ¾ cups
eggs	3
coconut milk	4 tbsp.
melted butter	1 tbsp.
honey	½ cup
heavy cream	1 cup

DIRECTIONS

1. Preheat the oven to 375 degrees F°.

2. Fit the pie crust into a pie dish or tart pan.

3. Sprinkle the shredded, unsweetened coconut evenly over the pie crust and set aside.

4. Begin creating the nut filling by first cracking the eggs into a bowl.

5. Add the honey, melted butter, sugar and two tablespoons of coconut milk to the eggs.

6. Whisk these Ingredients together until creamy.

7. Add the chopped macadamia nuts to the mixture and stir.

8. Spoon the nut filling into the pie crust.

9. Place the pie into the preheated oven and bake for fifteen (0:15) minutes.

10. Reduce the heat to 325 degrees F° and let the pie bake for an additional thirty-five (0:35) minutes.

11. Remove the pie from the oven and allow to cool.

12. In a small bowl, whip together the heavy cream with the remaining coconut milk.

13. Slice the cooled Macadamia Nut Pie and top each slice with a dollop of whipped cream.

14. Serve immediately.

NOTES

Nauru – Coconut Crusted Fish

On the small island of Nauru, most food items have to be imported but coconuts and fresh seafood are locally abundant. The country's national dish is Coconut Crusted Fish which is a succulent meal of fish fillets dredged in shredded coconut and fried in coconut oil. Pacific rockfish is usually used for this meal but tilapia can also be prepared instead of it. This dish is usually served with steamed rice.

SERVES 6

INGREDIENTS

fillets Pacific rockfish/tilapia	6
breadcrumbs	½ cup
shredded, unsweetened coconut	½ cup
large eggs	2
limes (thinly sliced)	1–2
Coconut oil for frying	
Salt	
Black Pepper	

DIRECTIONS

1. Season the fish fillets with adequate salt and black pepper, then set aside.

2. Whisk the eggs in a bowl until frothy, then set aside.

3. In a separate bowl, combine the shredded coconut and the breadcrumbs.

4. Dip each fish fillet into the egg mixture, then dredge them in the coconut and breadcrumb mixture.

5. Lightly pat the fillets to ensure the coconut and breadcrumb coating sticks to it.

6. Heat the coconut oil in a frying pan.

7. Shake off any excess crumbs from the fillets and then place in the hot oil to fry.

8. Fry the coconut crusted fillets for three (0:03) minutes on one side before flipping – time will vary based on the size and thickness of the fillets.

9. When the crust on the fillet becomes golden brown, it is done.

10. Remove the fillets from the pan using a slotted spoon and transfer to a dish lined with paper towels which will absorb excess oil.

11. Plate the Coconut Crusted Fish atop a bed of steamed rice and a dollop of tartar sauce on the side.

12. Garnish with lime slices and serve.

NOTES

New Zealand – Pavlova

Pavlova is considered to be New Zealand's national dish. It is in fact a sweet dessert made of a meringue base topped with whipped cream and slices of fresh fruit. It is believed to be named in honor of the Russian ballerina Anna Pavlova who visited the country in the 1920s. Pavlova is prepared for celebrations and holidays including Christmas.

SERVES 6–8

INGREDIENTS

eggs	4
cream of tartar	1/8 tsp.
cornstarch	1 tbsp.
castor sugar	1 cup
vanilla extract	1 tsp.
lightly sweetened whipped cream	1 ½ cups
fruit slices (kiwi, peaches, and berries)	1 cup

DIRECTIONS

1. Preheat the oven to 400 degrees F°.

2. Break the eggs and separate the whites and yolks.

3. Place the whites of the four eggs into a bowl and sprinkle the cream of tartar over them.

4. Beat the egg whites and cream of tartar until stiff peaks form, then set aside.

5. In a separate bowl, whisk together the castor sugar and cornstarch.

6. Add the castor sugar mixture to the egg whites one tablespoon at a time and beat until a stiff, shiny white meringue forms.

7. Use a wooden spoon to fold in the vanilla extract, then set aside gently.

8. Line up a shallow baking dish with a sheet of parchment paper.

9. Scoop out the meringue onto the baking dish and gently form into a mound measuring about six inches in diameter.

10. Reduce the heat to 200 degrees F°, then place the dish into the oven, and Bake for one (1:00) hour.

11. Turn off the heat but leave the meringue to cool in the oven overnight.

12. Top the meringue with whipped cream.

13. Arrange the slices of fruit over the whipped cream.

14. Slice the Pavlova using a serrated knife, then plate and serve immediately.

NOTES

_____
_____
_____
_____
_____
_____
_____
_____
_____
_____
_____
_____
_____
_____
_____
_____
_____
_____

Palau – Bat Soup

Bat Soup is regarded as a national delicacy in Palau. Fruit bats, also called flying foxes are the main ingredient in this dish. A serving of traditional Bat Soup consists of a whole fruit bat including its wings, fur and membranes. Its fur is chewed sucked on, then discarded. Some variations of the soup require skinning the bats and using the meat alone. This delicacy is popular at restaurants and tourists are encouraged to try the strange dish. Fruit Bat Soup is rumored to enhance sexual virility.

SERVES 4

INGREDIENTS

whole fruit bats (well washed but neither skinned nor eviscerated)	3 – 4
freshly sliced ginger	1 tbsp.
large onion (peeled and cut into quarters)	1
Minced garlic	
Chopped scallions	
Coconut milk/cream	
Soy sauce (to taste)	
Sea Salt (to taste)	
Water	

DIRECTIONS

1. Place the whole, washed bats into a soup pot.

2. Pour in enough water to cover the bats.

3. Add the onions, minced garlic and ginger to the pot.

4. Season the soup with sea salt.

5. Turn on the heat and bring the soup to a boil.

6. Allow the Ingredients to boil for about one (1:00) hour.

7. Pour the soup through a sieve or strainer and collect the broth in a saucepan.

8. Set aside the broth and skin the bats.

9. Remove the bones if desired, then add the meat and viscera to the strained broth.

10. Place the saucepan containing the strained broth and bat meat over low heat.

11. Add soy sauce if desired and a little coconut milk or cream.

12. Adjust the salt if necessary.

13. Generously add the chopped scallions to the soup and stir well.

14. Turn off the heat and ladle into serving bowls.

15. Serve the Bat Soup hot.

NOTES

Papua New Guinea – Mumu

Mumu is the national dish of Papua New Guinea. It is a slow cooked assortment of fruits, vegetables, root crops and meat. Mumu is also referred to as a method of cooking in Papua New Guinea where a makeshift outdoor oven is created using hot stones. In this dish, all of the Ingredients are layered in the pot and slow–cooked until everything is tender. Mumu is traditionally eaten with the hands.

SERVES 3-5

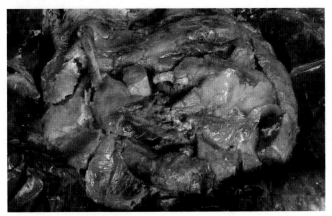

INGREDIENTS

assorted root vegetables (carrots, sweet potatoes, yucca root)	1 lb.
pork (cut into bite-sized pieces)	¾ lb.
chicken (cut into bite-sized pieces)	¾ lb.
pineapple chunks	¾ lb.
green vegetables (spinach, kale, green beans)	¾ 1 lb.
onion (peeled and sliced)	
cloves garlic (minced)	2
can coconut milk	1
Cooking oil	
Banana leaves	

DIRECTIONS

1. Peel and slice the root vegetables, then set aside.

2. Grease a large casserole dish or Dutch oven with cooking oil.

3. Line the base of the dish with banana leaves.

4. Place a layer of the yucca root, carrot and sweet potato over the banana leaves.

5. Place a layer of pork over the root vegetables.

6. Lay the pineapple chunks over the pork.

7. Place the chicken pieces over the pineapple chunks.

8. Arrange the green vegetables, onions, and garlic over the chicken.

9. Pour the coconut milk over the layers of Ingredients and then make a layer of spinach or kale leaves to cover everything.

10. Place a lid over the casserole dish or Dutch oven and place over a grated open fire for about fifteen (0:15) minutes to bring the juices up to cooking temperature.

11. Reduce the heat and allow the Mumu to simmer gently for about one (1:00) hour or until the vegetables and meat are tender.

12. Serve hot.

NOTES

_____
_____
_____
_____
_____
_____
_____
_____
_____
_____
_____
_____
_____
_____
_____
_____
_____
_____

American Samoa – Luau Palusami

Coconut trees and taro plants grow abundantly on the islands of American Samoa. Both coconuts and leaves of the taro plant are used to make the national dish; Luau / Palusami.

YIELDS 10

INGREDIENTS

Taro leaves (approximately)	40
coconuts	5
Onion (minced)	
warm water	1 cup
Salt	
Aluminum foil	
Baking Tin	
A thin cloth or tauaga (used to strain liquid)	
A coconut scraper	

DIRECTIONS

Preparing the Coconut Cream

1. Halve the coconuts and use a coconut scraper to remove the white flesh
2. Place the coconut flesh into the baking tin. Bake this until it becomes brown.
3. Pour a cup of warm water onto the brown coconut flesh.
4. Scoop up the mass of wet coconut flesh and place in a thin cloth or tauaga. Squeeze the cloth and extract the cream into a large bowl.
5. Add salt and onion to taste.

Preparing the Luau / Pulsami

1. Stack 4 taro leaves one on top of the other. Use a large taro leaf at the base and three smaller ones on top of it. Hold the stack of leaves together and shape it into a cone/bowl like container.

2. Once done, pour a small amount of coconut cream into the taro leaf container. Close the leaves by folding them shut over the cream. The enclosed leaf container will resemble a ball. Hold the top of the ball carefully so it will not become undone. Place the ball onto a square piece of aluminum foil and wrap the foil around the ball. Twist the foil at the top to seal it and hold it tightly.

3. Repeat this to create ten taro and coconut cream packages, each wrapped in foil. Place them in a baking tin and bake for one hour at 475°F°. Unwrap the foil and enjoy the delicious, gooey fusion of taro leaves and coconut cream.

NOTES

_____
_____
_____
_____
_____
_____
_____
_____
_____
_____
_____
_____
_____
_____
_____
_____
_____
_____
_____
_____
_____
_____
_____
_____
_____

Solomon Islands – Poi

Poi is considered to be the national dish of the Solomon Islands. Taro is an important food crop grown on the islands and it is the main ingredient in Poi. It is a simple side dish which is made by pounding cooked taro roots into a paste. Poi has a delicate flavor and is pale purple in color. It can be eaten as soon as it is made or it can be allowed to naturally ferment for a few days. This is called Sour Poi.

SERVES 3

INGREDIENTS

taro roots (rinsed)	1 ½ lb.
Water	
Salt	
Pepper	

DIRECTIONS

1. Fill a saucepan with approximately 2 quarts of water and bring to a boil.

2. Place the taro roots into the pot of boiling water.

3. Cook for forty (0:40) minutes until the taro roots are tender.

4. Drain and discard the water, then allow the taro roots to cool for fifteen (0:15) minutes.

5. Use a knife to peel the boiled taro roots.

6. Chop the boiled taro roots into large cubes.

7. Place the cubes into a blender along with a cup of water.

8. Blend the taro roots and water into a smooth paste.

9. Add more water and blend if necessary.

10. Transfer the Poi to a bowl.

11. Season with salt and pepper, then mix well.

12. Serve.

NOTES

Federated States of Micronesia – Chicken Kelaguen

Chicken Kelaguen is a marinated chicken dish that is famous in the Micronesian islands. It is marinated in a very spicy sauce called Finadene Sauce and then cooked in a delectable blend of lemon juice, coconut and peppers. Chicken Kelaguen is usually eaten with pita bread.

SERVES 4–6

INGREDIENTS

For Finadene Sauce

soy sauce	1 cup
lemon juice	1 cup
large onion (peeled and finely chopped)	1
hot peppers (finely chopped)	5

For the Chicken

whole broiler/fryer chicken (cut into pieces)	1
dried coconut	1
green onions (finely chopped)	4
hot peppers (finely chopped)	3
pita bread	4–6
Lemon Juice	

DIRECTIONS

For Finadene Sauce

1. In a large bowl, combine the soy sauce and lemon juice.

2. Add the finely chopped onions and the hot peppers to the soy sauce and lemon juice.

3. Mix well and set aside in the refrigerator for twenty four (24:00) hours or longer to allow the flavors to marry.

For the Chicken

1. Place the chicken pieces into the bowl of Finadene Sauce and mix well so that all of the meat is well coated.

2. Marinate the chicken overnight in the refrigerator.

3. Grill or broil the chicken, using any additional sauce to baste the meat.

4. After the chicken has cooled, debone and shred the meat.

5. Open the coconut and discard the water.

6. Grate the white coconut flesh and squeeze a little at a time to extract the milk.

7. Save the grated coconut and collect the milk in a separate bowl.

8. Add an equal amount of lemon juice to the coconut milk.

9. Chill the milk and lemon juice.

10. Add the hot peppers, green onions and the grated coconut flesh to the shredded chicken and mix in a large dish.

11. Gradually add the chilled coconut milk and lemon juice mixture to the chicken and stir well.

12. Fill the Chicken Kelaguen into pita bread pockets or use as a topping for open-faced pita sandwiches.

13. Toast the sandwiches and serve warm.

NOTES

_____
_____
_____
_____
_____
_____
_____
_____
_____
_____

Tuvalu – Pulaka (Fekei)

Pulaka is a type of corm that is grown in large, swampy pits in Tuvalu. It is similar to taro root. This meaty carbohydrate is a big part of the Tuvaluan diet. Unprocessed pulaka corms are toxic, so they must always be cooked. There are many traditional ways to prepare pulaka, but one of the most popular methods is to make it into a dessert called Fekei. Fekei is a mixture of grated pulaka and coconut cream. Toddy syrup (made from the sap of coconut flowers) is sometimes added to this dessert to achieve a sweeter taste.

SERVES 4

INGREDIENTS

medium pulaka corms/taro corms (peeled)	2
coconut cream	1 cup
Banana leaves (blanched)	
Toddy syrup (optional)	

DIRECTIONS

1. Chop the Paluka corms into large pieces.

2. Grate the Paluka corms and mix into a soft, thick paste.

3. Wrap the paste in banana leaves to make four bundles or packages.

4. Secure the leaf packages with string.

5. Bake the packages in an earth oven for about three (03:00) hours or bake in a modern oven for one (1:00) hour.

6. When cooked, remove the banana leaves and cut the Fekei into cubes.

7. Place the cubes into a bowl and add the coconut cream.

8. Mix and add the desired amount of toddy syrup.

9. Serve warm or cold.

NOTES

_____
_____
_____
_____
_____
_____
_____
_____
_____
_____
_____
_____
_____
_____
_____
_____
_____
_____
_____
_____
_____
_____
_____
_____
_____
_____
_____
_____
_____

Vanuatu – Lap Lap

Lap Lap is a baked casserole, predominantly made from grated root vegetables, bananas and coconut milk. There are many variations including vegetarian versions as well as others made with pork, chicken or flying fox meat. The casserole is wrapped in banana leaves and traditionally baked in an earth oven called an Uma. Lap Lap is considered to be the national dish of Vanuatu. This dish is usually prepared for special occasions on the island.

SERVES 6

INGREDIENTS

green bananas (peeled and grated)	2
large sweet potatoes (peeled and grated)	3
Chinese cabbage (rinsed and chopped)	1
bunch spinach (rinsed and chopped)	1
onion (peeled and finely chopped)	1
(1.4kg) chicken (spatchcocked)	1
vegetable oil	2 tbsp.
coconut milk	2 cups
bunch chives (sliced)	½
large banana leaves (spines removed)	5
cloves garlic (minced)	2
Salt	
Black pepper	

DIRECTIONS

1. Preheat the oven to 350 degrees F°.

2. Soften the banana leaves by blanching them in hot water or by passing them over an open flame for thirty (0:0:30) seconds.

3. Arrange the leaves on a large baking tray, overlapping them to create a base for a parcel.

4. Set aside.

5. Mix the grated bananas and sweet potatoes in a bowl, then season with black pepper and salt.

6. Mix the spinach and Chinese cabbage in a separate bowl, then season with black pepper and salt.

7. Combine half of the coconut milk with the onions and minced garlic cloves.

8. Set aside.

9. Season the chicken with salt and pepper.

10. Heat the oil in a large frying pan, then add the chicken skin side down, brown on both sides.

11. Set aside the chicken after cooking.

12. Assemble the Lap Lap by arranging half of the spinach and cabbage mixture in the center of the banana leaves.

13. Spread the sweet potato and green banana mixture over this.

14. Place the chicken, skin side up, on top of the sweet potato and banana layer.

15. Cover the chicken with the remaining spinach and cabbage.

16. Pour the coconut milk and onion mixture over the filling.

17. Wrap the banana leaves tightly over the filling, then secure with a string.

18. Place the package in the preheated oven and bake for about one (1:00) hour or until the chicken is cooked.

19. Remove the package from the oven and untie the string.

20. Unwrap the banana leaves and pour the remaining coconut milk over the top.

21. Garnish the Lap Lap with the sliced chives and serve immediately.

218

Calorie & Nutritional Comparison

MEAT AND PROTEIN

Meat/Protein 3Oz.	Calories	Fat (g)	Carbs (g)	Protein (g)
Scallops	74.8	0.6	2	14.3
Hormel Vegetarian Chili w/Beans	83	0.3	15.4	4.8
Lobster	83.3	0.5	1.1	17.4
Cod	89.3	0.7	0	19.4
Meatless Sausage Patty	97.3	6.9	3.7	7
Canned Tuna (w/water)	98.6	0.7	0	21.7
Pot Roast	104.6	3.1	0	18.1
Red Kidney Beans (1/2 cup)	108.8	0.4	20	6.7
Chicken Breast (no skin)	110	1.2	0	23.1
Lamb Chops	112.3	4.2	0	17.4
Black Beans (1/2 cup)	113.5	0.5	20.4	7.6
Morningstar Black Bean Burger (1 patty)	114.7	0.8	15.2	11.8
Pinto Beans (1/2 cup)	117.1	0.4	21.9	7
Turkey Breast (w/skin)	126	3.5	0	22.2
Salmon	126.7	3.8	0	21.7
Beef Liver	136.9	4.2	2.9	20.7
Hot Dog (1 small, no bun)	141.8	12.8	0.8	5.4
Mussels	146.2	3.8	6.3	20.2
Whitefish	146.2	6.4	0	20.8
Veal	148.8	5.9	0	22.4
Buffalo Wings (3)	152	9	1.5	16.4
Ham	155	9	2.6	14.9
Canned Tuna (w/oil)	168.3	7	0	24.8
Pork Chops	169.2	7.7	0	23.4
Sirloin Steak	171.7	6.8	0	25.8
Chicken Breast (w/ skin)	172	9.3	0	20.9
Bacon (5 slices)	182.4	15.6	0.2	9.6
Tofu, Firm	182.7	11	5.4	19.9
Breaded Catfish	195	11.3	6.8	15.3
Tenderloin	227.1	17.9	0	15.3
Ground Turkey	235	13.2	0	27.4
Chicken Tenders	253	16	15	12
Bratwurst	256	22	1.8	12
Ground Beef	263.7	22.6	0	14.1
Bologna	266	24.3	0.7	10.2
Fish Sticks	272	12.2	23.8	15.7
Babyback Ribs	314.5	25.1	0	20.6
Italian Sausage	346	31.3	0.7	14.3

VEGETABLE NUTRITION

Serving Size ½ Cup	Calories	Fat (g)	Carbs (g)	Protein (g)
Cucumber	6.8	0.1	1.4	0.4
Romaine Lettuce (1 cup)	7.8	0.2	1.4	1
Cabbage	11.1	0.1	2.4	0.6
Summer Squash	11.3	0.1	2.5	0.7
Radish	11.6	0.3	2.1	0.3
Celery, cooked	13.5	0.1	3	0.6
Eggplant, cooked	13.9	0.1	3.3	0.4
Cauliflower, cooked	14.3	0.3	2.5	1.1
Zucchini, cooked	14.4	0	3.5	0.6
Banana Peppers	17	0.3	3.3	0.9
Green Beans	17.1	0.1	3.9	1
Tomato	18.9	0.3	4.2	0.8
Green & Red Bell Peppers	19	0.1	4.6	0.6
Potato	19.5	0	3.9	1.5
Spinach, cooked	20.7	0.2	3.4	2.7
Mushrooms, cooked	21.1	0.4	4	1.7
Broccoli, cooked	21.8	0.3	3.9	2.3
Asparagus, cooked	22	0.3	3.8	2.3
Pumpkin, cooked	24.5	0.1	6	0.9
Leek	27.1	0.1	6.3	0.7
Brussel Sprouts	30.4	0.4	6.8	2
Onion	30.4	0.1	6.9	0.9
Carrot, cooked	35.1	0.1	8.2	0.9
Peas	58.7	0.3	10.5	3.9
Sweet Corn	66.2	0.9	14.6	2.5
Sweet Potato, cooked	103	0.1	24.3	1.7

SIDE DISH

Serving Size 1 Cup	Calories	Fat (g)	Carbs (g)	Protein (g)
Summer Squash (1/2 cup)	11.3	0.1	2.5	0.7
Collard Greens (1/2 cup)	30.6	0.4	6.1	2.5
Frozen Mixed Veggies (1/2 cup)	72.7	0.6	15.3	3.8
Corn on the Cob (1)	77.4	1.1	17.1	2.9
Baked Apple (unsweetened)	112	0.6	26.4	0.3
Sweet Potato (med plain)	117.4	0.1	27.7	2
Garlic Bread (1)	125	6	14	4
Mashed Potatoes (no gravy)	161.7	1.2	36.9	4.1
Wild Rice	165.6	0.6	35	6.5
Cabbage Roll	170	6	21	8
Baked Potato (med plain)	188	0.2	43.5	4
Onion Rings	195.4	12.8	18.3	2.6
Spaghetti Noodles (plain)	197.4	0.9	39.7	6.7
Spring Roll (1)	200	20	12	3

Plain White Rice	205.4	0.4	44.5	4.3
Chick-Fil-A Cole Slaw (1/2 cup)	235	18.6	15.1	1.8
Baked Beans	236.2	1.1	52.1	12.2
Hush Puppies (5 pieces)	256.6	11.6	34.9	4.9
Macaroni & Cheese	259	2.6	47.5	11.3
Pasta Salad	320	16	32	12
Au Gratin Potatoes	323.4	18.6	27.6	12.4
Stuffing	356	17.2	43.4	6.4
Potato Salad	357.5	20.5	6.7	27.9
Baked Potato (w/sour cream)	392.6	22.3	50	6.7
French Fries (med order)	458.3	24.7	53.3	5.8

FRESH FRUIT

Serving Size ½ cup	Calories	Fat (g)	Carbs (g)	Protein (g)
Watermelon	24.3	0.3	5.5	0.5
Strawberry	24.9	0.3	5.8	0.5
Cantaloupe	27.3	0.2	6.5	0.7
Honeydew Melon	29.8	0.1	7.8	0.4
Raspberries	30.1	0.3	7.1	0.6
Nectarine	33.8	0.3	8.1	0.6
Grapefruit	34.5	0.1	8.6	0.6
Peach	36.6	0.1	9.4	0.6
Apple	36.9	0.2	9.5	0.1
Blackberries	37.4	0.3	9.2	0.5
Pineapple	38	0.3	9.6	0.3
Apricot	39.6	0.3	9.2	1.2
Cherry	42.1	0.6	9.7	0.7
Orange	42.3	0.1	10.6	0.8
Tangerines	42.9	0.2	10.9	0.6
Plum	45.4	0.5	10.7	0.7
Pear	48.7	0.3	12.5	0.3
Mango	53.6	0.2	14	0.4
Kiwi	54	0.4	13.2	0.9
Grapes	56.8	0.5	14.2	0.5
Banana	69	0.4	17.6	0.8
Raisins (1/4 cup)	109	0.2	29	1.2
Dates (1/4 cup)	122.4	0.2	33	0.4

DAIRY

Product & Serving Size	Calories	Fat (g)	Carbs (g)	Protein (g)
Parmesan Cheese (2 tbsp.)	45.6	3	0.4	4.21
Low-fat Cheddar Cheese (1.5 oz.)	73.6	3	0.8	10.4
Ricotta Cheese (1.5 oz.)	80.5	6	1.4	5.2
Soy Milk	80.9	4.7	4.4	6.7
Non-Fat/Skim Milk (1 cup)	85.8	0.4	11.9	8.4
Light Whipping Cream (2 tbsp.)	87.6	9.3	0.9	0.7
Low-fat Cream Cheese (1.5 oz.)	96	1.4	5.8	14.4
Cottage Cheese (1/2 cup)	101.7	2.2	4.1	15.5
Butter (1 tbsp.)	101.8	11.5	0	0.1
Feta Cheese (1.5 oz.)	112.3	9	1.7	6
Goat Cheese (1.5 oz.)	114	9	0.4	7.9
Table Cream (1/4 cup)	117	11.6	2.2	1.6
Mozzarella Cheese (1.5 oz.)	119.5	9.2	0.9	8.3
2% Milk (1 cup)	122	4.7	11.7	8.1
Brie Cheese (1.5 oz.)	142	11.8	0.2	8.8
Kraft Free American Singles (1.5 oz.)	148	1	11.7	22.7
Cream Cheese (1.5 oz.)	148.4	14.8	1.1	3.2
Whole Milk (1 cup)	148.8	8.1	11.4	8
Provolone Cheese (1.5 oz.)	149.3	11.3	0.9	10.9
Blue/Bleu Cheese (1.5 oz.)	150.1	12.2	1	9.1
Gouda Cheese (1.5 oz.)	151.4	11.7	0.9	10.6
Gorgonzola Cheese (1.5 oz.)	156	12	2.7	9.3
Muenster Cheese (1.5 oz.)	156.5	12.8	0.5	10
Roquefort Cheese (1.5 oz.)	156.9	13	0.9	9.2
Monterey Jack Cheese (1.5 oz.)	158.6	12.9	0.3	10.4
American Cheese (1.5 oz.)	159.5	13.3	0.7	9.4
Swiss Cheese (1.5 oz.)	159.9	11.7	1.4	12.1
Pepper Jack Cheese (1.5 oz.)	167	13.7	0.8	10.6
Colby Cheese (1.5 oz.)	167.5	13.7	1.1	10.1
Yogurt w/Fruit (6 oz.)	168.3	2	31.7	6.8
Cheddar Cheese (1.5 oz.)	171.4	14.1	0.5	10.6
Vanilla Frozen Yogurt (1 cup)	229	8.1	34.8	5.8
Strawberry Ice Cream (1 cup)	253.4	11.1	36.4	4.2

NUTS NUTRITION

Serving Size 1/3 cup	Calories	Fat (g)	Carbs (g)	Protein (g)
Coconut	94.3	8.9	4.1	0.9
Chestnut	98.9	1	21	1.5
Almond	182.9	16	6.2	6.7
Pistachio	237.4	18.9	11.9	8.8
Hazelnut	240.5	23.3	6.4	5.7
Pine Nut	256.3	23	6.4	10.9
Walnut	261.3	26.1	5.5	6.1
Cashew, dry roasted	261.9	21.1	14.9	7
Pecan	273.8	28.5	5.5	3.6
Peanut, dry roasted	284.4	24.1	10.5	11.5
Macadamia	320.4	33.8	6.2	3.5

SNACK NUTRITION

Product & Serving Size	Calories	Fat (g)	Carbs (g)	Protein (g)
Cucumber Slices (1/2 cup)	6.8	0.1	1.4	0.4
Carrot Sticks (1/2 cup)	27.5	0.1	6.5	0.7
Tangerine Slices (1 large)	43.1	0.2	11	0.6
Applesauce (1/2 cup)	52.5	0.1	13.8	0.2
Celery Sticks w/ Cream Cheese (1 tbsp.)	54.4	5.1	1.3	1.3
Grapes (1/2 cup)	56.8	0.5	14.2	0.5
Dried Apricots (1/4 cup)	77.4	0.1	20.1	1.2
Apple Slices (1 med)	81.4	0.5	21	0.3
Pretzels (1 oz.)	108	1	22.5	2.6
Oil-Popped Popcorn (2 cups)	110	6.2	12.6	2
Graham Crackers (2 large)	118.5	2.9	21	1.9
Jelly Beans (30)	121.1	0.2	30.7	0
Raisins (1/4 cup)	123.8	0.2	32.6	1.3
Trail Mix (1 oz.)	131	8.3	12.7	3.9
BBQ Chips (1 oz.)	139.2	9.2	15	2.2
Tortilla Chips (1 oz.)	142	7.4	17.8	2
Cheese n Crackers (1 oz.)	142.6	7.2	16.5	2.9
Chocolate Pudding (1/2 cup)	150.3	4.5	25.8	3.1
Cheese Puffs (1 oz.)	157.1	9.8	15.3	2.2
Cashews (1 oz.)	162.7	13.1	9.3	4.3
Sunflower Seeds (1 oz.)	165	14.1	6.8	5.5
Peanuts (1 oz.)	165.8	14.1	6.1	6.7
Colby Cheese Cubes (1.5 oz.)	167.5	13.7	1.1	10.1
Beef Jerky (1.5 oz.)	174.4	10.9	4.7	14.1
Apple Slices w/Peanut Butter (1 tbsp.)	176.3	8.7	24.1	4.3
Chocolate Bar (1.55 oz.)	225.7	13.5	26	3
Chocolate Chip Cookies (4 med)	236.2	10.8	32.7	2.4
Doughnut (1)	250.2	11.9	34.4	2.7
Chocolate Ice Cream (1 cup)	285.1	14.5	37.2	5
Fig Bars (6)	334.1	7	68.1	3.6
French Fries (med order)	458.3	24.7	53.3	5.8

METRIC EQUIVALENTS

Liquid Ingredients by Volume					
1/4 tsp	=	1 ml			
1/2 tsp	=	2 ml			
1 tsp	=	5 ml			
3 tsp	=	1 tbsp.	=	1/2 fl. oz.	15 ml
2 tbsps.	=	1/8 cup	=	1 fl. oz.	30 ml
4 tbsps.	=	1/4 cup	=	2 fl. oz.	60 ml
5 1/3 tbsps.	=	1/3 cup	=	3 fl. oz.	80 ml
8 tbsps.	=	1/2 cup	=	4 fl. oz.	120 ml
10 2/3	=	2/3 cup	=	5 fl. oz.	160 ml
12 tbsps.	=	3/4 cup	=	6 fl. oz.	180 ml
16 tbsps.	=	1 cup	=	8 fl. oz.	240 ml
1 pt.	=	2 cups	=	16 fl. oz.	480 ml
1 qt.	=	4 cups	=	32 fl. oz.	960 ml

EQUIVALENTS FOR DIFFERENT TYPES OF INGREDIENTS

Standard Cup	Fine Powder (ex. flour)	Grain (ex. rice)	Granular (ex. sugar)	Liquid Solids (ex. butter)	Liquid (ex. milk)
1	140 g	150 g	190 g	200 g	240 ml
3/4	105 g	113 g	143 g	150 g	180 ml
2/3	93 g	100 g	125 g	133 g	160 ml
1/2	70 g	75 g	95 g	100 g	120 ml
1/3	47 g	50 g	63 g	67 g	80 ml
1/4	35 g	38 g	48 g	50 g	60 ml
1/8	18 g	19 g	24 g	25 g	30 m

DRY INGREDIENTS BY WEIGHT

(To convert ounces to grams, multiply the number of ounces by 30.)

1 oz.	=	1/16 lb.	=	30 g
4 oz.	=	1/4 lb.	=	120 g
8 oz.	=	1/2 lb.	=	240 g
12 oz.	=	3/4 lb.	=	360 g
16 oz.	=	1 lb.	=	480 g

LENGTH

1 in	=			2.5 cm		
6 in	=	1/2 ft.	=	15 cm		
12 in	=	1 ft.	=	30 cm		
36 in	=	3 ft.	= 1 yd.	= 90 cm		
40 in	=			100 cm	=	1 m

INDEX

225

227

ABOUT THE AUTHORS

Kristy Khemraj is a writer and artist who currently reside in the Caribbean. She is a graduate of the University of the West Indies.

Apart from recipes, Kristy writes short stories, reviews, and travel articles. She has written for both magazines and blogs in Trinidad and Tobago, USA, UK, and Australia. She is also a professional book reviewer and editor.

When she's not writing, she loves exploring new places, learning about new cultures, painting and testing new recipes with her family.

Henderson Daniel is a foodie and aspiring chef. Born and raised on the Nature Island of the Caribbean, there were no fast-food chain restaurants and every meal had to be cooked from scratch. Being the last born in the family, he spent a lot of time in the kitchen with his mother, learning about cooking.

In his late teens, he managed a small but very popular restaurant, which specialized in fresh fish and BBQ chicken.

He is also a graphic and website designer with HDTEN Media Group and started the site https://nationalfoods.org

Made in the USA
Las Vegas, NV
04 November 2020